MAN TRACKS

WITH THE MOUNTED POLICE IN AUSTRALIAN WILDS

ION IDRIESS

ETT IMPRINT
Exile Bay

This 24th edition published by ETT Imprint, Exile Bay 2024.

This book is copyright. Apart from any fair dealing for the purposes of private study, research, criticism or review, as permitted under the Copyright Act, no part may be reproduced by any process without written permission. Inquiries should be addressed to the publishers.

ETT IMPRINT
PO Box R1906
Royal Exchange NSW 1225 Australia

First published by Angus & Robertson Publishers 1935.
Reprinted 1935 (six), 1936 (two), 1937, 1938 (two), 1939, 1940, 1941, 1943, 1946, 1949, 1951 (two), 1956.
Published by Jonathan Cape in 1937.
Published by ETT Imprint in 2020.
First electronic edition published by ETT Imprint in 2020.

Copyright © Idriess Enterprises Pty Ltd, 2020.

ISBN   9781923205451   (pbk)
ISBN   9781922473363   (ebk)

Cover: *Tis a hot day on patrol and the water is scarce.* Frontispiece to the first edition.

Design by Tom Thompson

FOREWORD

THIS book of the life and work of the mounted police in Australian wilds is what the Mounteds would probably call a "patrol job." Well, the mounted patrols have helped open up much new country for our stockmen and miners. I shall be pleased if this "patrol" shows the way to some writer who can produce the complete story to which this fine body of men is entitled.

My principal qualifications for writing *Man Tracks* are: personal acquaintance with most of the men concerned, a share in a twelve-hundred-mile patrol through the last wild area of the Kimberleys, and twenty-five years' wanderings in the interior (often with the blacks) by which I have gained a knowledge of the country, and an understanding of the mentality of the aborigines, that can be learned in no other way. A recent trip of eleven thousand miles was taken to verify, as far as possible, the material in this book. As an onlooker I have seen all sides of the job.

The reason this book is not confined to "white" stories alone, is twofold:

Firstly, because I would hate to hurt the feelings of friends of any man who may have "kicked over the traces" – as might unintentionally happen if white stories alone had been selected. Secondly, because it would not include the general work and problems of the mounted men if aboriginal "hard-doers" were not included.

Regarding the white stories: I have been most careful to avoid hurting anyone by their inclusion. As for the aboriginal: at times he has speared my horses. Still, he is a lifelong friend, and would be tickled to know that "Watchel" had included his misdeeds in corroboree form.

I have sufficient material for several books such as this, and could name a score of men, retired and on active service, each of whose experiences would make a book in themselves. Unfortunately, in this book there is not even room to include the fascinating north-west and south-west camel patrols of Central Australia, the desert patrols of Western Australia, or the great rides of the northern Queensland "Mounteds." Then again, the records of every police outpost could supply material for a capital book. I am afraid this, often historical, material will have vanished before Australians are numerous enough to absorb it.

This book is written before the old order changeth.

Events are moving in northern Australia. With motor transport come roads, with wireless, isolation vanishes, distance too under the plane.

Already patrols are done by car in several districts. A portable wireless police plant has already been used in the Western Australian police expedition party to the Rawlinson Ranges; shortly, wireless will be installed at Timber Creek (Northern Territory), bringing that isolated post in touch with Darwin. Although horses will be used for years yet in the wilder districts, still the moving finger writes on. At present, in the Northern Territory alone, with its 523,620 square miles, there are only forty mounted men keeping order in a country larger than Great Britain, France, and Germany combined. This book is written before settlement and increasing population inevitably alter the adventure and romance inseparable to the job of patrolling these great areas of northern, central, and western Australia.

To every man who has helped me in gathering the material I tender my sincere thanks. For the photographs in this book, apart from my own, my thanks are due to Messrs W. L. Abbott, E. H. Wilson, J. Mahony, W. Coultas, W. J. P. Fitzgerald, M. C. Don, and Rev. A. Dyer.

Ion Idriess.

CONTENTS

CHAPTER

1. HALF-CASTE JOE	6
2. JOE'S LAST STAND	11
3. THE DESERT	18
4. THE BLACK CAMEL	24
5. THE SILENCE OF THE HILLS	27
6. THE IVORY WITNESS	31
7. THE PHANTOM RIDER	35
8. "YOU NO TALK!"	42
9. JACARRIE	48
10. JACARRIE'S LAST FIGHT	52
11. WHERE THE PROSPECTOR SLEEPS	56
12. THE TALE OF THE TRACKS	63
13. SEEKING MOODOORISH	69
14. THE NIGHT ATTACK	72
15. GRAHAM'S SECOND BULLET	77
16. A RACE AGAINST TIME	81
17. NEMARLUK	85
18. THE "BLACK INTELLIGENCE"	92
19. UNDER THE MILKWOOD-TREE	97
20. SEEKING THE TRACKS OF NEMARLUK	101
21. NEMARLUK'S VISITING-CARD	106
22. CROSSING THE VICTORIA	110
23. THE TRAP IN NEMARLUK'S CAMP	115
24. TWO TRAPS FOR NEMARLUK	119
25. THE CROCODILES AND THE RAFT	124
26. MARBOO	129
27. THE BOADICEA OF ARNHEM LAND	136
28. KING WONGO'S SPEARMEN	140
29. THE ATTACK ON THE JAPANESE	145
30. TIGER	149
31. THE CAPTURE OF NEMARLUK	155
32. THE SEA WANDERERS	160
33. THE DEATH OF McCOLL	166
34. THE LAW OF THE ASSAGAI	173
35. THE ESCAPE OF NEMARLUK	176
36. BUL-BUL MISTRUSTS CHUGULLA	180
37. THE ARREST OF TIGER	183
38. THE LONE PATROL	188
39. THE FLIGHT OF NEMARLUK	195
40. THE ARREST OF NEMARLUK	199

1
HALF-CASTE JOE

HALF-CASTE Joe was a dangerous man; handsome too. A first-class rifle shot, a boxer, runner, and swimmer. But what made him sought after by the crack stations of Queensland was his horsemanship; he could handle a horse with the best in a country where horsemen excel. And horses knew him; seemed to love him.

Tall, broad-shouldered and lithely built, with those clinging legs that seemed made to slip over a horse's back; a bronze-brown skin; eyes a slumbering brown under finely-chiselled brows; thin, close-shut lips shaded by a short, coal-black moustache; a well-shaped head of curly hair; beautifully shaped hands mesmeric with sympathetic feeling when fondling an animal – Joe was as near a coloured Adonis as one could find.

But he loved horses too much, speedy horses, pedigreed horses, other men's horses. He resented being a station-hand; hated being a half-caste; swore the whites owed him everything but gave him nothing. So, his mastery of animals he turned to his own private – very private – account.

This is his long story made short. He was arrested in the Queensland Gulf country for cattle-stealing and lodged in a cell at Normanton. Next morning the cell was found burned down and Half-caste Joe gone.

They chased him to the border but he beat them to it, choosing his horses as he sped through the bush. There the chase, for the time being, ended, because it costs time and money to extradite a man from one State to another. Time passed and the half-caste was almost forgotten in his old Queensland haunts.

Robert Stott was the mounted constable in charge of the Roper River police station, Northern Territory, an isolated police post bordering on Arnhem Land. With a companion constable he kept order in his wild domain, the civilized portion of it being the cattle country south and west.

Stott was a sturdily-built man, level headed, fearless, and a thinker. Returning from a bush patrol he called in at Hodgson Downs cattle station, forty miles south of the Roper, and there noticed a new hand, a smart half-caste, that Crawford the manager called Jack. After one sharp glance Stott took little notice of him.

Stott rested his outfit for a few days, as his horses had had a rough trip. Crawford, an athletic man who liked to keep himself in the pink of condition, challenged the other two in weight-lifting, jumping, swimming, running, and shooting. Stott proved the strongest, but the half-caste beat the whites in the other tests as well as at boxing.

Some time after returning to the Roper, Stott's policeman mate rode up with the mails. Mails only arrived once in ten weeks, and Stott opened his like a man famished for news. In a Queensland paper, old long before it reached Darwin, he read of the escapades of Half-caste Joe, and how he had broken from gaol. He felt positive that the "Jack" of Hodgson Downs was the wanted man.

Stott, unable to arrest him without a provisional warrant, wrote his inspector suggesting one be sent to Constable Haedge who should ride to Hodgson Downs via the Elsey, and arrive at a certain date five weeks hence. Stott would reach the station a few days before the appointed day and, by helping in any work on hand, prevent any suspicion arising in the mind of Half-caste Joe. When he saw Haedge coming he would seize Joe and hold him until Haedge rode up. He warned the inspector that if a police party simply rode up to the station Joe would shoot, then ride for his life.

Anticipating that the inspector would fall in with the plan, Stott, with a tracker and horses, in due course rode for Hodgson Downs.

When Stott rode up to the homestead Joe was handling colts in the stockyard. He glanced anxiously towards the house as Stott shook hands with Crawford. The policeman should not have returned until his next patrol six months hence! As the two white men walked down to look at the garden, Stott casually glanced towards the stockyard and called:

"Hullo, Jack."

When the Chinaman cook rang the bell for dinner Joe was not there, and at breakfast next morning he was away horse-hunting. The following day he was sulkily suspicious.

Two more days passed and Haedge was due. The half-caste had apparently become reassured. Stott lounged on the veranda with a book, but watching Joe as he moved about from the hut to his duties in the garden, at the house, or at the stockyard. Afternoon and the setting sun came, but no Haedge.

"Oh, it's a land of distances and time," thought Stott. "He'll come tomorrow."

He didn't.

"What is wrong?" pondered Stott. "The Queensland Government won't let the case drop. Haedge must be down with malaria on the track. I daren't wait later than tomorrow midday." That evening he talked it over with Crawford. "If Haedge arrives when I've gone he will try to arrest Joe and be shot dead. He will not stop to think; he is too impetuous; he will go straight for Joe. Not very big, he is game as a bulldog ant. Yet if I stay here longer Joe will disappear."

"Well, when you go tomorrow, what if I send Joe down the south end of the run for five or six days? Then if Haedge turns up I can hurry a blackfellow after you and you can nab Joe when he .returns."

"Right. But don't send Joe away until the following morning; he must see me go or he will suspect a trap is being set for him."

Next day after lunch Stott ran his horses in, said a cheery farewell and departed. Eight miles along the track he met Haedge coming with his plant.

"Where the deuce have you been?"

"I came around by the Roper to pick you up."

"The Roper! Didn't the inspector tell you to take the warrant direct to Hodgson Downs!"

"No. He forwarded the warrant and wrote I was to join up with you and arrest the man 'Half-caste Joe.'"

"Well, now we're up against it. Here's a dangerous man with suspicions that will become certainties immediately he sees us approach the station."

"How far is the homestead from here?"

"Eight miles."

"Well, let us go straight in and arrest him quick and lively."

"It *will* be quick and lively! This man is a tiger. He can fight like a thrashing machine, is as hard as nails, and active as a cat. He'll take to his guns and pick us off like emus in a bog; we'll hardly have time to hear the bullets whistling once he sees you!"

They sat under a tree and discussed the dilemma from every angle. Haedge was all for a set plan of action. A smart little chap, tough and dapper, he had been in the Prussian cavalry and looked it.

"It's no good our rushing in," said Stott. "If I could only get near enough to grab him it would be all right. But how can I do it with you on the horizon?"

"Well, you go into the station on your own and I will come along when you send up a smoke-signal."

Stott laughed.

"What will Joe be doing? No. Come on, let us ride along back. To turn up there again without you is almost as bad as arriving really alone. We will have to think of some perfectly obvious excuse, one that will grip his attention."

They rode on, Stott thinking hard.

"I heard a rumour that Harry and Steve Lewis have had trouble again with the blacks at Newcastle Waters," remarked Haedge cheerily.

Stott reined in his horse. Haedge stared at his alarmed face. Stott laughed:

"That's the excuse. Come on!"

An hour later Stott rode smartly up to the homestead, Haedge coming behind with the pack-animals. Crawford came out on to the veranda; the half-caste too. Joe's hand was at his revolver as he walked to the other end of the veranda.

"The blacks have attacked Newcastle Waters again!" called out Stott to Crawford. "They killed Steve Lewis and the Chinaman cook; Harry was wounded but he managed to get to the telegraph line and met a teamster who looked after him. They gutted the station and store-room and played merry hell." He hitched his horse to the horse rail and jumped up on to the veranda beside Crawford, highly excited, completely ignoring the half-caste while he gave elaborate details of the tragedy. Haedge rode up with the packs, nodded to Crawford, dismounted, and with the tracker commenced off-saddling. Joe still stood at the veranda end, keenly listening to Stott's description.

"Poor old Steve!" said Stott. "He was swimming in the lagoon and the niggers crept up behind the lignum. Then as he walked out to dress they put four spears into him. He never had a chance. By Jove! he would have put up a scrap even with his hands if he had only had a chance! The Chinaman was in the garden picking tomatoes for tea and looked up just in time to see Steve drop. He yelled blue murder. A station boy on his way to the lagoon looked up and spotting the killers yelled for Harry Lewis. Harry, rushing out with only a revolver, made for the lagoon, but they soon stopped him with a boomerang. The station boy then galloped up; Harry managed to climb on behind; and the boy made for the teamster's camp."

Stott was all excitement. "We've got to ride down straightaway. Can you let us have a bag of flour and some beef?"

"Anything you like," answered Crawford.

"Good! What about you coming with us?"

"I don't know," replied Crawford doubtfully. "We will have to get on with the branding soon."

"Oh, let the branding go. I'll give you a hand when we come back; I'll bring my two trackers and we'll put it through in no time! Jack can look after the place for you!"

But Half-caste Joe had been carried away by Stott's tale. With his slumberous eyes shining he came softly down the veranda. Haedge had walked to the house rail and was filling his pipe.

"Let me go with Mr Stott," volunteered the half-caste, "and Mr

Crawford can stop home."

"Good old Jack!" cried Stott. "That's the ticket!" and he playfully grabbed Joe around the waist. "Of course you can go. Can't he, Haedge?"

At the stress on his name, Haedge jumped straight towards the pair as the half-caste snatched his weapon; but Stott lifted him off his feet, pinning his arms to his sides. Haedge had the handcuffs on in a moment. But Stott still held his prisoner:

"The neck-chain now!"

Haedge quickly drew a neck-chain from a pack-bag and Half-caste Joe was chained to a veranda-post. With a long sigh Stott disarmed him and stepped back.

"This means that you are arrested for horse-stealing in Queensland and escaping from custody. You need not say anything. But I warn you if you do it will be taken down in writing and may be used as evidence."

The half-caste's face had gone a sickly brown; his narrowed eyes were furious as he turned menacingly towards Crawford.

"Well, Mr Crawford, *you* were in on this! Some day I will square accounts with you; and when I have finished you I will finish Stott!"

"Don't be silly, Joe," said Stott. "I've my job to do and I've got to do it. You will only get a year or two in Queensland and then you will be all square again."

"You've got your job to do, Stott. So have I. I've got a few years' stretch to do in Queensland, and then! Well, there'll be another job for me to do – finish Crawford and you. I'll do it. I might not do the stretch, but I'll do the other."

2
JOE'S LAST STAND

THAT night they slept beside Half-caste Joe and the next morning started for the Roper, Stott leading with the handcuffed prisoner riding beside him, the end of the neck-chain gripped by Stott, the reins fastened to the neck of Stott's horse. The packhorses followed along behind, driven by Haedge and the trackers. They rode the forty miles to the Roper in a one-day stage. The next stage was to Pine Creek, two hundred and sixty miles. Before leaving the Roper Stott said to Haedge:

"I will take care of the prisoner. If anything happens, your job will be to look after the horses. Remember, if this man gets loose and leaps on a horse, even handcuffed, we will never see him again!"

But Half-caste Joe was apparently resigned; he gave no trouble at all.

"Any water at the Waggon Waterhole?" asked Stott of Haedge on the second day's ride.

"Yes, plenty."

"Good. We'll make it at about five o'clock this afternoon and camp there tonight."

But when they arrived at the Waggon hole there was only mud at the bottom.

"I thought you told me there was plenty of water here!" said Stott angrily.

"Do you call this the Waggon hole? Why, Tracker Tommy told me the hole farther on is the Waggon hole."

"It will be dark before we get to water," answered Stott shortly. "Come on."

He pushed on as rapidly as possible, fully realizing the danger of travelling with a tough customer like the half-caste after dark. Night had just fallen when they arrived at the waterhole, Stott rode straight to a cleared patch among the timber, reined up and said:

"Get off, Joe."

The half-caste dismounted, naturally standing on the off side of Stott's horse, between the two horses. As Stott swung his leg over to dismount, the prisoner suddenly kicked the horse which plunged on Stott, jerking the chain from his hand. The half-caste was running instantly.

Stott picked himself up, yelling:

"Joe's gone! Don't let a horse off camp whatever you do!"

He leapt on his horse and galloped in the direction he had heard Joe running. A watery moon lit dimly the trees and the blurred cane-grass, the shadowy bushes that veiled the fallen logs, ant-hills, crab-holes and broken branches strewing the vine-covered ground. Stott wheeled his horse here and there peering everywhere for a fleeing shadow. What a disgrace, to have a man on a chain and lose him!

He would be lucky indeed if ever he got Half-caste Joe on a chain again. He stood in the stirrups, listening. My God! the man was really gone. Then, between the trees he saw a shadow cross a clearing momentarily bathed in moonlight. He spurred his horse among the trees, bending to dodge the branches. As he galloped into the clearing something leapt up ahead and ran for the timber on the opposite side.

Stott laughed aloud at the tinkle of a chain. If the half-caste had only lain still he would have ridden away and left him!

The half-caste ran like a man possessed, compelled to hold that nine-foot chain in his handcuffed hands. Even so, he reached the timber just ahead of the horse thundering to run him down. Then a limb caught Stott on the chin and knocked him violently from the saddle. The horse wheeled back out on to the clearing and stopped. The half-caste, crouched for a blow while running for dear life, glanced over his shoulder at the thud, guessed what had happened, stopped, gasping as he peered among the trees back towards the clearing. He located the horse. Stott groaned, but struggled to his feet. He guessed what the half-caste would attempt and staggered back towards the clearing. He fired at the outline of his horse; the animal leapt and bounded away to plunge around and gallop back towards Stott and stand again.

Then Stott saw Joe crouching in the moonlight, ghastly with rage, for he had been about to spring on the horse. Stott fired and missed, then ran straight at him. Joe ran back towards the timber, gained several yards but crashed over a stump, dropping the chain as he threw out his arms to shield his face. With a bitter curse he was up again, dragging in the chain, but the end caught in a stump and jerked him to the ground. Stott was almost on him when he bounded off again. Stott raised the revolver but as he pulled the trigger tripped over an ant-heap. In a breathless swearing he scrambled up. But Joe had gained the lead when down he crashed in a crab-hole. Stott's outstretched arm dropped as he too thumped down in the same hole. Spitting out grass and earth, he scrambled up with Joe in the lead again.

Stott fought to steady his breath and arm while he fired once more, but missed. He ran on rubbing his eyes, for now he was seeing two half-castes in the wavery light, and panting like a wounded bull. Then, frantic joy! he was gaining on the man. Gaining! Had he wounded him? The half-caste, unhampered, could run both longer and faster than he, and now he was running for his liberty. But he must be winded. Look! the beggar was not running straight ahead. He was dodging! Running towards the moon. Ah! Now he was crossing it; but he was doubling back past it; he was stumbling and staggering. Now Stott was almost on him! He raised the revolver – how many shots had he fired? Four? Five? Ah, the cunning dog! One more shot and the revolver would be empty. Then Joe would brain him with the chain, leap on his horse and away!

Stott sobbed in a great effort to calm his senses; he felt his heart was about to throb to pieces.

"I'll die if I don't get him soon," he thought. "Yet if I'm not careful he'll outwit me whether or no. Oh, how can I get closer to him? He's playing with me!"

He plugged doggedly on, gasping, as Joe wheeled drunkenly around in a curve. "He's keeping near the horse," thought Stott. "I daren't shoot the last cartridge; my hand is shaking and I can hardly hold the revolver. I'm almost done."

Then Joe ran into a thin, dead limb; it caught him on the chest and threw him backward. He scrambled up and leapt away, but the chain brought him down again. Groaning, he rose and staggered away, jerking in the chain. With two last long strides Stott was almost on him, and fired. Joe went down but half-rising, tried to swing the chain. Stott brought the revolver-butt down upon his head; grabbed the chain; tied it securely around his body; collapsed beside Joe and was violently sick.

An hour passed. Haedge at the camp stood in an agony of indecision, the trackers standing by, each holding horses. They had heard those shots away in the bush, and stood listening through the long, long silence. What had happened? Had the half-caste killed Stott? "If I don't go out and find Stott," thought Haedge, "he may be dying from injuries. If I do go, the half-caste may ambush me, seize a horse and escape. What can I do but obey Stott!"

After a long, long wait a tracker turned quickly to stare into the night.

"What name?" demanded Haedge.

"Horse come up!" replied the tracker. "Might be him come himself!" And Haedge knew a horse without a rider was coming.

"Man he come too!" said a tracker suddenly. "Two fella man!"

A cough sounded from the bush, the trackers started forward, the outline of a horse appeared, then the forms of men walking before it. Haedge rushed forward.

"Take him!" gasped Stott. And Half-caste Joe collapsed into Haedge's arms.

Stott sprawled forward to his knees, the half-caste's chain around him. "Tea!" he gasped. "Why haven't you the fire alight? Do you mean to say you haven't boiled the billy yet"

"We never thought of tea," replied Haedge, "not with you scrapping out there. Is he badly hurt?"

"I can't make it out. I shot him in the back and can feel the bullet on his chest; it must have gone right through him, yet he seems quite all right. How are you, Joe?"

"Pretty sore," answered Joe. "I'd like a drink of tea."

"Too right, you'll get a drink, old man – the best we have. Look slippy, you boys."

They drank pints of tea; neither could eat much. By the firelight they examined the half-caste's wound. It bled very little, nor did he look a dying man.

"The crack on the head is far the worst," he grinned ruefully. "If I was a full white that blow would have killed me."

"I am very sorry, Joe, but I must chain you up again," said Stott. "I can't afford to take any risks with you, as you know!"

Joe grinned, and submitted philosophically. The next day they just camped quietly, talking over events of the night before.

"That foxy beggar Joe was out to get my horse," explained Stott, "and he nearly trapped me."

The half-caste, leaning smoking against a tree, smiled reminiscently.

"I didn't know where the horse was, but Joe knew all the time. After I knocked him out I just lay helpless; I don't know how long we both lay there; I didn't care if we never had to move again. At last Joe began to move, then he sat up. 'It's no good, Joe,' I said, 'the game is up. Come on, where is that horse?' Do you know, the beggar staggered up and walked straight across the clearing to where the horse was standing in the timber with the reins caught in a stump."

They rode to Pine Creek, then by train to Darwin where a doctor examined Joe. "A narrow escape," he declared. "The bullet entered the back, struck a rib, and travelled right along it to the chest. It is only under the skin. I'll apply a local anaesthetic and remove it easily."

In due time Half-caste Joe was returned to western Queensland. Stott returned to the Roper.

Time passed. Then the inspector at Darwin received an urgent wire:

Half-caste Joe again escaped, riding for the Territory. Warn Crawford and Stott immediately.

But a Queensland patrol was riding fast behind the runaway and the border was not going to stop them this time. Joe could track with the best of them but he could not lose them. By tricks and doublings he misled them sometimes, but the trackers struck the trail again and again. He was travelling west on a thoroughbred-word was wired through to the young trooper stationed at Turn Off Lagoon near the border. Hurriedly he saddled his horse and rode east along the border, hoping to intercept the half-caste; the tracker watched him ride away. He had only been gone two hours when his horse came galloping back to the station. The tracker caught it, cantered back along its tracks, and found his policeman boss lying shot through the heart. He read the story of the tracks, saw where the policeman's horse had ridden straight to a horse concealed among the bushes, then wheeled around and galloped away. Lying in front of where the stationary horse had been was the policeman's body. The tracker followed that other horse's tracks right away to the river and there heard the voices of the oncoming Queensland patrol hot on the same tracks.

With the trackers on these tracks of a now hard-pressed horse the patrol rode hard too, and two hours ahead of them rode Half-caste Joe. In late afternoon he reined in his floundering horse by old Hann's rough slab homestead on Hann's Creek.

"Where's old Hann?" demanded Joe.

"Out on the run somewhere," replied the cook.

"Good. Get me a feed quick, old man."

The cook did so, and the half-caste ate hungrily. The cook asked no questions. At last Joe sat back from the rough table with a sigh.

"Good. Wish I could go to sleep for twenty-four hours, but I can't. Now, are there any rifles about? I want one badly. I hoped to get one from a policeman today but I only got a revolver."

"I don't know of any, but I'll have a look in the old fellow's room."

"I'll look!" scowled the half-caste and walked out of the kitchen into the tiny house. Just then Big Hann rode up. He had not intended returning that night but had met a black boy in the bush who, by "bush telegraph," already knew all about the shooting of the policeman. As he rode to the kitchen Hann saw a strange horse tied to a tree.

"Whose horse is that?" he roared to the cook.

"Half-caste Joe's!" replied the cook. "He's over in your room looking for a rifle."

"Is he?" roared Hann. "I'll give him rifle!" He strode towards the house, a huge figure of a man, a pioneer known throughout western Queensland and the Territory. With a rifle in his hand he neared the veranda as Half-caste Joe appeared at the door.

"You're a nice sort of a — man to go and shoot a policeman," roared Hann. "What the hell do you think you're doing? Think you can get away with things like that? Well, I'll show you you can't."

Joe never spoke.

Old Hann jumped to the veranda. Joe stepped out of the door with levelled revolver and fired. Old Hann staggered to his knees, dropping the rifle. Joe sprang forward and snatched the weapon but old Hann grabbed him and swung him right off the veranda, then collapsed. Joe landed on his hands and knees like a cat, sprang up, grabbed the rifle, jumped back into the house and slammed the door. The cook ran to old Hann and helped him into the kitchen.

"Are you really hurt, boss?" inquired the cook.

"'Course I'm hurt! Think I'm play-acting?"

"No, boss, but the bullet's gone right through you. I can feel it at your back!"

"Can you? Well, take off my damned shirt so as I can feel it too."

The cook obliged, and guided Hann's hand to his back.

"Yes, it's there right enough," growled Hann thoughtfully. "Feels like an onion; and my side is sore as a bundle of corns. Say, I've been shot right through the chest. Now how in the name of kingdom come did that bullet get round to my back!"

"Must have travelled there, boss," suggested the cook.

"Travelled me grandmother! Get a shears and cut this hair away and put on some Friar's balsam or cattle dip or something."

They ceased arguing at the sound of galloping hooves.

"The police!" said old Hann, staring at the cook. "*Now* there'll be a nice how-de-doo!"

With rattle of hooves and panting of horses the Queensland patrol reined up under cover of the kitchen. Hann told them the news. A tracker scouted around the hut, but there was no trace of recent tracks from it. The sergeant called on the half-caste to surrender but received no reply.

"Mr Hann, I do not want to risk the lives of any of my patrol by rushing the house. Do you mind if we shoot through it?"

"Make it like a cullender if you like," growled Hann.

The sergeant shouted warning to the half-caste that if he did not come out they would start shooting at once. Still no reply. Shots were fired through at all levels just before sundown. Then came rain, drowning the flash of a rifle now and again through the night.

At "piccaninny" daylight a tracker spied blood-stained tracks leading away from the house. They followed the tracks down to the creek, then into a broad patch of tall cane-grass. They surrounded it, waiting under cover for the sun to dry the grass. At midday it was fired. Slowly it burned, the flames pressed on by a morning breeze. A tracker saw away out in the middle the tall stalks moving as of some animal cautiously crawling through. He snaked out into the grass right ahead of those moving stalks, then lay down, levelled his rifle and waited.

Half-caste Joe crept on just ahead of the fire, the rolling smoke blowing over him and shielding him, the crackling of the flames drowning his crackling amongst the grass. He crawled right against a black face glaring over the black muzzle of a rifle. It is doubtful if he heard the crack of the rifle.

In Burketown the doctor examined Hann. He had hair on his chest which might gap an axe.

"My word, like a gorilla!" smiled a friend. "And as tough!" added a bystander.

"Yes," said Hann, "I'm tough, but those damned little ants do annoy me sometimes."

"You've had a narrow escape, Mr Hann," said the doctor. "A remarkable thing has happened; the bullet struck a rib, ran along it to the back, and is lodged just under the skin. I'll remove it in a moment without the slightest trouble."

Two bullets connected with the half-caste's case had done exactly the same thing.

Was old Hann tough? Well, he works today from sunrise to sunset out in the bush of the tough nor'-west.

3.
THE DESERT

JAMES WHITE thought he could beat the desert: where a blackfellow could live he could; furthermore, he could locate a goanna hole with the certainty of a "desert rat."

But no white man is quite so good as that.

His friends were more than dubious; they reminded him that the desert natives are men born to it, through centuries of environment that even they sometimes died beside a dried-up goanna hole.

White laughed. A cheery fellow White; a youngish man, a bushman, too, though not "desert wise." His mania was a mountain of gold. "East it is, east," he insisted. "There's six hundred miles of country out there no one knows anything about. If a man just keeps walking east he's bound to strike it, just like Merton did when looking for lost horses."

Thus, indeed, Merton found his famous mine with the gold sticking up out of the ground. But such mines are rare indeed.

White did all his prospecting on foot, carrying neither food nor tools. He would disappear into the bush for months at a time, and really could live like a blackfellow. But the bush is not the desert.

The tiny mining-town of Laverton, six hundred miles inland from Perth, has the farthest east police post in Western Australia. The men who have manned that outpost have helped make history in the State since the first of the roaring days of gold: helped in exploration; helped the water-finders whose job was more precious by far than that of the finders of gold. From the time that their spades helped to bury those first twenty men of Burtville who died with their boots on, that little police outpost has carried on with one job after another. As the years passed, bringing their hardly-won advancement in pioneering life, Laverton has seen historic expeditions start out north, north-east, and east; has seen the Kookynie and Darlot warriors come raging down to the massacre of the Lancefield tribes; has seen gold come and go, and cattle come and gold come again. East of Laverton lies four hundred miles of sand and spinifex, while south-east, for nine hundred miles, is – desolation.

Across the Eastern Desert lie the Warburton, the Petermann, the Rawlinson and other ranges. These possess some strange lure. But only the best of desert men, well equipped, may cross that arid region; and then only after heavy rain. For there comes an occasional year when rain falls, which fills the gnamma holes-holes in granite rocks. And these granite intrusions only occur among the sand and spinifex at distances of about thirty miles apart. Miss a line of these tiny rock holes and you fare like the Arab who has missed his oasis, never to return.

It was after one of these heavy storms that White laughed farewell to Jimmy Mitchell and started east for his mountain of gold.

He carried two days' food, a water-bag, a compass and a Bible inscribed "Mascot White."

"He will never return!" prophesied Frank Hann the explorer.

Months passed. The Laverton aborigines travelled desertwards on their annual "walkabout." They returned several months later with news from the spinifex natives of the tracks of a white man a hundred and. fifty miles out. The Laverton police calculated the distance by the number of "sleeps" it would take the natives to reach that vicinity. The spinifex men had stated that the white man was living on wild peaches and lizards, and that there was water where he now was roaming. Months later, the wild spinifex men again met the natives of Laverton and told that now the body of a white man lay two hundred miles east.

A job for the police. A dead man in the desert.

Find him!

In December 1915 Constable Hunter set out from Laverton accompanied at the last moment by a white man, Preddy (a good camelman, curious to see this country out east); Old Peter, who was a "desert man"; Kilyu, a police tracker; and a spinifex boy, Billy, who could not speak a word of English. This lad was supposed to have seen the dead man lying on a peculiarly-shaped hill. Events proved that he had not, but his tribesmen had given him a really good description of the locality.

He was the only spinifex man that the Laverton aborigines could coax into the "white man" town. He was very frightened and would only mumble answers to Kilyu the tracker's questions.

For twenty miles east the camels padded through mulga bush, then out on to blazing sand tufted with coarse grey spinifex. And the soft crunch of their pads, their throaty gurglings, the creak of saddles, was the only sound. With corrugated brow walked Old Peter, a dirty feather in his hair, Kilyu the tracker following, with the spinifex boy behind him. Hunter noted their glum looks, and with Preddy tried an occasional joke. But the desert was before them, and this had been a dry season. On the evening of the second day they came to the big native rock hole Woolger. Woolger was dry!

Old Peter stared across the sands with an expression as fixed as the Sphinx. With frightened looks Kilyu and the native boy "hoostha'd!" the camels down to unload. For Woolger was a "spirit" hole, a deep hole, a good hole for the blacks. They sang it in corroboree as a hole that never went dry.

Next morning the worried-looking trackers were talking in low tones amongst themselves. Hunter cheerily inquired; eagerly Kilyu explained. They were afraid to go on. Old Peter said they would all die, for now that Woolger was dry the rock holes farther east would surely be dry. Which eventually proved correct.

Hunter was determined to push on and they did so. He assured them there was plenty of water in the water-drums, and not to be afraid. Obviously they were. He cheered them all he knew while sharply watching against desertion.

Then the desert face broke into chasm-like wrinkles that were "breakaways," rocky cracks, enormous channels one after the other down into which and across the labouring camels had to be coaxed and driven.

In the heat of this exhaustive work Old Peter vanished. Nor could their quick efforts find him. Kilyu, who did not know the country, stared in sullen fright. Billy, who could not speak English, just stared at Hunter. Hunter looked at Preddy and both men laughed and shrugged.

"We'll have to turn back," decided Hunter; "return quickly to Logan's Well. From there I'll send the tracker into Laverton for Thin Peter; he is due back in Laverton to-day with Constable Thompson from patrol. He knows the desert, and Billy can explain to him where the body is supposed to be. Our camels are thirsty and we've a two days' trip back to Logan's Well. Here's where we hurry."

They secured Thin Peter, left Kilyu the tracker behind, and faced east again. Billy the spinifex boy with guttural detail explained to Thin Peter the direction and locality in which he had been told the little hill lay. The old aboriginal glared from wrinkled eyes, shrugged his bony shoulders, then walked on.

Thin Peter was a real son of the desert; wiry as a mulga stick, lean and dry as the spinifex, tireless as a hawk. Cheerful in his own dry way, dogged as the sand-dwellers needs must be. They pushed on, the camels alone complaining. For these were town camels that missed their daily drink; they groaned and slobbered and became groggy at the knees. A dawn came with the sun a ball of molten gold and they pushed straight on towards it seeking, water! water! water! At midday they were leading staggering camels, their own mouths open seeking air. As far as the eye could reach was sand dotted sparingly with dry grey spinifex. In the dancing distance was a smudge that might be a clump of mulga. Leading the patrol, like a long black crane was Thin Peter striding doggedly farther and yet farther ahead. Hunter marvelled at the man's bare feet, for he felt the heat of the sand through the soles of his boots.

This was Christmas Day, Hunter's third Christmas in the desert. It might be his last. He thought what a heavenly present water would be for his patrol. He thought of all the gold, of all the lovely things he would like to have, but he could think of nothing so much to be desired as a waterhole. He trudged doggedly on, hiding his growing fear. Had he - endangered the lives of his patrol?

A fine type, this man of the Western Australian Mounted Police. Tall and strong, clear of eye and firm of jaw, a type that hates the very thought of turning back from a job.

In mid afternoon he was deeply concerned, for they were too distant now from water to turn back and he thought the end had come when Thin Peter stood stock still away out there, swaying as a reed might sway in a mirage. With tug! tug! at the noserope, with the squelch! squelch! squelch! at their feet they dragged the groaning camels on until Hunter stood beside Thin Peter and wondered had his mind really weakened from thirst. Below him the ground fell away in a gorge and down there were three waterholes like bluish silver reflecting trees and grass. He listened incredulously to the screech of galahs; saw the flight of bronze-wing pigeons; and, yes! the white of a rabbit's tail! He was sure, then, he was seeing things. But Thin Peter pointed downward and grinned as he chuckled "Naneri."

Thus was found an oasis in our Australian desert mapped now as "Hunter's Falls."

Next morning, with the camels' bellies rumbling to the water they held, they plodded away again and in one short mile trod again on sand and spinifex.

In the cool silence of a desert night they sat grouped together, the smoke of their pipes rising in the starlit air. This was another dry camp, familiar enough in the yearly story of the desert patrols. During some patrols the camels have had to go a week without water when travelling from rock hole to rock hole. But this patrol was into country where the waterholes were unknown; daily they had to take their chance of finding another hole. For two days and nights the camels again had not had a drink. Stony country had made these town camels footsore; they were hungry, too, because there was little desert bush for them to eat. Plain in the starlight they squatted there with snake-like heads suggestive of prehistoric monsters leering above the spinifex. From blankets spread on the sand the men lay gazing up at the stars.

"We daren't travel farther than another day and night if we don't find water," said Hunter. "I dare not risk the patrol again. To-morrow evening will mean three days without water; three days back to the oasis will mean six. These camels will only just manage to do it."

"Well," puffed Preddy, "it's a hard thing to find, you know. A tiny hill, a queer-shaped one carrying a dead man's bones. And all around it four hundred miles of desert."

"He sleeps in a rather awful peace," said Hunter towards the beautiful sky. "And if we don't find him to-morrow he will sleep so till doomsday."

A black hand appeared in the sky; it smudged and spread into a blanket that rapidly grew to a cloud swiftly swallowing the starlight.

"A thunder-storm!" exclaimed Hunter, "by all that's wonderful! If it will only break and rain!"

"We'd better tie the camels down," advised Preddy, "and quickly."

For, even as they watched, the black cloud was already creeping over them. They hobbled the camels and side-lined them, securely tying each nose-line to a bush. That line is connected to a wooden peg in the tender nose and a camel will not pull back on that.

Thunder came and earth space was all roaring and growling. Lightning flashed and the desert jumped up sickly white and shimmering, then black night came with the sky blotted out.

A red flash came and the spinifex leapt up dancing in a shimmer of orange. A wild yell answered from the dark and in the next flash there was Thin Peter dancing mad, his naked body prancing with arms flung to the sky, shrieking sounds like apemen make. The Storm God knows what prayer this was, born in the hearts of desert men ten thousand years ago.

They stood by the frightened camels as thunder rolled and lightning came again to play with that wild figure leaping amongst the spinifex. But the dry storm rolled away, leaving not one drop of rain. The sky shone out a gorgeous blue, glittering with stars.

Next day the abrupt roughness of the Virginia Range arose from the desert. Drought had driven the wild tribe away from here three months before. The patrol passed through a break in the range, walking again while tugging at their labouring camels. There was just sufficient water swishing in the canteens to get the humans back to the oasis if they turned back now. Then they had luck-the bright green of kurrajong-trees; the camels quickened their pace for those leaves are moist and camels love them. They allowed them their fill, and started again, the camels munching.

Away ahead Thin Peter pressed doggedly on, his skinny body dully glowing under the sun, heatwaves dancing before him; Hunter walking behind, staring ahead, trying not to remember that every step he took carried the patrol another step from water.

"Just one hour more," thought Hunter. "One hour might find him. We can't perish if we push on just one hour more."

They pressed on, staring over the sand and spinifex for a peculiarly-shaped hill to appear out of the haze. The hour dragged by, bringing Hunter yet another excuse, a smoky clump of mulga-trees emerging out of distance. He would go just as far as those trees, make the boy climb one and see if he could see the hill farther out.

They reached the trees. Billy climbed and had not reached the top when he yelled, waving excited arms.

It was eight miles farther on, a lone hillock surrounded by spinifex and sand. Only thirty-five feet high, flat topped, it had a circumference of hardly a quarter-mile. An insignificant thing in itself, yet it was a landmark in this awful monotony, a something that might arrest the eye of a perishing man.

They spread out over this forlorn hillock and searched without success until Hunter found a cave half-way up. And in there slept White with his Bible beside him, a compass to show him the way, and matches, too, for a light. A few little odds and ends, several small gold specimens, and empty food-bags.

The patrol had done its job. They started back for water, taking White with them. But that night for some reason the camels were more than usually restless; moaning distress and uneasiness in the middle of the night, they abandoned camp and set off across the desert. Though Hunter was wakeful it meant a chase of miles before they were recaptured and forced back to the pillar of flame that marked the desert camp.

Men have perished when their camels have faded away in that manner. And men have never returned who have failed to mark their camp.

On the sixth evening with no water they again neared Naneri (Hunter's Falls). The camels smelt water, but the party were ready and quickly roped the frantic animals to the earth. They carried them water in buckets lest they kill themselves by drinking.

So – White came back to Laverton.

4
THE BLACK CAMEL

WILD country, harsh country. Craggy, rock-bound hills, and nearly waterless, with broken gorges and abrupt ravines scoured by the floods of ages. And a silence down on the sparsely-timbered creeks disturbed only by the hoarse croak of a crow. Up above, among the rocky crests, a foraging wallaby thumped along the ledges seeking scanty pickings on the sides of steep spurs. The valleys poorly grassed, with but little herbage.

A forbidding area this, harbouring scanty animal life and, yes – a silhouetted camelman!

Up on that ironstone ridge, a dark shape upon a black camel. Not really black, for the animal stood in shadows among rocks tipped a dull red by the setting sun. The rider was gazing down into a grey pocket already lined with shadows, a pocket of some thousands of acres of open valley lands enclosed by practically impassable hills. There was one entrance to that pocket, a gorge. And in that pocket cattle, just the beginning of a herd, sought a meagre existence.

The camel rider's face was grey and frowning as the rocks, his cold grey eyes suspicious and vengeful. A small, thin man, with that sunburned wiriness that hints at surprising strength. A real bushman, but soured by isolation and unfounded suspicions. Calculatingly his glance lifted from the darkened hollow to sweep the rim of hills. He jerked his head erect as a startled animal might, for across the skyline rode a horseman who vanished even as the watcher's hand clutched his rifle.

In bitter chagrin he jerked his camel's nose-peg and the obedient animal turned and lumbered back down the hill-side. He who watches may also be watched! Too late to intercept the lone horseman now, and soon too dark. Who could he be, riding these ranges where man so seldom rode?

Then the camel rider cursed with a sudden "hoostha!" that brought the camel lurching to its knees.

He leapt off and stepped forward to a dark mass lying among the stones.

His riding mule! He bent over it, seeking for the bullet wound. There was no wound, no bullet, but he was convinced there was. He who suspects evil is hard to convince that no evil has been done. This man imagined some mysterious one was stealing his few poor head of cattle, whereas they were dying naturally of age and starvation. He mounted his camel and rode down into the darkening valley with thoughts as black as the gathering night.

An extraordinary animal, this camel that could pick its way among rocks; that could climb ranges. For a camel's pads are tender, born only to tread upon sand.

Day came, fiercely bright. There had been no rain for many months, the trees stretched motionless branches, their sparse leaves drooping. A hot, parched silence crying aloud for rain enveloped this loneliness, seldom broken by the call of a bird.

Afternoon came slowly, then evening, then hot, black night. Rain-clouds slowly gathered, blotting out stars, smudging the sky. In the breathless silence a thousand ears seemed listening. Imagination? No! It came again, a faint thud like the limp body of a rabbit falling gently to the ground.

A flash of lightning illuminated rock and gorge and weird gnarled trees, and the staring eyes of a man and his white, lined face, bluish in the flash that lit up the giant camel he was leading, and the limp body of a man dangling across its hump. Then darkness with thunder that crashed and rocked until those valleys shuddered. Wind came whistling around the crags, snapping with reports like rifle-shots the dead limbs of tree. Again that flash, as if heaven's bombs were lighting the devil's path of the pair toiling below.

He was laughing, with a ghastly laughter, as he glared at the lightning-lit heavens above. Rain! That washes out things! Rain! On this night of all nights!

He vanished in darkness and his camel with him.

Surely the Black Camel of the Arabs on which rides the Angel of Death!

This man was doing an uncanny thing, travelling through black night amongst the roughest of mountains and not on a track. And with a beast whose touchy pads crave for the softness of sand!

Yet there was a track nearby, a wild donkey track that wound faintly among the boulders. This bushman could have kept to it by cautiously feeling out step by step with his foot. Instead, he turned sharply away and down into a rough, dry creek impeded by boulders. He tugged at the nose-rope, intent on creeping up the creek, cursing the camel whose great legs were all askew. A dry creek that would be a torrent if only the rain came! Presently he left the creek and began climbing a steep ridge, and the rain did come, sleety and icy cold. He laughed aloud and tugged and cheered his camel now slipping as it clumsily put sore feet groping amongst slippery rocks. For miles he travelled, up and down, then up again and along ridges, then down again into some black pit.

Before grey dawn came he had staggered to where a grey drizzle covered the ghostly peaks of No Man's Land. Around him – shadowy desolation. He was working his way up a dry timbered creek searching for what he found – a big heap of driftwood caught between tree-roots, evidence of floods long past. He hurried away up the creek-bank into a dwarfed scrub and tied his camel to a bullock bush, then unlashed its burden and staggered with it back to that long tangled pile of driftwood. He laid his burden on it and set the pyre alight. In the light of those leaping flames he hurried among the trees and added log after log to the pyre. It roared and hissed under the fain as it lit up the strange scene and the toiling fireman.

He stood bolt upright, his heart thumping; then ran to quieten his camel, for the cursed thing was terrified of the thunder and the fire and him toiling down there. He stared in dismay at its tracks churned around the bullock bush. He glared up at the leaden sky-the rain would wash those tracks out! But he led the camel away, tied it to a wild apricot bush, and hurried to complete his work. He made a great job of it. Then he took the camel to that edge of the world and, turning it loose, hunted it far down. It would slowly clamber down to flatter country; never climb back again over these rocky crests. He watched it awhile as it stumbled on its painful way; then returned to gaze earnestly at the mass of sizzling coals. Soon the ravines that fed this creek would begin to run, then would come the flood that would wash the coals of this fire, and all trace of everything in it, away forever.

He rubbed his blackened hands on his trousers, and with a sigh vanished the way he had come.

And the rain stopped. It had rained heavily right to the range top. It would almost seem that God had stopped it from coming up over the hill.

5
THE SILENCE OF THE HILLS

BRUCE RANDELL rode with worry on his brow. His brother had not returned, despite urgent work awaiting him. Besides, he had promised to return in time for the send-off to that grand old station man McTaggart. The brother had left Angepena Station on 12 August for his own place, Yancanninna Station, some twenty-five miles away, promising to return on the twenty-fourth. It was now the twenty-sixth; so Bruce Randell rode to Yancanninna. It was just a station track along which Randell's searching eyes saw a faint buggy-track, his brother's. He knew those tyre-tracks-one wheel of the buggy was not perfectly round and this slight peculiarity was reproduced in the track upon the ground. Only highly-trained eyes would have noticed those tracks, for recent rain had almost blotted them out. Those buggy-tracks were going towards Yancanninna Station, but-they had not returned. Randell arrived at the Yancanninna homestead late in the afternoon. It was locked up and silent. Randell sought his brother as the bushman searches, examining the doors locked from the outside; the barred windows; then the path that led from the living-door down to the stockyard. He walked thoughtfully beside that path. No boot had been on it since the rain. He searched at the stockyard rails; no horses had recently been taken from the yard. Then he searched along the pad leading from the yard-the pad along which a saddled horse would be led before the rider mounted. There were no tracks. It was slow work because of that earth film which rain had showered over all tracks days before. He walked slowly beside a horse-pad that wound away from the stockyard leading into the hills. But the hard-pressed earth of the pad told him nothing. No one had been at this homestead for at least a week. At sunset he walked thoughtfully back to the house. What could possibly have happened to his brother? If an accident, it must be a serious one, for Fred was exceptionally strong, a noted bushman too, with plenty of initiative. A champion rider, a breaker in of the wildest horses, it was almost impossible his horse could have thrown him. Even had he been thrown, unless killed, he would crawl doggedly for miles. He was the sort who never gave in while life lasted.

At sunrise Bruce Randell saddled his mule and rode out along that pad – it led to Worturpa, twenty miles deeper in among the hills. Worturpa was old Jock Grice's place. Grice was Fred's father-in-law. Fred might have ridden over there and been detained by something urgent and unexpected.

With eyes carefully scanning the ground he rode some miles, then was relieved to meet a station-hand seeking timber for fence-posts. Just a chance meeting, for there was no white man between Yancanninna and Worturpa. But the man, an employee of Fred's, could tell the brother nothing; was surprised to hear that Fred was not at Angepena Station.

"Last time I seen him," he said thoughtfully, "he'd just returned from the muster at his old father-in-law's. He'd put a slipper on the off hind-hoof of that little brown gelding he often rides. Must have put it on in a hurry, because when he rode away I noticed four head-prints of the nails in his track."

Randell asked him to keep a look out for tracks as he worked through the bush, and rode on. He had ridden several miles when he abruptly reined in, peering down over his mule's neck at four evenly placed dots pressed into the earth with the faintest suggestion of a "frame" around them.

Those dots were the heads of four new nails protruding from a horseshoe recently tacked on the off hind-hoof of a small horse. He dismounted and carefully examined that track. It was heading towards Worturpa hut; it had been made before the rain ten days ago. He could tell that because the imprint of the horseshoe was blotted out by a fine dust spat up by raindrops. The four little holes made by the protruding heads of the horseshoe nails were dull little holes with rounded edges, not quite filled in by the dust disturbed by the raindrops. The firm clay just here had preserved those four dots; elsewhere their fellows were quite filled in or blotted out.

Very carefully Randell rode and the nails showed here and there; just where the earth could receive and hold an impression, those four little dots had sunk in. He found others as he wound in and out among the hills, traces of a horse-track, and in one soft place traces of a mule and a camel-track. But no track of any sort returned from Worturpa. Repeatedly he rode out on different sides of the track on to any piece of flat country he came to, and searched for any sign of a hoof-mark coming from Worturpa.

Always the hills pushed him back on to that one negotiable path. From sunrise to sunset he rode and searched; at dark he camped.

Next morning he set out on the tracks again. His brother had not ridden back. Why? There was no habitation beyond Worturpa, and this was the track back.

He reached the lonely hut in early morning. It was locked up; old Grice was away. Randell searched all around the hut, circling out to a wide radius. But there was no trace of those four nail-heads; no trace of any track. Rain had fallen heavily here.

Old Grice might be out on some distant station mustering; he might be away for days. Randell sat his mule, thinking, staring at the immemorial hills. The only man within miles was a lonely copper gouger, John Allen McPhail, about nine miles east of Worturpa hut. He might be working at the Donaghue Castle copper show; on the other hand he might be away prospecting. Then there was a wandering dingo-shooter somewhere out in the hills.

Randell shook his bridle rein and hurried back in the direction of the nearest town, tiny Copley, seventy-five miles away. He had ridden a hundred miles in the last twenty-four hours. When he arrived at Copley, he was dead tired. He rang up Mounted-Constable Waterhouse at Beltana, then went across to the hotel and there found Grice, just arrived in town.

"Hullo, where did you leave Fred?" asked Randell.

"At the hut."

"What day was that?"

"I don't remember exactly; memory's not too good. Why?"

"He hasn't turned up yet and I can't find any tracks going back to Yancanninna."

"You don't mean it! He may have gone across to Umberatana."

"He hasn't turned up there; he had no occasion to go anyway."

"Miller told me he wanted to take over the sheep, and Fred said he thought he would. I left him saddling up his horse."

"Have you any idea which way he intended going home?"

"None at all. I've followed his tracks into those hills before, but I've never been able to find where he comes out again."

"Well, I'm worried. I've reported the matter to the police. Constable Waterhouse is on his way to Angepena now. I'm to get Albert the tracker in the morning and we'll be at Worturpa hut tomorrow night. I've sent the word around for a search. When are you coming out?"

"I'll get a start tomorrow night."

Randell nodded and set out on the long ride to Angepena to meet the police (Thursday, 29 August). The following night he was at Worturpa hut.

Waterhouse organized his forces as the men arrived – several station owners, and the half-dozen scattered bushmen to whom word could be sent. It was a serious job the men discussed around a blazing fire in the lonely hut, for their only hope of finding Fred Randell was to track him. A difficult job indeed in such country, for rocks tell tales only to the keenest eyes in traces far apart. And in those ranges there were a thousand

thousand places where a man could lie with a broken leg and never be found again. Worse than all, rain had fallen since Fred disappeared, probably washing all traces away. Then again, they had to find tracks to start on. His tracks led to Worturpa hut, but none led away. In which direction had he gone?

Their only hope lay in themselves. Besides the trackers, each white man here was an experienced tracker; several were experts. Owner or station-hand, their living practically depended on it. Perhaps in no other part of Australia is a man's living so dependent on his tracking ability as in those remote ranges.

Two teamsters there had more than a hundred and twenty donkeys in their teams. They could let these animals go in the night in a locality infested by wild donkeys. In the morning any man could name anyone donkey in the teams and they would go out, pick up that particular donkey's track, and get the animal despite the tracks of its hundred mates. Further, they would never once get the track mixed with any of the numerous wild donkeys' tracks. When these two men heard of the lost man they simply left their teams and came straight across bush to the rallying-place.

With men such as these as trackers, if the police could not find Fred Randell he would never be found.

The "black" camel.

6
THE IVORY WITNESS

THEY arranged to work in parties of twos; to circle the hut and continually work out wider and wider until one party or the other picked up the tracks of the horse with the four protruding nail-heads in the shoes.

Three miles from the hut one party found the tracks of the muster of a fortnight ago. The track of the four nails was amongst them; they followed them the rest of the day only to be led back towards the hut at dark. Miles farther away another party picked up muster tracks, including the tracks of the little brown horse, and followed them all day. Fred had ridden the horse; few other men would have gone where these tracks went. They saw where he had been chasing one big-footed bullock, and where he had put it down with the mob. These tracks also returned towards the hut.

Yet another party found the horse nail-tracks; yet when these tracks had been made the horse had been riderless! They knew this because it had gone under limbs of trees so close to its back that a rider would have been knocked off. They could see also that the horse had not gone there of its own accord for there was no grass to entice it there and the country was so fearfully rough that no horse unguided or unled would have faced it. Before sundown they proved by the tracks that the horse, then left to its own devices, had been trying to make its way back to Worturpa.

What had happened to Fred Randell after he had finished the muster? He had ridden part of the way out into these hills, then apparently had dismounted and led or driven the horse into this forsaken area, only to turn it free. Why?

On the third day they got the horse. It had neither saddle nor bridle. What had happened? If an accident, the horse would almost certainly have still carried the remnants of a bridle. But if it had been unsaddled and then let go deep in those fastnesses where it was not expected to make its way back, then why had Fred let it go? And why had he not returned?

Well, what next? They had found the nail-tracks, and, though only visible now and then, had followed them throughout the muster, then on that inexplicable ride and walk into the hills; then found the horse, and so had pieced together part of the story. And what next? Turn again to the only book they knew that held the story, the book of the earth.

The days slipped by. Then miles from the hut they found a camel-track. Strange! They followed it until a tracker noticed a strand of tow caught on a bush. That strand had been torn from a tow rope. Now, what was a camel with a saddle on doing there? A camel would never go in such a place as this unless ridden or driven or led. It had been led, as that strand from the tow rope proved. Their curiosity, keenly alert as is that of any man who has successfully read the book of the earth, was aroused.

Next day all parties concentrated on the camel-track, each man tracking by the side or ahead of another to save time. Had the rain of a fortnight before been just a wee bit heavier, had it lasted ten minutes longer, all these faint traces would have been washed out. That camel was carrying something, but there were no tracks of a man leading it, and yet it had been led by a tow rope! No one believed a camel would willingly go where these tracks were leading. Presently they realized that such had been the wish of the man who had guided the camel. With grim cunning he had taken the animal where tracks would never have been suspected. He had not ridden; he had led the animal; yet there were no tracks of a man! Had he worn moccasins? They began to feel that this camel-track had something to do with the disappearance of Fred Randell. The feeling became certainty when they found where the man could have used a wild donkey track, but had deliberately chosen the roughness of hill-side and gorge instead.

With long delays as again and again they lost the tracks, and marvelling how the camel could have kept its legs among those rocks, they held determinedly on, finding the still visible pressure of a grass tuft here, the pressure of a twig into the ground there, a dislodged stone where the weight . of the camel's big pad had pressed the stone away. At night they camped on the tracks; all hands searching again at sunrise.

In late afternoon they saw where at last the man had taken advantage of a wild donkey pad, but only because that pad was a continuous long ledge of perfectly bare rock on which no hoof of unshod animal would leave a trace, let alone the soft pad of a camel. They marvelled at the ominous luck that so persistently dogged this careful man; for there never would have been a trace had it not been for that rain which had rained neither too hard nor too little, but just sufficient to wash, here and there, a few grains of sand into some hardly noticeable depression on the rock. And on these moist grains had been stamped a faint impression of part of a camel's pad, an impression hardened under the sunlight that so quickly followed the rain.

By some uncanny adjustment of nature a faint trace would be left in some unbelievable fashion just where they seemed to have hopelessly lost all sign.

But a day came when they stood by the last trace, cornered in a rough creek among tumbled stones, twisted roots, uprooted trees and the debris of storms long gone by. They scattered wide, circling almost without hope of again cutting the tracks. All except Treloar. He stood there by the last faint impression, studying earth and stones and grass and trees around. The camel could not have flown, nor disappeared into the earth. It must have gone over it. Stooping, sometimes on his hands and knees, he searched the ground inch by inch.

At last, a distant shout called the party together, all but Treloar. Tracks had been found out there, leading right into No Man's Country. They stared at tracks as plain almost as of yesterday, for these had been imprinted when the late rain was lessening into a drizzle. But what of the gap between the head of the creek, where the tracks had disappeared, and here?

They looked at one another then stood gazing back. Somewhere back there they felt was the secret of the camel and of Fred Randell. Down in the creek Treloar was searching; and away from the creek he found the bullock bush. All around it the ground was churned up where a tied camel had been walking around that bush in the rain. Pieces of the bush had been chewed off too. Carefully Treloar followed tracks back towards the creek and he saw where the camel had been tied to an apricot bush. From there, at last, were the tracks of a man, leading down into the creek. They must have been made just when the rain was beginning to hold up. And in the dry bed of the creek were the ashes of what had been a long, fierce fire. He gazed at it. It was a "made" fire; that was obvious by the way logs had been torn from the undergrowth to feed it. That one glance showed, also, that it had not been a campfire. A campfire is round; but here was the charcoal and ashes of a long and narrow fire.

And diligently had this fire been tended; otherwise there would have been short ends of charred wood about it.

Treloar stood reading what that fire told him.

The rain had put it out before the big coals had had time to burn right down. It also proved the date of this fire. That rain! Had it continued a little longer the creek would have been in flood.

Silently all grouped around the ashes while Constable Waterhouse carefully raked them. He unearthed a few charred fragments of bone which crumbled to powder at his touch. Then he raked out something that would not burn away – the twisted, blackened, "Eye Witness" knife of Fred Randell.

So they returned to Worturpa hut. Mounted-Constable Kerin of Farina was hurrying across country to join in the search for the missing man.

When eighteen miles beyond Mount Lyndhurst Station he noticed a forlorn looking camel standing in a corner of the netting fence. Curious to know what such a beast was doing there, he rode across. The camel gazed at him. He noticed at the back of the hump on the off side above the loins a large dark stain. It looked suspiciously like dried blood.

That camel belonged to old Jock Grice.

Later, Fred Randell's saddle was found hidden among dry wattle sticks a mile and a half from Worturpa hut. The girths were done up; so it could not have been thrown from the horse.

"What have you done to Fred Randell?" demanded Constable Waterhouse one day of Grice.

"Nothing."

"What kind of a horse was Fred riding when you saw him last?"

"A dark-brown colt."

"I arrest you on suspicion of having murdered Fred Randell."

When Detective Wylie Nation sifted the ashes of that fire he found one good human tooth. Dr Angas Johnson declared it to be all that remained of the body of a man.

Body of Sailor, the giant Aboriginal.

7
THE PHANTOM RIDER

SIDI BEN MAHOMET rode with gloomy brow. Bitterness glowed in his coal black eyes. Three score years in age; his manhood wasted in this foreign land, vainly seeking fortune to buy a Moroccan home. Once chief of a mountain clan, now a wanderer accursed, riding heavily in debt with a black devil at his elbow. He glowered ahead to where momentarily, like a gallows in the sunset, towered the windmill above the Spinifex paddock of Mount Minnie Station.

By the side of the Moor rode Sailor, a gigantic aboriginal, his rugged, chocolate-black face innocent of expression. Sailor too was dreaming, morosely but resigned. Before the white man had come, Sailor's gigantic physique and phenomenal strength would have made him a king among his people. But now he rode as a hired hand with not even a white man for master. Obediently to Sidi's beckoning arm he rode around the mob to open the gate into the Windmill paddock. Perfectly he rode, instinctively easing his great weight on the horse, guiding it almost by pressure from the knees.

As the mob swung in through the opened gate, the Moor shepherded them through. Through the dust-cloud he too, tall and heavy, sat his mare to the manner born. She was his delight, this fine upstanding mare, fiery of eye, perfect of barrel, her hind legs peculiarly marked with a white splash extending up the inner side. Built for speed she was a weight carrier too, of the breed that would travel until she dropped.

On this peaceful afternoon of 15 June 1925, the Moor made camp near the windmill, in this vast paddock of sixteen thousand acres. A bare paddock but for the long, thick, coarse tufts of spinifex grass that spread into the distance like a grey-green sea.

It was lonely too, until from the homestead the owner (R. L. Richardson) came riding down to learn their business. Now the Moroccan was no longer Sidi Ben Mahomet, but Alex Hughes, the Moor horse-dealer, known as such in the Onslow district of Western Australia these fifteen years past.

"Good evening, Mr Richardson."

"Good evening, Hughes. That's a serviceable looking mob of horses you've got there."

"Yes. I am travelling them through the station country for sale. A spell would do them good. Can I camp them in your paddock for a week?"

"Not that long; three days if you like. I'll be wanting the paddock after that."

"Thanks. I'll push on then to Hooley's station; it is eighteen miles nearer Onslow and I hope to sell the horses there. I camped in Dead Bullock corner near the Cane River on the Peedamulla boundary last night. I could have got a paddock at Red Hill Station, but came on here instead."

"Right. You can spell your horses in my paddock for three days."

The Moor again thanked him, while attending to his saddlery of which, like every good stockman, he was very particular. He folded his saddle cloth neatly and hung it up, then placed the saddle on top of the cloth, folded the stirrup-leathers and irons over the saddle, folded the bridle and placed it also over the saddle.

"That's a handy poley saddle," admired Richardson with the stockman's regard for these things.

"Yes," answered the Moor complacently, and placed his big brown hand upon the well-oiled saddlery.

After an hour's talk of station news near and far Richardson rode cheerily away nodding "So long!" to Sailor. And the campfire twinkled behind him.

Each morning the Moor and Sailor would ride away into the big paddock, and mustering the hundred and twelve head of frisky horses, drive them to the windmill troughs for water. At such times Richardson would invariably ride down to the mob for a yarn.

He was sympathetic, as stock-owners invariably are in another's misfortunes; and the hungry Moor found himself unburdening his troubles, telling of his worrying over present and past financial losses, of how his ill luck still dogged him until now he was afraid he would never get back what these horses had cost him. Richardson nodded understandingly; he had suffered losses, too. The Moor grasped at this sympathy; eagerly he spoke of other troubles until his brow grew black as fate. One morning, in that deep voice of his, while his brooding eyes grew serious, he complained of pains about the heart, frightening little pains that stabbed like the cut of a knife should he become excited or exerted. He told, too, with glowering brow (and he watched the station man cunningly) of trouble with his stockman Sailor. He could not induce Sailor to do what he wanted him to do; Sailor was stubborn, and foolish in the head; and he was always giving the horses sore backs.

"No wonder!" ejaculated Richardson. "He must weigh seventeen stone. Why don't you go into Onslow and engage a lighter man. It is only a forty-four-mile trip. I'm going to town shortly and I'll drive you in in my car if you like."

But a stubborn repulse clouded the face of the Moor. And they did not go away on the appointed day, for some of the horses were missing. One evening the Moor asked Richardson for the loan of a shot-gun and cartridges.

"I've seen some big kangaroos about. I'd like one for meat; I'm tired of beef." Richardson lent him his Cashmere gun. Casually the Moor asked the loan of a sheath-knife, too, with which to cut the kangaroo up.

Next day the Moor asked Richardson if he would draw up an agreement between himself and Sailor to the effect that should Sailor desert he would forfeit all claim to his accumulating wages. Even though he owed Sailor money, he was afraid, so he explained, that Sailor was planning to run away into the bush and leave him with all the horses on his hands.

Richardson refused. He was rather puzzled.

Judging by their camp-life, the two men seemed to get on well together, never bickering or quarrelling. While dismissing the matter from his mind he put it all down to the Moor's worries. He certainly looked worried, this big old chap with brooding eyes set under deep-lined lids, his big hooked nose standing out over thin slits of lips. He was an upstanding old fellow in his Norfolk jacket, grey moleskin trousers, felt hat with the black band, and elastic-side boots deeply spur marked.

Spur-marks on a boot rarely escape a stockman's notice. The Moor frowned down at his boots as if at some premonition.

That evening Richardson came again. He admired the Moor's mare and rode her around the horses, minding them while the Moor prepared Sailor's supper. As with practised hands the onetime mountaineer bent over the cooking utensils, his face was a brown study. In the almost still evening air the smoke from the galley wreathed around his shoulders like a shroud. He and Sailor would be driving the horses away the following day, taking them along the bush-track to Hooley's station, eighteen miles nearer Onslow.

Next morning, at sunrise at the windmill, Richardson bid the Moor farewell.

It may have been late afternoon when the Moor and Sailor drove seventy head of horses to the lonely gate which leads into Dead Bullock corner in Corranoolly paddock on Peedamulla Station. With a nod the somber-visaged Moor motioned Sailor to open the gate. The Moor carried a gun. "We will shoot a kangaroo – coming back," he growled. Sailor looked at him with expressionless eyes and grunted.

They drove the horses in the direction of the Cane River where the animals would find their own good feed, then turned their horses back for camp. Sailor opened and shut the gate as the sun was slowly sinking.

"Where kangaroo?" he growled as they rode back towards camp.

"Down there!" replied the Moor throatily, pointing with the gun. "I have seen one down there every morning-a big one! Watch-and see where he falls-if he rolls over in the long spinifex grass he might not be found-for a long time!"

A puzzled frown corrugated the brow of Sailor.

He stared down the rapidly dimming paddock.

"You ride out that way," pointed the Moor. "I will ride along the fence and shoot him as he runs towards it."

With a flick of his bridle wrist Sailor turned to obey and as he rode away the Moor lifted his gun and fired. With a startled "Ugh!" Sailor flung his arms high and his great body rolled convulsively from the saddle. The Moor was at the gallop with the report of the gun and wheeling the riderless horse snatched its trailing bridle, leapt off, and with lightning action whipped off saddle, saddle cloth, and bridle. The liberated horse sped away to tell no tales as the Moor slung the saddle into hiding; then with haste, but neatly, he folded the saddle-cloth and placed it underneath, and folded the stirrup-leathers and irons over the top of the saddle. For a while he stood in a trembling crouch, his eyes more fearful and nearly as wide as the accusing eyes of his mare. There was a breathless hush over the spinifex paddock, everything listening to the hooves of Sailor's horse galloping into the distance. His heart thumped violently as there arose the mournful, wailing cry of a curlew.

Sidi Ben Mahomet went mad. He leapt on his mare, spurring deep as she bounded away straight towards the dying sunset. Her thudding hooves pounded in his mind as he leaned over the saddle while his gripping knees and hoarse cries urged her to gallop her life away.

"Oh, Allah! has it come to this, that I should be hung like a dog in an alien land!"

He came to the fence. In a second he realized that to gallop to the gate would mean "they" must see his tracks. He reined the mare on her haunches, leapt off and whipped off his belt. As bushmen do, he strapped the wires tightly together, then led his mare over. Undoing his belt the wires rebounded with a twang. Then leaping on the mare again he galloped away.

Night came down, the stars shone out and faster the miles sped by, and the mare's hooves thud, thud thudded with his madly racing brain. The gnarled cadjibut-trees were ghosts and Sidi Ben Mahomet shrank from their clutching hands as the branches swished by. Instinct urged him towards far away Morocco; he sped to reach the coast and the pearling luggers that come for water with the high tides at the full moon. But Time raced with him, and his steed was Fear. Time passed the Moor, and racing just ahead leered back and showed him what a month later would bring: Richardson travelling to Onslow and reporting to the police the disappearance of Hughes the Moor, and Sailor! Ah! How much faster Time then moved – Police-Constable Gulson and black trackers in the spinifex paddock! Trackers, black like Sailor! Sidi Ben Mahomet spurred his mare until her flanks dripped salt blood on the sands. Fool, frenzied at his own mental pictures though he had a month's clear start! – More! it was two months before Detective-Sergeant O'Brien found Sailor, But Time raced with him on Fear while his mare's hooves thudded through him until he screamed as he galloped down the bushes that were black men, and they swished-to behind him and snatched back at him and wailed just like the curlew.

"That shot in the night! Hark! Oh, Allah!"

It was only the memory of his own – Richardson's Cashmere gun.

But the Moor did not hear the panting of his mare! Nor could he lose the Phantom Rider by his side, nor blot his mind to the fearful pictures that he showed. The air swept the veins that stood out cords on his temples. Terror spurred him, as he spurred his faithful mare. Fifteen panting miles sped by imprinting the drag of her faltering hooves, in the sand. He didn't notice those betraying marks until the Phantom Runner leered-then Sidi Ben Mahomet hit the ground and stars seemed to explode in his brain. He lay there dazed until hearing galloping hooves that were but the thumping of his heart. He sprang up and reefed at his mare and screamed and kicked. But her heart was thumping too; her deep, long-drawn sobs and the piteous appeal in her eyes stirred his own self-pity as he glared at her. In frantic haste he whipped off the saddle (Sidi Ben Mahomet's poley saddle), the saddlecloth and bridle, slung them across his back and ran on through the night towards the sea. A saddleless mare might tell no tales.

At last he came to a fence and clutched it; slobbered as he swayed there, just like his floundering mare had slobbered. And he did a strange thing: folded the saddle-cloth neatly and placed it across the wire; lifted the saddle on top of the cloth; folded the stirrup-leathers and irons over the top of the saddle; and hung the bridle neatly over all.

And Time raced ahead in his mind and showed him how, many weeks later, the poley saddle would be found by Thomas Napier, boundary-rider on Peedamulla Station, who in turn would show it to Police-Constable Gulson and to Detective-Sergeant Michael O'Brien. Sidi Ben Mahomet saw mounted trackers Morrie and Harry, their faces turned to bloodhounds' jowls, as they stooped under the fence and peered for tracks where he stood.

Where he stood! Oh, Allah!

The Moor turned and again ran wildly towards the sea. He panted into the coastal sand-hills so weird in the fading starlight with their scrubby bushes casting black shadows that leered as the squelching sand hissed up from the tracks he made. Tracks! And the trackers coming months behind, coming, sure as Time, on the tracks of Sidi Ben Mahomet!

Poor fool! Time did not show him that in his beloved poley saddle O'Brien would ride relentlessly day by day, eating kangaroo meat when his rations gave out, deviating for nothing on earth while he clung to faint traces left months ago by a frantic man. But Time showed the Moor other dreadful things in a flash: the long patience of Detective Sergeant O'Brien at last finding Sailor's body right in the centre of the spinifex paddock; then his tracking over thirty miles of lonely country after rain and wind-blown sand had blotted out almost all trace.

At last the Moor heard the murmur of the sea and laughed with joy for its soothing sympathy. It was the chilly grey of dawn when he ran down and far out on the wet sands and held out his great arms to the waves. He ran into the water in hysterical joy that they could not track him here, then paused in agonized fear-his boots! They would know him by his boots-the spur-marked boots of Sidi Ben Mahomet! He tore them off with a wild cry and flung them far out. But his triumph died with the splash as they sank-the treacherous tide would wash them back again!

He turned and ran crying into the sandhills, And again Time ran before him and showed him William Bandy, the windmill repairer, picking up the boots on the beach at low tide on 7 August and, on recognizing the spur-marks, showing them to the police. And Tracker Morrie – Morrie was on his tracks now! Now! Oh, Allah! Was this the infidel's month of June, or was it the month of August?

He stumbled on into the sand-dunes where sheep-pads wound in and out among the spinifex tussocks. A sob of utter relief shook him. He would run upon a sheep-pad, and sheep by day would tread that pad and blot out his tracks. At last! At last he would beat them!

But – Time eventually brought O'Brien! He stood frowning, staring, thinking. For he had lost the tracks upon a sheep-pad. Presently he went on. He had tracked the fugitive for over thirty miles where wind and driving sand and weather and rain and time had again and again obliterated all trace, to be beaten now. Grimly he walked slowly along the pad.

Now, wherever a big, drooping tussock of spinifex barred the way, the sheep had gone round. But Sidi Ben Mahomet, moaning with exhaustion, his fevered eyes and racing mind conjuring visions, planted his stumbling feet under the drooping grass that occasionally overhung the track.

Long afterwards Detective-Sergeant O'Brien lifted a drooping tussock. A smile spread over that grim, set face. There, freshly preserved by the thick, drooping grass, as new made almost as if it were only yesterday, was the footprint of Sidi Ben Mahomet.

The Moor laboured on a little farther. The sound of the racing hooves of his mare was his pounding heart. He was riding for his life when he stumbled to his knees. He would give his life for just one long, long sleep. That sudden stab in his heart-it made him think of Richardson's sheath-knife. He laughed aloud at the thought of cutting up a big kangaroo; then weakly pulled out the knife and cut some spinifex grass. Now, that big bush just ahead! He would make a bed of the grass and go to sleep under the bush. A long, long sleep. He smiled queerly and threw the knife away. There-it had gone now. They would never find it . . . never find his poley saddle . . . or his spur-marked boots . . . they would never find him . . . Ah! that pain again . . . he must go to sleep before it woke him.

He crawled anxiously forward. He spread out his bed of grass. Then his left arm clawed the sand as it slithered weakly from under and he sank down with his face in the grass he had cut.

So Sidi Ben Mahomet, alias Alex Hughes the Moor, died of fright.

The body of Sidi Ben Mahomet (Hughes the Moor).

8
"YOU NO TALK!"

DUNCAN'S wife, Mary, was working for the magistrate at Derby. Mary was a dutiful wife and a good housewoman. Unusually clean, she had even been known to polish her teeth. A merry soul, she enjoyed a joke whether in "English" or "Native." On Sundays, to see her all dressed up and being escorted to church on the arm of Duncan was dimly to realize to what heights our black brother can rise. Mary was an acquisition to the magistrate's household, and particularly so to Duncan. Much rich food, plenty clothes and tobacco, did she bring home to the aboriginal camp to him. He was relieved of all the responsibilities of life. All he had to do was to sit around and smoke, and take her to church on Sunday.

Mary fell sick. A peculiar illness; she would fall ill suddenly; return to camp for several days; then reappear at work, quite bright. But she fell ill more frequently, even more suddenly. She fell ill for the last time.

Duncan brooded. Then he disappeared. Bushmen who knew the native mind simply shrugged. These few realized that Duncan had gone bush to seek out the Old Men.

Now Duncan was a highly civilized "boy." He had grown up in the little West Kimberleys port of Derby; had before marriage been in white men's employ, when he designed to work, ever since a boy. He understood the white man, his ways and customs-and the Law! While Mary worked at the magistrate's house, Duncan often yarned with the police sergeant. He had always been on friendly speaking terms with the constables. The haughty police trackers he had cultivated assiduously. He could speak excellent English for an aboriginal; and what he did not know about the white man's queer mentality was of no interest to any native.

Yet, in this crisis of his life, he sought out the Council of the Old Men. In secret conclave they sat, shadows of tall rocks about them, an eagle wheeling in the blue above. They carried the dead woman's body by the Secret ways of the Dead, an almost unbelievable distance. And they came to Mount Marmion, a grim cliffy hill where owls roost in weather-beaten caves. By the last Path of the Dead they skirted the iron-brown cliffs and reached the fiat, barren crests where a few gnarled trees stand out like spectres. Coarse, tufted grass grows scantily there. Desolate, wind-blown platforms like fouled eagles' nests were hanging from the trees.

They built a new burial platform, toiling naked, their scarred, deep-lined faces serious as the immemorial rites of their tribe. In low chant they "sung" the body up on to its eyrie, then around it on the ground carefully arranged a circle of ochred stones. While the Old Men squatted silent with bowed heads, the witch man painted his body with the sacred symbols, then muttered an incantation handed down from past ages by the spirits of the dead. While he did so the Old Men clawed each stone christening it by a "secret" name. Each stone now represented a known and living man.

While these stones that now were men were standing quietly in their places and waiting, the Old Men squatted around, hunched up like withered crows, keeping vigil for many hours in a silence broken, rarely, by a whispering breeze or spirit breath through the pyre above, sometimes by a sibilant hiss, the sharply indrawn breath of a watcher as he invoked the Spirit of Vengeance. The Spirit answered through the hot sun as a drop of grease fell from above and splashed on the stone of Clabby!

The grim Old Men squatted sharply erect, their eyes staring at the greasy stain slowly spreading on the warm stone of Clabby.

With one accord they twisted on their heels and stared from under beetling brows far out over the grey Kimberley bush towards the country of Clabby.

That spot of grease told that, by malign influence, Clabby had poisoned the wife of Duncan.

Clabby lived in the gunyahs of his people near Kimberley Downs Station. He was a lad of twenty, a bright laughing lad, a favourite with the white stockmen as with his tribesmen. Few aboriginals have friends as Clabby had. He even called the birds his friends. There was only one temporary shadow in his bright young life, the absence of his mate, Tommy, employed as stockman on Kimberley Downs.

But soon Tommy would return from the muster; throw off his "white man's" clothes, then stripped and ochred and with feathers in his hair, would seize his spears and go laughing with Clabby on *pinki* (walkabout).

Duncan returned to Derby. No one asked questions. The men smoked and talked as usual at the aboriginal camp but their real talk was in questioning , silences. The women chatted as women do, but their fleeting glances spoke volumes.

Duncan and Paddy, his friend, prepared for a journey, none asked whither or why. They discarded their "white man's" clothes with a gesture creepily suggestive of the triumph of the primitive. They anointed their bodies in the Secret Time and the Secret ingredients were symbols of Life and Death. Then they picked up war-spears and vanished.

As they travelled, they seemed to be what they really were, a part of the bush itself. They spoke but seldom; then only in an interrogative grunt. And the hot bush was silent; no bird called as they passed; their feet made less noise than the fall of a leaf in dry grass.

Back at the Derby camp the tribesmen and their women went about their daily life as usual. Not to a white soul did man, woman, or piccaninny mention the departure of Duncan and Paddy. Surprised ignorance would have answered any question referring to it.

The primitive men stole on. Paddy, like Duncan, was a Christianized native, and an employee of white men. More, by the craft of his bushmanship and his endurance, he had once saved Pollett's life when that constable was perishing of thirst. But now...

At Kimberley Downs they appeared among the gunyahs of the local tribe under the big old trees of the creek that meanders away below the homestead on the hill. After due formalities they squatted down, and after one glance none asked their business. They met Yankee here, as if all three were drawn together by instinctive understanding. So they were, for Yankee had been ordered by the Council of the Old Men to make the third to carry out the Law. Yankee also greased his body with oils which the witch doctor had charmed, then thoughtfully examined the points and barbs of his spears.

The three stayed several days, just yarning among the people as visitors do. They carried war-spears – but travellers in the bush must do that. Then one morning Duncan stretched himself lazily in the sun.

"I think we go walkabout. Might see wallaby." He picked up his spears and leisurely walked away. Paddy followed. "Coming?" grinned Yankee to Clabby as he too stood lazily erect. Eagerly Clabby ran for his hunting-spears. They followed Duncan into the bush.

Coming to a waterhole, a beautiful mirror to the white trunks of the paper-bark trees, Duncan stood idly looking down on the peaceful pool. Paddy sat down and tossed his spears beside him, while Yankee knelt by the pool edge pointing out the little fishes to Clabby. Clabby sat beside Paddy, and Yankee sat back and squatted on the other side of him. It was pleasant, being free men with nothing to do but go out and hunt and kill things. Duncan squatted down-behind Clabby. A dragonfly of brilliant green shot across the pool and hovered over a lily-leaf. Duncan fitted a long spear to his woomera, jerked back his arm and sped the spear straight into Clabby's back.

Clabby leapt high, spun round, and ran screaming as that long-hafted spear wobbled in his back.

"Kill him!" hissed Duncan, "or take this!"

They gazed at the threatening spear then leapt up and raced after Clabby. They killed him, carried the body quite a long way and buried it deep in sandy soil among thick bushes. Then with their fingers and bent knuckles, with soft fluffy grass, by the blowing of their breaths, by the touch of heel or toe, and with the palms of their hands, they carefully obliterated and disguised their tracks right back to the water hole.

Duncan turned to his confederates with an ominous twitching of his spear.

"Don't you talk!" he muttered.

The threat in his bloodshot eyes made the command sink in.

Duncan turned and they followed him back towards camp. When nearing the gunyahs they met a stooped old man, walking with one hand clasped behind his back as the old and bent often do. He smiled a toothless greeting. Duncan stood, his shadow men behind him. The old man's eyes wavered uneasily.

"There is blood upon your spear!" he cackled. "What have you killed?"

"Clabby!" grunted Duncan. "Don't – you – talk."

In the speaking silence the old one's glance wavered, fell. His half-laugh froze to a dull, close-shut face. He slouched quietly away.

They strode into camp and squatted among the gunyahs. No notice was taken of their return; the chattering went on. An old lubra was squatting, grinding grass-seed. Suddenly she peered around.

"Where's Clabby?"

Duncan stared her in the eye.

"He has gone to Napier Downs Station," he said slowly.

In the hushed silence they waited until the old woman's glance fell; with trembling hands she rubbed the stones that grind the grass-seeds into flour. Then the whole tribe knew that Clabby had "gone to Napier Downs."

Several days later the three left camp. They walked bush for half a day without a word. Then Duncan turned on them.

"You two men go *pinki*," he said deliberately. "Stay away a long, long time. And ... don't – you – talk!"

They gazed a moment, then abruptly turning strode away south-east towards the desert fringe. Duncan watched them until they disappeared away into the Pindan. Then he turned towards Derby and civilization.

Time passed by in the dreamy way of the bush.

Tommy, the friend of Clabby, returned from his station job and eagerly sought his mate.

"Where Clabby?" he asked soberly.

"He go Napier."

Tommy looked the man in the eye; a hush came upon the camp.

Eagerness vanished from Tommy's face. Slowly he walked across to an old lubra squatting on skinny haunches as she ground grass-seeds into flour.

"Where Clabby?" he demanded sharply.

"He go longa Napier!"

"No more!"

"Maybe. Maybe something happen!"

In the silence the grinding of her stone sounded harsh and loud.

Tommy turned abruptly and walked "bush." He returned at evening and squatted among the gunyahs. The life of the camp went on. But in the days and nights to come the silent Tommy learned many things; never directly; no one ever told him a word. A chance remark here, a grunt there, a long silence there, an innuendo from one lubra to another, the handling of a weapon as a warrior sat absent-mindedly by the fire, the flutter past of a spirit bird and the interrogative raising of eye-brows. No one ever told Tommy a thing, but presently he knew everyone who had visited camp during his long absence, everything that had happened-that anyone there knew. But-no one talked!

By day Tommy sought tracks, finding none. Instinct guided him to a waterhole. Water plays a vital part in every aboriginal's life, all things start from, or end at-water. Round this hole he circled in ever widening circles, patiently, day by day. The cunning of the guilty, the wind and weather, had washed out all tracks. But he knew, by the time that elapsed between their leaving the camp and return to it, the distance the four blacks had probably walked that day. So day by day he searched carefully in ever widening circles. His eyes never left the ground; his nostrils were ever smelling for things. He found his mate.

Now Tommy was civilized too; but he discarded the tribal law of a life for a life and hurried to civilization for his revenge. Eventually the station people saw a police patrol travelling through Kimberley Downs: Constable Hawes with his horses and packmules and trackers.

Paddy and Yankee were still "bush" on their *pinki* staying bush a long, long time.

But the patrols of the white man's law can reach to three thousand miles in the back country; and they, too, can stay bush a long, long time.

Duncan again cast off his clothes and went *pinki* from Derby. On feet of sinew and leather he travelled the seventy miles to Kimberley Downs in little more than a night, and came to the gunyahs of Clabby's people. The life of the camp went on; everyone thought of something else when Duncan squatted amongst them. They did not talk.

But one old gin could hold out no longer. She had loved Clabby. The arm with which she ground her grass-seed flour was trembling as she croaked at Duncan:

"Pleeceman come! He dig up Clabby! He look longa tracks. Maybe he look longa *you*!"

Duncan slowly fitted a spear to his wommera while he glared down into the bleared old eyes.

"You – no – talk!" he hissed. She waited with trembling lip but the spear thrust did not come. Duncan wheeled on his heel and strode swiftly away.

He hurried back to Derby, this highly civilized Duncan. At Derby he washed off the goanna fat and ashes and ochre; put on trousers, shirt, coat, and boots; washed and combed his hair. Then strolling along to the police station, he marched straight into the sergeant's office.

"You know me long time now, Mr Tuohy?"

"Yes, Duncan, I have."

"You know my wife Mary belonga me, she work longa magistrate before she die."

"Yes, Duncan."

"You know me good boy, me good citizen!"

"Yes, Duncan."

"You know me no more killem man, me civilize man?" He hung on the sergeant's answer:

"Yes, Duncan, you civilized man."

"Those feller longa Kimberley Downs say I kill Clabby. He friend belonga me! You no believe that Kimberley Downs nigger!" he added scornfully.

Sergeant (now Inspector) Tuohy is a highly civilized man. He put down his pen and leaned back in his chair yawning. Mopped his brow for it was a hot day. His clear blue eyes gazed speculatively at Duncan.

"No, Duncan, me no more believe him. You want him job Duncan?"

"Yes, Mr Tuohy."

"Right, Duncan. I get you job longa hospital. Good job there."

The patrol found Paddy and Yankee far out in the Pindan. And Tuohy arrested Duncan just when he wanted him.

Duncan only got a short term in gaol, the killing was "tribal," and civilization let him off lightly. Duncan lives at Derby now. But the spirit folk are whispering for vengeance: "He who slays, must be slain." Duncan clings close to the police station. Gloomy dreams have warned him of a sitting of the Council of the Old Men.

9
JACARRIE

THERE was no doubting Jacarrie's gameness and resource. From being a lone wolf he had gathered fifty spearmen around him, and to hold them had launched out into cattle-spearing on a wholesale scale.

And at nights around the cooking-fires, to the odour of good roast beef, he boasted that as the whites had taken their country to feed cattle, he would take the cattle to feed them! Their throaty approval was music to his ears. Soon he would be leader of the largest band of cattle-spearers that had ever harassed the Kimberley stations.

A powerful buck Jacarrie, with the savage face of the fighting aboriginal. There was some justification for his complaint too, but it was not all just. There is ample country for the blacks in the Kimberleys. And plenty of work; some stations feed one hundred natives each. Along the entire length of the Fitzroy River the aboriginal likes work.

Men of Jacarrie's breed from the ranges though, seek work spasmodically. No blame to them. At nearly every station a beast is killed regularly for these "bush blacks," so that they may have no excuse for interfering with the cattle. Besides, the Western Australian Aborigines Department keeps three stations for the feeding of aborigines alone. Jacarrie was quite justified in saying that in the dry season the stations desired the waterholes for their stock. But not *all* the waterholes. And he could have added that there is no lack of animal and plant food in the Kimberleys. It would have been against his wild ambitions to have done so. Instead, he sought new recruits, and the discontented and adventurous came dribbling in with shovel-bladed spears and tomahawks and knives of iron. Well-equipped men these of the "modern" aboriginal age – no stone knife and wooden spear with its point hardened in the fire.

Those shovel-bladed spears (shovel-nosed they are generally called) are by far the most efficient weapon the aboriginal has evolved. They are assagais, as deadly as any handled by the Zulu. The long iron blade is firmly attached to an eight-foot haft. The blade is sometimes eighteen inches long and often six inches broad, point and long edges craftily sharpened. Such a weapon will easily kill a bullock, its great cutting blade simply ripping him up, shearing the organs wide as it passes into and sometimes right through the body. If not mortally hit he quickly bleeds to death once the blade enters his body. Needless to add, these assagai blades make an awful mess of a man. Among the bush natives, the demand for iron is very keen. They will travel long distances to obtain by threat or barter any old scraps of iron from the station natives.

But Jacarrie was riding for a fall. It only wanted a white stockman to ride on this crowd while at a killing and they would fill him with spears. In that way many a Kimberley native outlaw has started on his career.

Such, in October of 1925, was the fiercely avowed intention of Jacarrie, fighting man of the hills. He swore he could defy any number of police when once in the caves honeycombing the big limestone ranges, as Pigeon did for three years. Such men as Pigeon, Lillimara, Captain, Banjo, Major and others fought not only with the spear but the rifle too. Daring horsemen, they were familiar with the life of the isolated whites and the methods of the police patrol.

No notice is taken of the natives spearing an odd beast now and again. But when they start on a wholesale scale and that within cooee of the homestead ...

It would be better for all concerned if a police patrol could catch Jacarrie in the act and put him in gaol a few months for unlawful possession of beef. The band then would probably break up and scatter and no lasting harm be done.

And now Constable Walter's patrol was hot on the trail. Lansdown Station had sent word to Fitzroy Crossing police station of a very serious raid. With Trackers Moses, Junucubine, and Joe, the patrol rode on through a beautiful Kimberley day; bright sunlight bathing the rugged Sir John Range, the melodious call of a butcher-bird ringing through the timber, the horses plodding along as old stagers do.

Tracker Joe reined in his horse to point at the paunch of a steer lying in the bed of a creek.

"Plenty feller men been spear 'im," said Moses pointing to the tell-tale tracks. "Plenty women and piccanin too – That one feller Jacarrie!" he pointed triumphantly to a footprint.

"This feller one Daylight!" added Joe as he leaned over his horse's neck.

Walter stared down at the imprints that to his trackers betrayed the owners as plainly as a fingerprint betrays a white identity.

"Which feller way you know him track belongs Jacarrie?"

"I know him alright," grinned Moses confidently. "Can't miss him that one Jacarrie. I know him long time. That feller toe belong him more big than nother one! I know him that one track belonga Daylight, and that one belonga Larry," pointing as he spoke.

"Three notorious cattle-spearers," mused Walter, as he read the story of the broken spears where the steer had put up a great fight.

He gazed around. They were in a wide valley between rocky ridges grey with scrub. This valley seemed to lead into the deeper mountains. In there, he knew, was ideal country for a game of hide and seek, of ambush and defiance. Still farther back were the King Leopolds and once in that jumble of precipices and caves, pursuit would be hopeless.

A wild shout came ringing through the trees from behind a ridge to the south. The trackers sat bolt upright, the horses listening prick-eared as an answering shout came joyfully from the east. Walter immediately rode his horse towards a cadjibut thicket, the trackers hurrying the pack-animals deep in among the trees. They listened then as, fainter now, there came hulloaing voices from the east, west, and south. The patrol had come from the north. Listening, they sat their horses, ready for a gallop should the alarm come. But the voices all passed by. The hunting band, unsuspicious of a travelling patrol, were gathering for the feast.

They secured their outfit to handy trees, then sat listening to the diminishing hulloaing. Those echoes carried a ring of triumph, of security, of anticipation. Alertly Walter listened lest a changing timbre in the voices betray that some latecomer from the north had discovered their tracks.

They spoke in whispers; no smoking, for the aborigines possess a sense of smell keen almost as animals. One whiff of tobacco-smoke might carry betrayal a mile, even the odour of a sweating horse may cause alarm.

Within that dense thicket, evening brought tormenting mosquitoes. Silence otherwise, save the rustling of some native cat, the movement of an uneasy horse. Both horses and men suffered thirst, but dared not seek water lest they stumble on a waterhole occupied by Jacarrie's band.

At nine in the evening a chant of voices filtered dimly through the cadjibut leaves.

"Blackfeller corroboree now, boss!" whispered Moses. "Plenty blackfellow have big corroboree, eat him plenty beef."

Which meant that the confident Jacarrie had thrown caution to the winds. The patrol crept out of the thicket among ghostly trees to hear the roar of men's voices, the shrill chant of women, the snarling of dogs over bones.

"Blackfeller busy now, boss," muttered Moses.

"All he thinkem been eatem bullock! He have em big fellow tuckout; by an' by he knock up longa corroboree, too much tuck out *longa* beef. He sleepy feller by an' by."

The patrol crept through the timber, over fallen logs and down into the blackness of gullies towards those growing voices until a shadowed wall seemed to blot out the very night. Fronting this cliff, fires illuminated dancing figures throwing gigantic dancers in shadow form on the cliff face behind. Stamping thunder of feet, hoarse defiance of men's voices emphasized with the drumming of the women. Appetizing smell of roasting beef.

Fronting this cliff was the wide bend of a creek, big trees lining it in rosy relief. From the shadows, Walter and his men crept out towards the creek and found that it entered the wall of the gorge. To run down the creek into this gorge, would mean escape for Jacarrie's men. Walter must make two of his men creep down the creek among the boulders and cadjibut saplings and worm their way past the feasting people, while he blocked this end of the gorge. They could not escape up the cliffs to either side. He strained his eyes towards the shadows behind the fires, mentally placing his men. He whispered his instructions and they nodded understandingly, well versed in native ambuscade. Then in the blackest shadows they settled down to wait until repletion and exhaustion would send the dancers into sleep.

10
JACARRIE'S LAST FIGHT

GRADUALLY the stamping eased down; the singing lessened in volume; the clacking of the wommeras then the drumming ceased altogether. The fires burned low, stars twinkled from a cold blue sky. The night grew chilly; silence enveloped the camp; there sounded a gnawing somewhere followed by the throaty growl of a dog. A frog in deep bass croaked from the rock hole, an owl hooted from away down the gorge. Sleep claimed all things of the day except the patrol, lying there among the cold logs and rocks, shivering the night away.

Just before sunrise, the aboriginal sleeps as if he were dead.

The patrol crept out, each man creeping down into the creek and away to his place, moving in the blackest shadows, alert for any prowling mongrel. Down below the cliff coals glowed like dull rubies. The only sound the rustle of a bandicoot; later a grunt as a cold native sleepily kicked his lubra to poke the family fire together.

Dawn broke, ashen grey. The sky lightened gradually, all wispy with still, grey clouds. Earth shadows dissolved to grey, the cliff face became grey, the trunks, then the branches of trees formed in shape. A bird twittered grumpily only to relapse into silence. A night hawk whistled softly twice and shadows leapt into the camp shouting every man to hurry to the centre and "sit down quiet fellow!" Alarmed howling of dogs then pandemonium in the leaping away of shouting figures to screams of women as Moses shouted "Him Jacarrie! Daylight! Thulonga!" and the scuffle of the trackers springing at the men they knew while the others scattered like monkeys from a broken cage, some even leapt to climb the cliff.

Walter was well satisfied with his prisoners. Jacarrie, Daylight Thulonga, Meerinwunga, Windimie, Poolaplee, well-known cattle-spearers for long past. He made each man point out his camp, in each of which was fresh beef. He charged them with unlawful possession. They listened stonily, their deep-set eyes unwaveringly regarding the patrol man. From shaggy brows they glowered at the trackers as the light police chain was put around their necks. Sturdily built men, health and strength showing from their ash covered bodies. Jacarrie with his deep-set eyes restlessly moving, a swift cunning in his deeply lined face. A taker of chances, this man.

His prisoners secured, Walter looked around in the fast growing light.

The camp was like a butcher's shop, the heads of cows and bullocks, legs and slabs of meat hanging from the trees. Gnawed bones lying among the ashes of every lukewarm fire, numerous stone ovens with meat cooking for the morning. The trackers grinned as they sampled the contents of an oven.

Walter ordered them to collect and destroy a hundred and fifty spears that had been left behind in the hasty flight. He did not like the look of things, and if there was to be any trouble the natives would be handicapped by the loss of these weapons.

A volley of howls from the top of the cliff caused him to stare up at men in wild silhouette shrieking to the captives to fight and make a run for it. The prisoners glanced uneasily around as up there on top a dozen men like painted spiders struggling around a marble were rolling a huge stone to the brink of the cliff. It came toppling over to crash among the trees. The black men had the numbers but above all advantage of position; they were working up their courage for an attack. Walter moved his men well out from the cliff face as smaller stones came hurtling down to a chorus of yells, while the dogs up there seemed about to hurl themselves over the cliff, so berserk was their rage. Walter felt glad he had smashed those spears. The patrol started back for the cadjibut thicket and the horses and the natives followed, running along the parallel ridges with wild leaps culminating in defiantly insulting gestures, shouting encouragement and promise of rescue to the prisoners, the women and piccaninnies running along with a shrill screaming of abuse. Walter breathed easier when his patrol walked *out* of that gorge.

The horses and mules showed prick-eared joy when the patrol arrived and led them from the cadjibut thicket. They had been tied there since three o'clock the previous afternoon and plainly expressed delight on being led away to an open patch and unsaddled. With relieved snorting and shaking of coats they rolled and kicked on the sand then trooped briskly away for a drink. While they were feeding, the patrol watched them sharply while enjoying a longed-for meal themselves. It seemed days since they had watched the billy boiling.

The shouting of the tribesmen had now died away, but they were still visible up on the ridges which lined both sides of the valley. Walter was anxious to get out on to the open country. He had a hundred-mile trip now to the little Fitzroy Crossing police station. As they were saddling the pack-animals some native women and children came diffidently out from the bush and asked permission to accompany the patrol to Lansdown Station. Walter nodded permission.

They rode out towards the open country, and at midday halted by a soak in a creek where the prisoners were fed and all hands enjoyed a rest for an hour. When on the march again Walter ordered Trackers Joe and Junucubine to ride on ahead but away to the right, to a spring at the back of a range and see if there was any horse feed there, preparatory to the night's camp. If not, they were to ride straight for the station homestead, and the patrol would travel straight on without deviating.

The two trackers rode away, watched by the prisoners. But they grunted no remark, just walked stolidly on through the grass ahead of Walter with the pack-animals stringing along behind, Moses away at the rear. Straggling among the trees still farther back followed a score of native women and children. The afternoon shadows came; the bush grew cool. Walter, riding along cheerfully, noticed that one of the pack-saddles was slipping. Calling to the prisoners he motioned them to wait under a shady tree. He caught the pack-mule, dismounted, and commenced restrapping the pack. His horse, in the manner of old bush stagers, mooched away towards the shady tree and commenced cropping grass near the prisoners.

Walter readjusted the pack, and walking towards his horse, motioned the prisoners to move on. They rose to do so and moved off as Walter caught his horse. As he put his foot in the stirrup they sprang at him, Jacarrie shouting "Kill him! Get revolver! Knock him! Kill him!" At the rain of blows from sticks and stones the horse plunged away while Walter's elbow jabbed Daylight's chin and loosened his grip. Walter ducked to dodge that encircling chain while leaping back from their clutching arms. He snatched out his revolver shouting "Back! Back! or I shoot!"

"Kill him!" screamed Jacarrie. A stone split Walter's forehead and he fired amongst their feet, but they still plunged forward jumping to encircle him with the chain as he sprang back and back and back. A stone loosened his teeth and he raised the revolver and – it misfired! With distorted faces they clawed at him while he kicked and punched and twisted to keep that chain away. They ripped his coat and snapped the buckle off his belt. Through the ringing in his ears came thundering hooves as Moses galloped up and hurled himself upon the shrieking men. They grabbed his throat and pulled him down and savaged him while clawing at the desperate Walter struggling to get his revolver to work, to brush the blood from his eyes. Into the fight screamed a native woman Jennie who brought a stick down upon the men throttling Moses, screaming:

"You stop! No more kill 'im policeman; no more kill 'im!"

She warded off a stone but missed a stick which thumped heavily on

Walter's head. He went down and the revolver exploded, Jacarrie falling heavily across him as Moses wrenched free and with the lubra rained blows on the men fighting on Walter's body. They beat them back, they crouched there at bay on the chain, Jacarrie gasping his life away across Walter's legs. But he was game. Walter regained consciousness to dimly feel Jacarrie stir; then heard his hoarse gaspings:

"Kill him! Him close up dead feller! ... Finish ... him! Gun ... no ... good!"

But the dying man's comrades had not his pluck.

They shivered there on the chain, snarling up into the bloodstained faces of Moses and the woman.

Jacarrie had killed his last bullock; fought his last fight.

The Patrol.

11
WHERE THE PROSPECTOR SLEEPS

THIS job would need the very best trackers available. Mounted-Constable Birt of Beltana wired Smith at Farina to meet· him immediately with Tracker Fred. Then Birt sent for Claypan George and Little Bobbie, and treated the patrol horses to corn and oats.

Beltana is a little town towards the north of South Australia on the north to south railway, three hundred and fifty-three miles inland from Adelaide. Farina, a tiny place farther north still.

"Charlie the Mailman" had driven into Beltana with news that old Harry Hemming was missing. Charlie ran the mail out east to the scattered stations. Past Frome Well Station, by a big old gum-tree beside the lonely track was the rendezvous where Hemming used regularly to meet the mail and receive his stores. But on this last outward trip the old man was not there. Charlie had hung the rations up in the tree out of the way of dingoes, then proceeded on his way. On his return trip the rations were still there.

Riding out to the tree, the police discussed Hemming. A quiet old chap with a fixed purpose. Years ago, while still a young man, he had claimed to have discovered a rich gold-reef out in the McKinlay Ranges. Partly because of its inaccessibility in those days, but finally owing to the drying up of water, he was forced to abandon his find. He started back for Beltana, but was picked up unconscious on the mail-track and carried to Frome Well Station. There he was nursed back to health. He promised his benefactors that "someday" when the country was opened up a little more he would return, relocate the reef, and reward his good Samaritans with a share in the find,

Well, he had returned after many years. He was nearly sixty now. Some of his rescuers had crossed the Great Divide, still he was determined to repay his debt to the living and to the descendants of those who had gone before.

Hemming's camp was at a spring somewhere in the hills. He had made arrangements with people at the Frome to forward his rations and meat with the mailman every Sunday. And along the track somewhere near his camp he used to wait for Charlie the Mailman with the regularity of clockwork.

When the police arrived, the rations were still up in the tree; a goanna scuttled away from the meat-bag.

"This looks serious!" said Birt.

"He has fallen ill and died in camp," suggested Smith, "or else he's met with an accident out in the ranges."

"Which means the same thing!" replied Birt as he gazed at row after row of parched, barren hill crests.

A shower had blotted out all tracks. Half a day passed before Little Bobbie's shrill hail sounded from away in the bush. He had found an old heel-mark imprinted in soft, retaining ground. Eagerly the scattered trackers converged on that heel-mark. There is no human being on earth that can follow a trail with the insight and patient tenacity of the Australian tracker, once he puts his mind to a job.

That dim trail led them to a maze of stunted, half-burned tea-trees. No trace could possibly be left in this blackened desolation, so the trackers worked by deduction. He must have gone straight through this scrub before a passing fire set it alight. The trackers went straight through too.

The police chopped a way for the horses through the charred and tumbled mass leaving the trackers to worm their way ahead and be free for the task of picking up the tracks on the farther side.

One quiet afternoon they came to a tent on a grassy rise overlooking a quiet pool fed by a spring. Around the tent the undergrowth had been cleared away. Nearby was a neat bough shed, and kitchen of brush. An air of deathly stillness pervaded this lonely camp. The tent-flap was fastened.

"He will probably be dead on his bunk," murmured Birt as he unlashed the flap.

But the neatly made up bunk was empty, the blankets spread and tucked in without a wrinkle; his clothes were clean and neatly folded; the floor was swept; everything was tidy and scrupulously clean. They walked back to the kitchen and saw that here, too, was "a place for everything with everything in its place." Only the man was missing.

One billycan was missing from the neat set, and they could find no prospecting dish and pick. But the most careful searching failed to reveal a clue as to which direction he had gone from his camp.

"He has taken some rations, his tools, probably also a blanket and water-bag, and gone searching for his El Dorado," decided Birt. "And from this trip he has not returned."

"Evidently made this spring his base camp," said Smith, "and from here searched in all directions, carrying enough food for four or five days during each trip."

"Yes," mused Birt, "he was at the tree every Sunday to meet the mailman. Allow him another day per week in camp for cooking, etc. That would leave him five days at most. He would not be away from camp more than five days on anyone trip. If he has broken his leg, he would ration what food he had left. Missing over a fortnight now, there is a faint chance that he is still alive."

Smith added: "Apparently he was a good bushman, or he would have been lost before this. It looks like an accident. If so, he would have to be able to crawl to a waterhole. Few and far between in this country. If not near enough, then he died of thirst more than a week ago."

"I'm afraid so. Still, there has been that storm which washed out his tracks by the tree at the road. It may have left a few days' water in shallow depressions in the rocks. There is the faintest hope."

"This probably is the very water hole he was camped at years ago. It must have been a particularly dry season that dried this spring up."

"We'll make this water our base for the horses," decided Birt. "There is good grass here. It's going to be a job!"

They gazed around at the low, steep hills, massed battalions of them spreading away to the plains. Far distant could just be seen the majestic blue of the Flinders Range. A flock of birds came whirring to the spring to drink.

"I would not care to be lost anywhere out there!" said Smith. "We'd better put the billy on."

All hands searched in the morning, going in different directions and gradually circling the camp in an attempt to cut the tracks. At sundown each man returned tired and a little bow shouldered. The prospector had disappeared as if the earth had swallowed him.

"Never mind, boss," said Claypan George cheerily, "we find him that fell a track tomorrer alright!"

But it was a week later before an excited shout came faintly through the trees. Scattered among the timber each man listened, then hurried towards that echoing shout.

It was four miles from camp, half-way up a stony ridge, just the scratch of a boot-nail on a flat ironstone pebble. The three trackers grouped around this tiny clue were as delighted as the police. It was the start; it gave them direction. No bloodhounds in the world could have located that nail-scratch with all scent of the track washed out by the storm.

The country was impossibly rough for horses; the entire job was done on foot. Day by day the trackers led the police down into precipitous gorges, up razor-back spurs, across scrub entangled gullies and slippery ravines.

"Surely no white man has ever been here before!" exclaimed Smith as one day they gazed over a tangle of nature at her maddest.

"There's no telling," replied Birt soberly. "The white race have wandered all over the globe. I shouldn't be surprised at anyone finding an empty meat-tin at the North Pole, or an empty tobacco box in the loneliest jungle in Malaya."

Days later they found the plainly read story of the search for the lost reef. Every outcrop of quartz, "blow," lode formation, or ironstone had pieces broken from it by the prospector's pick. On any likely looking auriferous locality he had left his mark in the shape of broken stone; searching doggedly; trying to call back the memory of years. Where quartz or ironstone cut out there would frequently be a long blank, just bush and hills, rocks and trees and gullies but not one trace of the man. At such times the trackers would sit down and talk and smoke, discussing among themselves as to which direction "that feller been go!" Occasionally they would sit so for an hour and more; the police never disturbed them; when on such a particular job it is wise to leave the trackers entirely alone. To interfere with their methods or to hurry them is to turn them into sulky dullards intent on failure.

They had lost the trail for several days, when, one morning, descending a steep range, the trackers sat down to pull out their pipes and discuss the latest probabilities. Birt and Smith, climbing the range behind them, suddenly stopped as wild laughter rang out from over the spur ahead. They found Little Bobbie almost in hysterics.

"Old man been tumble down!" laughed Fred showing a matchbox and pointing at a faint scratch on the bark of a protruding root. This, the toe of the old man's boot had struck, he had tripped and fallen and on picking himself up had dropped a box of matches. So again they moved off on the trail, Bobbie still laughing at that weather-stained matchbox in his hand.

"Poor old chap," murmured Smith. "I'm afraid he's a goner."

In another place it was a twig he had snapped that led the trackers on. They stood and gazed all around, then walked carefully on, choosing the easiest way along which a man would have probably walked. Again and again they would pause, to choose eventually one side or the other around a clump of boulders, one detour around a prickly patch of scrub, one most probable way that he had climbed a ridge ahead. Presently they came to a root he had grasped to help pull himself up. Claypan George pointed out where his tugging weight had loosened a little the red earth around the root.

The signs one day led them down into a steep valley paved with stones. There, an occasional boot-nail scratch on a stone led them up this rapidly narrowing valley right to the mouth of a cave. The trackers entered, striking matches. Claypan George then came out to say:

"Old man been camp longa cave three day," holding up three fingers.

"How do you know?"

The tracker pointed to a tiny heap of dried tea leaves outside the cave mouth. It was one heap, emptied from the meticulous prospector's billycan. But on looking closely they saw that the heap was really three heaps emptied one on top of the other.

"Only boil 'em billy one time one day!" And Claypan pointed to the charred stick-ends of a fire, and showed by those charred fragments how they had gone to the making of three different fires.

From this cave the trail led up a rough stony creek for two miles. Only in every two to three hundred yards was there the blurred scratch of a boot-nail upon a stone, but the trackers spread out across the creek and walked confidently ahead scanning the ground.

"They're pretty right going straight ahead," nodded Birt with a glance at the precipitous walls. "The old chap apparently walked straight ahead to find a way out of this creek."

But at two miles up the creek from the cave all trace disappeared as cleanly as if a pterodactyl had swooped down and carried the man away.

For four days the trackers searched the country, while the police returned to the waterhole camp, and trudged back heavily loaded with provisions.

The trackers had found no sign but had drawn their conclusions: "We think um old man bin come back longa tracks then bin go *that* way!" Claypan George pointed south.

Correct. The old prospector had evidently decided that he was too far in this direction for his reef. He had returned down the creek. But where had he left it?

The trackers climbed up opposite sides of the creek, clinging to tree-roots, worming their way around overhanging slabs of rock. It was Little Bobbie with the perfect eyesight who late on the fifth day yelled in that gleeful crescendo of his. Clinging to a root he reached down and held up a little flat stone. Imprinted on it were two faint nail scratches. The other trackers scrambled across to him then tracked right back down into the creek, proving the prospector certainly had come from there. Birt and Smith, looking up and over the steep spur which there formed that bank of the, creek could just see, far away, the hazy outline of mountains.

"My heavens!" exclaimed Birt, "Has he gone over *there* looking for his reef!"

"He is giving the country a thorough scouring," mused Smith. "After all, no man could come back to a tangle of hills like this and after twenty years walk straight to one tiny reef. A needle in a haystack would be easier to find."

They climbed the spur, so rocky that nail scratches were detected here and there right to the top, then plainly saw the mountains looming behind the low, rugged hills.

"Well," decided Birt after a spell, "we'll scramble along behind with all the tucker we can carry, and leave the trackers unloaded to carry on with their job."

With infinite patience and complete certainty they tracked right across to the mountain range, sleeping, as from the start, on the tracks. Of nights now the ranges rang to the howls of dingo packs.

"Fancy a man camped alone in a place like this!" said Birt. "Those wild dogs all around him."

"If they haven't driven him crazy it is a wonder," replied Smith as he stirred the fire. "He seems to have been a steady, methodical old chap, though; not easily ruffled."

The first spurs of the range rose straight up, a barrier forbidding in its desolate loneliness.

"'Abandon hope all ye who enter here!'" quoted Birt as, away below the trackers, he and Smith toiled slowly up. With many a "breather" they reached the top of the range to hear wild yells, then see the silhouetted trackers with waving arms and kicking legs pirouetting in a fantastic dance.

"They've found him!" exclaimed Birt as they hurried forward to renewed antics from the trackers who slung their arms around one another and stamped and yelled in corroboree. They wheeled around and three arms shot out pointing straight across a canyon.

From a ledge high up on the opposite wall there drooped a red blanket!

They climbed down into and crossed the canyon, but to reach that blanket they had to scramble a long way down the canyon then climb a zigzag course. They got a long way up, marvelling at a man climbing such a place as this, when suddenly Tracker George yelled and from the twisted roots of a tree snatched up a hat and waved it.

"Old man bin come longa this place after sun bin go down," he explained. "Rain come; plenty wind! Old man loseum hat. Can't find 'em. Get him dark time! Old man bin crawl along big fella hill, try find 'em place look out camp."

They worked their way along the canyon side until it formed a ledge, a rocky hill-side rising on their left, a cliff rapidly forming to their right.

"It must have been an awful night!" said Smith.

"Evidently sunset came before he could reach the top. Probably sunset was blotted out by the storm, and it grew suddenly dark leaving him away up here. Apparently he groped his way along this ledge. What a miracle he didn't fall over!"

"Ah!" exclaimed Birt. The ledge ended, blocked by a boulder. There was the red blanket, lying half over the cliff face. Here was where the old prospector had lain himself down for his last sleep. Blocked in every direction, his groping hand feeling only vacancy on one side, in the wind and rain he had spread his red blanket and sought sleep. At break of a grizzly day he awoke, threw back his blanket, sat up, yawningly rubbed his eyes, stood up – and with one step plunged down into eternity.

They worked their way back along the ledge to seek him, leaving a tracker to direct. They had to go far down the canyon and make a detour through tangled scrub to get below the cliff, taking their direction while in the scrub from the shouts of the tracker above.

Below the cliff bottom was a steep slope. Here the old man's body had struck and shot straight through bushes as he thumped down the incline. Following the trail of the broken bushes they picked up a pocket-knife, then a pipe, tobacco, and a box of matches, then a torn waistcoat in a broken bush. Scrambling still farther down, broken bushes mutely directed them into a precipitous gully. And there, at the foot of a huge tree whose gnarled roots had caught the debris and flotsam of many a storm, was the writing on the earth where Hemming had finally landed.

He had not been killed outright, for there lay a badly torn flannel, an undershirt, and a belt. Here, after recovery, he had propped himself against those big old roots and taken off these clothes to see the extent of his injuries.

There were the marks too, the trailing roots of a vine, a pulled out tuft of grass, a broken bush where he had dragged himself up out of that gully, and there was the trail through long coarse grass where he had tried to drag himself down into the canyon. Presently they came on those signs which showed where he had died. But the body was gone. The trackers pointed across the canyon.

There, plain upon the rocks and at the entrance to caves, sitting up watching them were many dingoes, mothers with puppies among them.

They followed the trail downward for quite a distance where the body had been dragged, until they saw the skeleton gleaming white, clean picked. The legs had been fast caught between the roots of a leaning tree.

One leg-bone and arm were broken; the skull was uninjured.

His bones lie buried there on the canyon side.

Perhaps his spirit awaits to guide some earthly prospector to the mine.

12
THE TALE OF THE TRACKS

THE good folk of Oodnadatta were retiring; every here and there a light would go out in the little whitewashed town. A black night and very cold. A dog barked at a wandering camel lumbering past somebody's backyard.

This South Australian township, six hundred and eighty-eight miles inland from Adelaide, would soon no longer be railhead. Construction gangs were building the line two hundred and eighty miles farther north to Alice Springs, capital of Central Australia.

An urgent knocking aroused Constable Virgo. It was the station master calling:

"Train robbery, Virgo! Frank Jones, manager for Wallis Fogarty, has been robbed of a kit-bag containing over £3000, apparently at the Sixty-one Mile Construction Camp. Word has just come through by portable telephone from Wire Creek. No particulars."

"And the train is travelling on?"

"Yes."

Virgo pulled his clothes on over his pyjamas, hurried outside and dragged Tracker Bob from his bed.

"Quick! Put trousers on!" he ordered. "Man been stealem money longa train. We got to catch him. Find him quick!" Virgo ran inside for pistol and handcuffs as the roar of a racing car came straight for the police station. Constable Spilsbury leapt out shouting: "Robbery, Virgo, from construction train Sixty-one Mile Camp. She stops next at the Twenty-one Mile."

"Beat her to it!" ordered Virgo as they leapt aboard.

That was a wild drive in pitch darkness: over a bush track disappearing among sandhills to emerge on stony flats, then suddenly break up in the boggy ruts cut by the drays and trucks and camel-wagons of abandoned construction camps. Twice they screeched around into their own dust as Spilsbury dodged logs in front.

"Make haste slowly fast as you can," urged Virgo.

"Tracker Bob's eyes must be nearly falling out!"

"His brains will fall out," answered Spilsbury grimly, "if we hit a tree!"

They pulled into the Twenty-one Mile as the train steamed in, leapt off the car and boarded her. Searched the train and passengers' swags, without avail.

The crew told Virgo that Jones had left his kitbag a moment unattended in the guard's van at the Sixty-one Mile. When he returned it was gone. Jones was waiting there now, the train had come on.

A construction material train was due going on up the line; Virgo and the tracker jumped aboard leaving Spilsbury to follow in daylight with the car.

The Sixty-one Mile Camp was situated in a deep hollow between the Hamilton sandhills and the engine-driver dare not stop his labouring train. He slowed down to ten miles an hour and Virgo jumped out rolling down an embankment with the tracker on top of him to hear a surprised:

"My God! how did you get here? I *am* glad you came!" And there was the shadowy form of Jones bending over them telling his story, with no inquiry at all as to whether they were hurt. Virgo listened, made his inquiries, then turned to Tracker Bob:

"We have got to find the men and we have got to find that money. Understand?"

The tracker shivered sulkily.

"We find 'em alright," he growled. "Daylight we see 'em tracks!"

In a shivery dawn Virgo was searching the camps close by the line when the tracker came and mumbled:

"Me been findem tracks belonga two fella. Him been go dat way (east) and den dat way (north). One fella he carry somethin'."

Close beside where the guard's van had stood the previous night he pointed out the tracks. Peering at the ground he walked the faster as the warming sun rose and the tracks showed their clear impression in detail on the sand. They were sandshoe tracks; one had been made by a new pair of shoes with rough crepe soles; the other impression betrayed ordinary rubber soles almost worn out, several pieces of the soles and heel being broken away.

"He been puttem bag down here," pointed the tracker. "Two feller men been open him!"

There was the impression of the bottom of a kitbag with on each side of it the deep-trod tracks of a man. Delightedly Virgo nodded "Go ahead!" With quickness and just a little luck they might soon finalize this job.

They ran along those tracks for half a mile; then the tracks doubled back to the railway line and there showed that the men had leapt to the sleepers running from sleeper to sleeper and on the iron rails too. This necessitated real tracking. On the sleepers was a layer of dust, fine almost as mist, which occasionally showed a faint imprint. But most of the sleepers showed no trace; the bright iron rails none.

Tracks or no tracks, it was all the same to Tracker Bob. He kept swiftly on, eyes scanning the ground on both sides of the rails, watching for where the tracks would leave the line. A mile farther on he pointed saying:

"Shoes been hurt 'em this feller man! He sit down, takem off shoes. New shoes."

There was the hard-pressed imprint where a man had sat down, the heel-edge marks too where his bending weight had been on the heels.

"He carry 'em shoes now!" said the tracker. They pushed on for two miles, the tracker pointing occasionally at a barefooted track:

"Change him bag here! Arm he tired!" and pointed to two impressions: a heavy right-foot imprint and a heavy left where the men had leaned across the rails, one to hand over the bag and the other to receive it. Several times Tracker Bob showed where they had swopped the heavy bag while still at the run. He showed too, by the difference in depth of imprints between the tracks of the left and right foot, where the barefooted man had changed the bag from the right hand to the left.

It was a fascinating chase, so hot on the quarry and seeing every move as though watching the robbers' actions in a movie-picture show. No matter what these flying men did it was here to be seen as plainly as if carved on rock. Two miles farther on Tracker Bob, becoming better humoured in the warming sunlight, pointed to where "barefoot" had sat on the rail and put his shoes on again. Even though he had been careful this time to place his heel edges on a wooden sleeper, still there were the marks, the faint heel-marks on the dust of the sleeper that betrayed the bent forward weight of a sitting man while he laced up his shoes. When about three and a half miles from the Sixty-one Mile, the tracker suddenly stopped, glancing north then up along the line. The slightly deeper, firmer, and "steadier" tracks of the man wearing the old shoes showed he was carrying the bag, and here were his tracks leaving the line and going north-west towards the sandhills while the "new shoe" man went straight on along the line. They followed the tracks of the bag-carrier across hills covered in places with mulga scrub, eventually coming right down among the gums and box-trees of Hamilton Creek. There on the sandy gravel of the big dry watercourse the tracking was simple and there Tracker Bob pointed:

"That one bag been heaby. That one man him close knock up, him bin all a time change him hand. Him only little bit long way now I tink, might be him close up longa creek!"

Virgo pressed eagerly on, eyes now roaming for a possible sight of their man among the timber. But the tracks crossed the creek then continued west up the bank only to enter the creek again where Bell's Creek junctions.

Three hundred yards farther on Tracker Bob pointed with a triumphant grin. Virgo, staring down at marks proving the ground recently disturbed, felt like a man about to win a fortune. He dropped to his knees, dug with his hands, and felt joy when he touched a kit-bag and dragged the gravel-covered thing out. With thumping heart he opened Jones's bag. It contained a loaded automatic pistol, a number of letters, a few shillings in silver and copper, and £5 9s. 6d. in postal notes.

Where was the £3000?

Swiftly they followed the trail now leading to the east bank of the creek. There they stared at tracks of new shoes; the second man had rejoined his mate. The tracks showed that they had stood a very short time and talked, then turned and walked straight across country.

Virgo and the tracker followed, and hearing the creak of huge wheels saw, just ahead, a camelwagon loaded with water-tanks. To the directing shout of the teamster the lumbering beasts were pulling up under a box-tree. Virgo followed the tracks right to this camel-wagon where they had been stamped out under the camels' great pads. While Virgo made inquiries of the teamster, Tracker Bob walked to the head of the camels and picked up the tracks again. North-east over low stony hills the tracker walked slowly, with thoughtful expression studying the ground. Virgo followed in an agony of silent impatience, knowing that for the first time the tracks were lost.

The now hard ground was thickly paved with stones. Tracker Bob stood, his eyes intensely concentrated and with the lids all screwed up staring out over the bush-covered ground ahead, inch by inch, foot by foot, yard by yard, to his limit of close vision. Then he walked as a stalking cat might while staring at the ground right and left. Again he halted and stared ahead. Onward again; then turning left he slowly moved in a half circle, and after twenty steps pointed to the ground.

He had cut the tracks! A little stone lay there nearly turned over; the weight of a man had forced it from against its fellows, leaving exposed its light under brown part where previously it had rested upon mother earth. Again and again Tracker Bob lost the tracks; again and again he cut them. Sometimes a faint mark between two stones would betray where toe-tip or edge of heel had just touched the ground between and slightly displaced the stones. Then the trail would be lost for one hundred yards or so, until Tracker Bob found a little stone quite turned over by the hurrying weight of a man; he would lose it again only to point to a stone showing a distinct break away from the firm soil surrounding it where a slipping foot had pushed it out of position. He would lose it yet again, then find a pebble pressed into the ground where the soil under it was softer than the surrounding earth. Eventually they tracked down a hill and saw below them the gleaming ribbons of the railway line; beside it a single row of tents with black dots of men working on the line. Plainly there came up to them the clang of the blacksmith's hammer. The tracks led straight to this camp, then between two tents, and turning, disappeared under a closed tent-flap. When Virgo entered, the first things he saw were two pairs of sandshoes, one a new pair freshly worn, the other old, frayed, and very much worn. Red dust adhered to the soles of both while grains of sand were caught between the cracked soles of the older shoes.

Virgo found out who slept in this tent and the one adjoining, and had both men brought to him separately. The first man told a fearless and good story of where he had been with his mate the night before; he told the time and the directions they had taken which entirely disagreed with what Virgo had been told by the tale of the tracks. Virgo showed him the new shoes. Yes, they were his; but he denied wearing them the previous night. His tent floor was dug up unavailingly, only £7 was found in his pockets. He was sent back to work and the second man brought up. He was fearless too and told a plausible story; but it did not agree with his mate's and was totally at variance with the story told by the tracks. He denied, too, ever owning or wearing the old shoes. (How could he decipher the grin on the face of the tracker standing near by!) A search of his tent realized only 16s.

Then Virgo questioned them both together, with facts that he knew, and they looked startled and soon were confused and could only answer "I don't know," or "I forget." Virgo sent them both back to work. He felt sure of his men but he had to prove they were responsible for the robbery; he had to find the money too.

"That money is about here somewhere," he said to Tracker Bob. "They have taken it away and hidden it. Find their tracks where they left the tents."

The tracker grinned.

"I know him now alright, I been see em boot young feller been wear!" He walked around the tent and pointed: "Two feller go this way boss."

They followed these tracks back over stony ground all the way to Bell's Creek then up along the creek to a sturdy box-tree. And here were knee and toe-marks where men had been kneeling by an old rabbit burrow. Virgo lay down and reached his arm far into the burrow and his clutching hand closed on £1684 in £10, £5, £1 and 10s notes. They followed the tracks leading away from the tree, and these led them across country right back to Hamilton Creek and there, under a gum-tree, were impressions on the ground where two men had sat down, and one, wearing old sandshoes, had changed them for boots.

"This one same man you talk to longa camp, boss," said the tracker pointing towards the boottracks. "That long feller man, you ask him question last time."

"Yes, but where is the rest of the money. We have only found half!"

"Tracks go back longa camp," said the tracker thoughtfully. He was leaning against the gum-tree, his black brow wrinkled, dreamy eyed, his lips tight shut. Suddenly he laughed at the trunk of the tree then pointed to the boot-tracks. "He dam fool, he been climb tree. Money along tree alright!"

Virgo gazed at the boot scratches on the bark of the tree. Tracker Bob climbed up to a hollow and put his arm in while Virgo smiled to the assured laugh on the face above.

"Him here alright!" And the tracker threw down £1414 3s. 6d. in bank-notes and cheques. This made a total of £3103 18s. 8d.

But there were still some tobacco-tins containing silver missing. They followed the tracks back and these led them to where they had seen the camelwagon pulling in early that morning. The big beasts were lumbering about under the trees and had obliterated the tracks again but they picked them up farther on and followed them right back to the camp.

But that £35 in silver Virgo could not find. He arrested his men when Spilsbury arrived with the car, and brought the money and prisoners back to Oodnadatta, just nineteen and one-half hours after the robbery had been reported. His little police band had travelled a hundred and sixty miles by car, train, and foot.

The prisoners were convicted and sentenced.

Virgo, when the release of the first man drew near, was called away on a job and only returned some hours after the man was discharged.

A man went to Bell's Creek, and from a hollow in a box-tree, and from under a large stone, took four tobacco-tins full of silver.

The empty tins were found by the police, hot on his tracks; but this time there was no camel-wagon to blot out those tracks.

13
SEEKING MOODOORISH

HOFFMAN stared around – seeking – listening. Near by grew a gigantic banyan from whose overspreading branches aerial roots like grey snakes writhed down to grip the earth. Around its base and as far out as its branching rootlets could reach, the fantastic tree had throttled every vegetable thing. Silent menace quickened the twist of those grasping roots. Hemming in the banyan-tree as if to choke it in turn grew this jungle of giant-bamboo. Hoffman jerked around at a thud! thud! thud! Breathing relief, he listened to the crackling in there among the dry leaves.

"A river kangaroo!" he mused. "This labyrinth sounds alive with them."

A rasping shriek then a flutter above made him gasp. He swore in relief as a crane flapped heavily away. Cautiously he wormed his way farther in among the cold stalks while a breeze up above slowly rattled and swayed and creaked the mast-like bamboos. With his senses on edge he crept farther into the maze. What an awful place! Fancy hunting wild men in this! Naked men, with bodies as slippery as the gleaming bamboos. Shadow men, in a hide-out where never a ray of sunlight came to cast a shadow. He might stand right beside a man; a spear might thrust out between these bamboos any second; or some hairy arm clenching stone dagger come groping out behind. Shivering, he crept on, trying to hear all around him, to see all around him.

Mounted-Constable Hemmings's patrol, operating on the upper waters of the Daly River, Northern Territory, were seeking Moodoorish and his shadow Nujooloo for the murder of Renouf at Point Blaze, a hundred miles farther north-west. Young Renouf, wandering around the north seeking material for a book, had chummed up with Jim Nichols, a bushman holidaying in Darwin, and buying a tiny launch had sailed south-west along the coast. Springing a leak, they beached the launch at Point Blaze to repair it. One day while Nichols was walking the shore crab-hunting young Renouf was cooking. From the scrubby bush behind him the tribesman had crept out right, up to Renouf's gun, levelled the weapon at the bending man, and shot him.

And now Hemmings's patrol had been seeking the slippery Moodoorish for quite a time, this last week on foot searching the bamboo thickets of the Upper Daly. But Moodoorish and his shadow man were always just a little ahead. Then the trackers were whispered that

Moodoorish was travelling swiftly back towards Anson Bay, near Point Blaze. Hemmings mounted his patrol and rode fast down into the wild lands.

Hemmings, with Hoffman and Trackers Splinter, Kit, Fred, Charlie, Bogey and the two dogs. Enjoying the time of their lives those dogs; every breeze brought some scent of animal, reptile, or bird to their sniffing nostrils; every mile showed track of wonderful things to chase. A dog's life in this country was life indeed.

Little smoke-puffs occasionally rising signalled the coming of the patrol, the Black's defiance to the White.

Among the plains and scrub thickets by the coast they rode on a hunting party of Brinken tribesmen, who told the trackers that Moodoorish had reached the coast and that his tribesmen had threatened to spear the police. They added with scarcely veiled satisfaction that he and Nujooloo, Cambit, Nudjic, Nanynyah, and others of the band had sworn to cut the kidney-fat out of every tracker they could catch!

"The usual boast," laughed Hemmings when the double threat was interpreted.

They soon found signs that Moodoorish's band had located a prolific hunting-ground and showed no inclination to leave. In various directions were tracks of large bands of hunting men, invariably returning to favourite camping-grounds among the sand-dunes each evening. The patrol established camp beside a grassy creek sheltered by scrub and from here, day after day, rode out on their quest. Several times the coming of night alone saved Moodoorish. Still, he would not leave the locality.

On the evening of 9 June 1929 the patrol rode into camp. While a tracker put the billy on, and Hoffman prepared the evening meal, the others Unsaddled and hobbled the horses out on a little grassy plain, then walked back into camp and hungrily ate a late meal. They stretched out on their blankets with sighs of relief. It was glorious after a hard day's ride to smoke and lie there gazing at the stars, listening to the joking voices of the trackers gossiping around their fire a few yards away and the tinkle of horse-bells out on the plain; inhaling the faint smell of flowers and grass and watching the deepening shadows of the sheltering trees. Away down the creek the deep hoot of an owl was answered after a pause by his mate up the creek.

Between restful silences they discussed the tragedy of young Renouf, the chase, and the probabilities of catching Moodoorish on the morrow. Instinctively, as bushmen do, they listened for the tinkle of a bell to tell them just where their horses were. The aborigines knew they were there, so it was useless silencing the bells. After a refill of pipes they wondered what the boys would be doing in Darwin; whether there was any excitement in town, or out in the back country. Then they wondered how their own people were faring "down south," three thousand miles away. After a musing silence Hoffman yawned, glancing towards the greyish white of his mosquito-net stretched low down between the trees. Then there gradually rose a prolonged, quavering howl that died dismally away. The two dogs rose whimpering uneasily.

"That was a peculiar howl," said Hoffman. "Seemed unusually high pitched for a dingo."

With a growl that rose to a bark the dogs ran out into the night.

"They are more than a match for any dingo," said Hemmings, "but they'll never see him, unless it is the glow of his eyes." Presently the dogs came quietly back. "Think I'll turn in," added Hemmings, "there is a long day's ride ahead of us to-morrow."

The trackers were peering out among the trees as the two white officers settled down under their mosquito-nets. They didn't speak above a whisper again that evening. Bogey smothered the fire to a glow, then the trackers turned in. By and by the patrol slept. The two dogs lay in the ashes, their heads upon their paws, their nostrils occasionally distending, their eyes glowing out into the night. Coldness crept down over the dim camp.

Trackers and "friendlies".

14
THE NIGHT ATTACK

THE stars showed only shadow branches like writhing black snakes, dead brambles, and coarse tussocks of buffalo grass. Then something moved and a starray illumined terrible eyes like an owl's, encircled by broad white rings. No mouth – yes, teeth gleamed from blackness enclosed by a broad white band. The lips closed and the band vanished, camouflaged by the grass. Then the teeth showed again; they opened, and the eyes glared up at the stars as long, quavering howl moaned out over the plain, suggestive of a soul in distress.

It was the signal howl of Moodoorish calling his pack to the attack. The pack listened, and registering the exact position of their leader, snaked forward to encircle the camp.

They were invisible. The Australian aboriginal had learned the secret of camouflage centuries before the Great War taught us the primitive necessity. These men were snaking their way through bush: some crept on a plain out from both banks of the creek; others moved in scrub nearer the creek; some crept among the creek timber itself. But no matter where each man was he was invisible. Feather-tufts in their clay-daubed hair, bars of white and yellow ochre encircling black bodies, broken stripes down their limbs, broken yellow bars made the black ash-daubed bodies melt into their immediate surroundings. The most jazzily painted ship upon a foggy ocean was not so indistinguishable as these.

And they had plastered various parts with mud to smother the body-odour lest the nostril of some wideawake tracker detect them.

In the dreamy silence from down the creek the old howl hooted again, deep and solemn. One could imagine him sitting there all fluffed up believing that the earth was holding its breath waiting for his mate to answer. She did answer, from up the creek. But both owls had drawn much closer to the sleeping camp.

So did Moodoorish know the exact position of his men closing in on the left and right flanks.

It was almost midnight.

Hemmings struggled back to awakening; some urgent, growling warning would not be denied. Heavy with sleep he opened his eyes, lying motionless. His ears registered a thumping-his dogs' tails! He turned his head, the two dogs were crouched beside his net; but seeing him awake they arose and snarled out to the night, lips curled above threatening fangs, bristles erect upon arching backs.

Hemmings listened, wide awake. Hoffman Was breathing heavily close by. Cautiously he half rose to his elbow, peering through the net. Dull, like vague grey air-spaces below the trees, were the mosquito-nets of the trackers, sound asleep. The dogs growled with an increasing, gurgling rumble that threatened to break into fury. Hemmings gripped his rifle, cautiously lifted one side of the net, and wormed his way out. Cool night caressed his face. He listened to a deathly silence, except for the deep breathing of Hoffman, and the renewed snarling of the dogs now mincing out into the bush as a spiteful cat steps out.

"Who's there?" called Hemmings sharply.

Twenty spears came hurtling in answer; splintering of barbed points striking trees; thud of an assagai blade within six inches of Hoffman's head. Furious charge of the dogs; spits of flame with the sharp cracking of Hemmings's rifle. Billowing thumps of trackers leaping straight up through blankets and tearing mosquito-nets; snaky hissing of spear-hafts clattering between branches and twigs. Startled "Whough!" of Charlie then "Whough!" again as he crashed down amongst bushes. Hoffman leapt out with automatic in hand staring past the flash of Hemmings's rifle.

"Arrh!" grunted Bogey, and writhed low down at the butt of a tree.

Then silence, broken by the soughing hiss of the last spear, answering crack of fire arms, distant barking of enraged dogs. A long silence.

"Who is hurt?" called Hemmings. A moment's pause then Kit's urgent voice.

"Charlie got 'em two spear longa leg. Bogey got 'em spear too!"

Noiselessly alert, they clustered around the wounded trackers: Charlie with a spear through the thigh and another through the leg; Bogey through the arm. His was only a flesh wound, but Charlie's case was serious. While Hemmings and the remaining trackers kept watch, Hoffman cut out the spears and bathed the wounds with Condy's. Not daring to strike a light, for the remainder of the night he was groping for, and pulling by touch, long splinters of mangrove spear-head from Charlie's thigh.

When the dogs returned, growling low, they received such praise as made them again want to charge out into the bush.

"Thank God!" said Hemmings. "There's the tinkle of a horse-bell. The horses are all right so far anyway. If they keep quiet for too long or if they plunge away you will have to stay here with the wounded boys while the rest of us run out and do what we can to save them."

Hoffman nodded. But the horses remained contented all night.

In the dawn they stood among the trees looking in a speaking silence at the bedraggled camp. Six spear-hafts were sticking up through Hemmings's mosquito-net; one broad-bladed spear was buried within six inches of Hoffman's pillow; two long hafts stood at an angle midway down beside his blankets. Spear-hafts stuck up from the ground between the whites, and the trackers' torn nets; several were sticking in the trees; others lay splintered.

Charlie was in a bad way, his eyes drawn and bloodshot, already semi-delirious.

"It might be blood poison," said Hemmings.

"Mangrove wood is poisonous. We will abandon the patrol for the time being and take Charlie to the nearest point on the railway, then return with fresh trackers."

Hemmings took the badly hurt man to Brock's Creek a hundred miles south-east, while Hoffman remained at Tipperary Station shoeing the horses in preparation for the continuation of the patrol.

Hemmings returned with Constables Don and Sargeant and fresh trackers. The much strengthened patrol rode straight back down to the coast.

Moodoorish was over confident. Crowds of natives were hunting in the vicinity, performing triumphal corroborees illustrative of the killing of Renouf and the subsequent defeat of the police. From near and far tribesmen were arriving to witness these stirring corroborees.

Arrived at the coast, the patrol camped on clear country out from a saltwater arm of the sea which, as usual, was hedged by dense mangroves. Next morning over a hundred spearmen collected amongst the mangroves, their howls increasing to a roaring welcome as more excited tribesmen came hurrying in.

With a war-cry out they pranced in war-paint and feathers, leaping and howling as they brandished wommeras while rattling spears and chewing their beards.

Behind the patrol the horses, feeding on an open plain, lifted inquiring heads at this fanatic exhibition.

The warriors leapt into separate, compact squads, stamping in circles, advancing and retiring and advancing again; hoarsely chanting killing threats to the growing thunder of savagely stamping feet that warmed their blood. A horrid, rhythmic thud beat out across the plain from those two hundred feet. Then with one concerted yell thrice repeated they fanned out and from stamping squads were leaping men spreading out swiftly in a crouching race to encircle the camp.

The patrol stood firm; the trackers, big-eyed, shivered a little.

"Now!" ordered Hemmings, "you have not to shoot at men – not unless I shout the order. Aim at the ground six feet in front of them and when I say 'Fire!' then fire rapidly. Ready!"

The rifles rose coolly towards the oncoming warriors.

"Fire!"

Smoke-puffs and quick reports; whistling bullets that chipped the ground then ricochetted and whistled past as sharp reports again whipped the dust ahead. That boomerang line seemed to sway, momentarily hesitate, as some broke and, leaping around, sped back to the mangroves. With hideous yells others turned, followed by yells of frustrated hate as spears sped curving through the air. Then the die-hards turned and fled. In a few moments all had disappeared into the mangroves.

"A bloodless victory!" said Hemmings, smiling

"I thought there was going to be something doing!" laughed Don. "What a mess they would have made of us if they could have got to close quarters!"

Sargeant turned round to the trackers, laughing at their excited faces. They opened their mouths and the watching horses out on the plain listened, big-eyed, to rolling peals of laughter.

The patrol arrested Moodoorish for the murder of Renouf, and Nudjic, Nanynyah, Cambit, and several others for the spearing of Charlie. The tribesmen dogged the patrol for seventy-five miles, but the rear party was not caught napping.

The prisoners were tried in Darwin, but were dismissed and sent back to their own country on the grounds that as they were all implicated and could not be identified in the dark, they could not be witnesses against themselves.

Moodoorish and his band returned in triumph, and the fame of their exploits spread in corroboree from the Daly to the Victoria. Which is quite as it might be. But I could not help thinking in September 1934, how simply an inexperienced man could be bludgeoned to death on that coast. Cochrane and I had rounded Point Blaze and anchored in the mouth of the Finnis River. Canoes almost immediately came off and Moodoorish and his crowd invited themselves aboard the little *Swanee*. Hefty, cheeky bucks, smelling of grease and stale war-paint, their naked bodies a glowing red, polished by powder of the little burnt ant-bed. No cringing aborigines these fellows; savage-faced, their sharp eyes roamed all over the vessel. We were crocodile shooting and were well armed, Their expressive faces noted the fact. All the same, we took no risks night or day.

One afternoon I rowed ashore intent on a shot at a big, old-man crocodile that habitually dozed on a mud bank in a gloomy mangrove creek. I had hardly stepped ashore when Moodoorish strode out from the mangroves. "Tabac," he demanded with outstretched paw. We had already issued the natives with tobacco and food for services rendered during our crocodile-shooting that day. Half a dozen of Moodoorish's band came along to stand grinning on each side of me. Moodoorish hoarsely insisted for more tobacco and his hairy paw seemed threateningly close. I stepped back, swung the rifle unobtrusively to keep his hand from my throat, and glanced swiftly around to see if Cochrane was watching. He was, sitting on the cabin top with a military rifle across his knee, eyeing Moodoorish's companions endeavouring to edge behind me and the dinghy.

The thought then flashed across my mind how easy it would be for any inexperienced man to be murdered along that coast.

The "Swanee" at the mouth of the Finnis River.

15
GRAHAM'S SECOND BULLET

JOE MOODY was so by nature, they said. Actually, so long as money was not in question, he was a normal bushman; a good man too, knew his way about the country. Tall and wiry with tight-shut mouth and unwavering eyes, his gaze became a somewhat disconcerting glare at times. But no one had anything against him, and had it not been for that unfortunate money delusion he would be working now. To this day he firmly believes that Kimberley people owe him £196,000. He staggered the local sergeant by a claim for £40,000.

"Forty thousand pounds!" exclaimed old Sergeant Tuohy. "Forty thousand grandmothers!"

Some of the boys assure me that it all started over a game of "two-up." I believe it started long before, in those mysterious recesses of a man's mind. However, that two-up game was played back in 1926.

Bob Graham then kept the Club Hotel in Derby.

Graham is a happy-go-lucky bushman, a care-free type ready for laughter or sport or fight as occasion necessitates. A man who would lie down and smoke and read on a rainy day rather than walk the veranda and curse the weather. Bob carried a bullet in the lung, a souvenir from the war.

"I only remember it," he would say with a laugh, "when it feels out of plumb. If I had an ounce of lead in the other one it would balance better."

When I saw him in Derby last year he had that balance; but the lead had not shifted the balance of his smile.

Moody had blown into town with a £150 cheque, intent on a drinking holiday. He handed the cheque over the bar:

"Here, will you take this, Bob; the bank is closed. Bank £100 of it for me in the morning, and I'll get busy with the change now."

Graham obliged.

Moody paid a number of debts then started on his spree. It was a thorough one. He was suffering recovery when that two-up game was played. There was a crowd of hard-cases in town and the game speedily rose to bets of hundreds of pounds at a spin of the kip. Moody had a phenomenal run of luck. At the end of the game it would have taxed the resources of a bank to pay him so they paid him with cheques drawn on the "Bank of the Billabong."

When ready to go back to the bush Moody approached Graham for a settling.

"How about that money you owe me, Graham?"

"What money?"

"That £1200."

Graham stared; then laughed, thinking it a joke.

Derby is noted for its practical jokers. But Moody soon convinced him that he was in deadly earnest. Graham then produced his books and proved that instead of him owing Moody £1200, Moody was in his debt to the extent of £13.

Shortly afterwards Moody was sent to an institution for mental observation. There is no telling how that obsession became conviction there. However, in the Kimberleys the incident was forgotten. Time passed and fate brought misfortune to Bob Graham.

"Oh, well, I'll have to grease the old straps again, I suppose!" He rolled up the swag and rode away droving.

Droving in the West Kimberleys is almost all down the great Fitzroy Road. That is the one and only road, anyway. It comes from Wyndham in the East Kimberleys to Hall's Creek, where it meets the road coming from the Northern Territory. Together they meander between rough harsh hills to Fitzroy Crossing and down along the "Old-man" River to little Derby. Most of the West Kimberleys stations are on the banks of this ancient river whose sandy bed is dry during six months of the year.

After a considerable time Moody returned to the bush. Observation had proved him normal except for some harmless delusion of large sums of money owing him.

One day in 1931 Graham was working on an outstation of Upper Liveringa Station when Moody rode up, carrying a rifle.

"Hullo, Tom!" exclaimed the surprised Graham.

"Hullo, Bob."

"Where did you come from?"

"Down river. I'm doing a bit of dogging."

"Any luck?"

"Not bad. Got a good few scalps," answered Moody grimly. "Since that new regulation came in about cutting their ears off I've got to take a strip right down the back now."

"Where's your plant?"

"Down along the river on good grass. The black boy is minding them."

"Well, you'd better stay and have some dinner." Moody accepted, further, he camped there that night. And again he asked Graham for a settling.

Now, Graham had his books with him. He had set his mind on being the proprietor of the Port Hotel, Derby. (He is now, by the way.) He produced these books and went over them carefully, proving again that Moody still owed him £13.

Moody left next day when the droving outfit came riding into camp. They discussed his strange delusion.

"You'd better be careful, Bob," warned the drover.

"Bosh! He's harmless."

"No man with a kink and a rifle is harmless," growled a station-hand; "not in these parts anyway!" And he glanced around at the wild loneliness of the Kimberley bush.

Time passed and Graham was camped at Noora Noora, an outcamp of Liveringa, fifteen miles from the homestead. His offsider was a black boy with two lubras. The little building down among the ridges is of two main rooms with a cemented path around it. One morning Graham was yawning himself awake when he heard a stealthy footstep on the cement. Not the bare feet of a native. He listened and sensed the menace in that tiptoeing step. He leapt up, slung off his pyjama-coat, put on a flannel, snatched his towel, then opened the door.

Moody stood outside. "Hullo, Tom."

"Hullo, Graham."

"Where did you camp last night?"

"Down by the fence. A hell of a camp; ants crawling all over me. Never had a wink of sleep."

"Well, if you wait while I have a bath, we'll have breakfast."

He walked along the house towards the bathroom, feeling a bit grumpy, still hearing the menace in those steps. He was cleaning his teeth when Moody called from outside:

"I came for a settlement, Graham!"

"What settlement?"

"That £1200!"

"Go to hell!" answered Graham definitely, and went on brushing his teeth.

The door was pushed open, Moody stood there with a levelled revolver. Graham saw the look in the man's eyes. Instinct jerked his arm across his chest as he collapsed with the world reeling black. It seemed hours before he awoke, but it was hardly minutes. Moody was fumbling about for something.

"I'll sham dead," thought Graham. "He's not going to shoot again."

Then he felt Moody bending over him, his heavy breath on his face, felt a hot hand grasp his wrist.

"Something's wrong!" thought Graham. "He should not hold my hands like that!"

He struck out, leaping to his feet, hurling Moody backwards. Then he charged with lowered head straight into Moody's stomach.

Moody collapsed, and Graham, leaping over him, ran as he had never run before. Lying on the bathroom floor were two fish-hooks tied together with a short length of line. Moody had intended burying these hooks in Graham's wrists to "handcuff" him.

"I'll sham I'm mortally hit," thought Graham as he ran, "just like that wild bull I shot a month ago. I knew he was mortally hit so I didn't chase him any more. There was no need to."

He staggered to his knees, then leapt up and ran erratically. He staggered again and wheeled at right angles, running drunkenly towards the stockyard fence. As he slipped through he saw Moody coming behind with drawn revolver. He ran up along the fence rails to keep them between him and bullets; then as Moody drew level he slipped through the rails and ran for the shelter of the goat-yard. He shammed collapse there, gazing under his arm at Moody running through the stockyard to get him. He leapt up and ran across the goat-yard and saw the two lubras running for the bush. He shouted frantically; they stopped, gazing behind, ready to run. Moody saw the lubras, hesitated, then stood, uncertain as to how many blacks might be about and how soon they might run to some nearby stockmen. He gazed searchingly at Graham huddled across there against the rails, evidently dying. Then he turned round and walked past the house out into the bush.

Graham collapsed – in earnest.

16
A RACE AGAINST TIME

THE lubras carried him to the house and laid him down. He frothed blood. "Shot in the lung!" he thought. From war experience he directed them to prop him in an easy chair. He felt better so. He scrawled a note to the manager at Liveringa Station; the black boy, just in with the horses, took the note, leapt into the saddle, and was off at the gallop.

Then Graham examined his wound. The bullet had struck the forearm, gone through the upper arm, and pierced the right lung.

"Robert is a gonner this time!" mused Graham as he watched the blood welling out. "What's the odds! If I've got to die, this is a nice way to die. I feel no pain!"

He could do nothing for himself – only wait.

The station car should arrive in three hours at the latest. Then would come the hundred-mile drive into Derby.

"I might bleed to death before we reach a doctor," he murmured. "It's not bleeding very fast, just steadily. If they don't come in time I'll just grow fainter and fainter, then go right out to it. I don't want to, but it will be a pleasant death if it must be."

The hours dragged by; three hours went.

He was beginning to feel faint. The lubras bathed his forehead and limbs with cold water. Another hour dragged by . . . then another long, long hour . . . He began to give up hope.

At Liveringa Station Kim Rose, the manager, had gone on to Lulugai Station when the black boy galloped up, so they marked the unopened letter "Urgent" and sent it by black boy galloper to Lulugai. But Kim and Ken Rose, still travelling, had already left for Mount Anderson Station. Douglas Moore, manager of Lulugai, received the letter. "I'll keep it until Rose returns," he said to Frank Weir, the bookkeeper.

Later he took the letter from his pocket and gazed uneasily at that "Urgent." "I don't like to open another man's letter, but this may be urgent business, and Rose may be away for days at Mount Anderson."

"Open it," suggested Weir. Moore did so, and jumped up;

"Good God, Bob Graham's been shot!"

Weir raced a car to Noora Noora, expecting to meet a dead man.

"Have you brought a pick and shovel, you old pen and ink?" laughed Graham. "Because I won't need it." Then his stomach seemed to tear his lungs out; he stretched in awful pain. A man shot through the lungs learns what hell means if he laughs or sneezes. And Graham learnt yet more of lung wounds during that nightmare drive to Derby.

Mounted-Constable O'Neill, of Derby, thought quickly and acted quickly. A uniform to a demented man might be like a red rag to a bull, so he jumped into a car with his trackers and sped along the Fitzroy Road in mufti. Typical sample of the Kimberley Mounted Police, this O'Neill. Tall and almost boyish-looking, yet with twenty thousand miles of bush experience already to his credit. Just then he was trying to reason out what the wanted man would do.

Moody had camels. A continent was open to him; if he travelled south he could vanish into the desert. Or he could strike south-east through the spinifex and enter the vastness of Central Australia. Or he could go east and lose himself in the big distances of the Northern Territory. North was rocky mountain country. He would never take camels there; nor west, for that meant Derby and the sea. If he decided on the desert, and given only two days to reach it, his capture would mean many months.

He was a dingo-shooter, cunning in the ways of the bush, cunning in the ways of the wild dog; many a one had he scalped. Now, apparently, it was on his mind to scalp men. What if he was mad enough to put up a fight! He would have plenty of ammunition. What if he travelled out to some far-away desert rock hole and just waited for the police – waited for them as many a time he had waited for wild animals to come and drink. It would become a fight for the water and whoever lost would perish.

Instead of fleeing immediately, he might be hurrying now to square accounts with some other victim of his delusion.

O'Neill reached Upper Liveringa Station in the afternoon, and mustering a strong plant of horses, started them out with the trackers towards Noora Noora. Then, with Rose and Moore, he raced there by car. At Noora-Noora natives showed him Moody's camel-pads following a fire-ploughed track leading to a boundary-rider's camp. This lonely man told them that Moody had called at his camp several days before and said he was going to handcuff Graham and Leed and cut their ears off until they paid him the money.

"My heavens!" exclaimed O'Neill, "there is no possible way of warning Leed in time. If Moody has pushed on without camping he will just about reach Leed before us."

They jumped in the car and sped on until it was too dark to see the tracks, then camped. At dawn they were following the tracks, now making, apparently, for the Fitzroy Road.

"If he crosses the road he'll be heading for the desert," said O'Neill, "and Leed will be safe. But if he hasn't camped, and turns straight up the road, then –"

"Press the car all you can to the Fitzroy Road. If he goes bush and we miss him it won't matter so much. You can hurry word to Leed while I return with the trackers and pick up his tracks. But if he's gone up the Fitzroy Road then we're bound to see his tracks on the road."

At Mount Hordiman tank they saw where he had filled his water-drums.

"It looks like a desert trip!" said Rose.

"Yes, but he mightn't travel south until he settles with Leed."

A few miles farther on he had camped for the night.

"Thank heaven!" exclaimed O'Neill. "We can warn Leed now, anyway. By camping here he has lost all his start."

That Moody was not anticipating such swift pursuit was proof in that night's camp, and in that he kept his camels all the time to country along which a car could follow. This was the bush, and the police were a long way away. He never dreamed of police pursuit in a motor car.

They followed the tracks then right to the Fitzroy Road and here they turned sharply up along the road in the direction of the Fitzroy Crossing.

"My lucky stars!" breathed O'Neill. "If only he sticks to the road!"

"Looks as if he is really out to settle another account before he takes to the bush," said Rose grimly.

"Push on!" urged O'Neill. "If he leaves the road now, I'll follow on foot while you chaps return to the trackers and tell them to hurry the horses after me. We've got him, anyway. He's too late now for the desert; he will never reach it."

The car sped on, following very fresh tracks, for a misty rain had fallen there the night before. On that layer of moist dust the big camel-pads were plainly visible from the car. Those tracks told them something else, too. "That explains why!" exclaimed Rose.

"Yes," replied O'Neill, staring at the tracks.

"His camels have got sore feet. He has shod them with greenhide pads. That is why he did not go straight bush after Leed, country too stony. He's our man now!"

Nine miles farther on they saw Moody ahead, riding a camel and leading another.

"Go straight past him," said O'Neill, "before he has a chance to see who is in the car. If he recognizes you two he will guess something is doing."

They raced past and the camels shied violently.

The car pulled up well ahead.

O'Neill climbed out leisurely, as if as an afterthought.

"Don't let him see who you are!" he whispered. He strolled back towards where Moody sat his restive camel, a rifle across his knee.

"Good day," smiled O'Neill. "Sorry we startled your camels."

"It's all right," growled Moody. "They're not used to cars."

He stared at O'Neill, who noted the revolver strapped to the pommel of the saddle. If he snatched at the rifle Moody would simply cling to the butt while he drew the revolver with the other hand. It's a ticklish job for a man on foot to arrest an armed man who is gazing down from the top of a camel. Harder still to think out a trivial conversation that will deceive the suspicious man above and induce him to sit his camel down.

While O'Neill was rolling a cigarette in drawling conversation while waiting the slightest chance to leap up and seize the man, mistake came to his aid, Moody mistook him for Sam Thomas, the well-known bookmaker, *en route* to the Fitzroy races. Moody imagined he had certain business with Sam and it was with a crafty glint in his eye that he sat his camel down.

Immediately the camel lurched down O'Neill sprang at Moody, knocked his breath out in the quick struggle and handcuffed him.

"So you *are* a policeman!"

"Yes."

Moody looked around to his rifle lying on the ground.

"Had I known in the beginning I would not have been taken so easily."

The car turned back to them and Moody was invited to step in.

"These bracelets hurt!" he growled.

"Can't help that," answered O'Neill.

"Oh, well, I'm probably more comfortable than Graham, anyway. By the way, is he dead?"

"He was alive when I saw him last," answered O'Neill.

Thus was an account quickly squared. Sundry jokers and several who had not joked at all breathed a fervent:

"Thank God!"

17
NEMARLUK

A WILD, long-drawn cry rang out over plain and billabong; an aggressive, challenging cry.

An old bull buffalo lifted his fly-bitten head and peered from bleared eyes. For this was the triumph call of Nemarluk, King of the Wild, undisputed leader of the Cahn-mah. The tribe sprang to their feet with howls of *"Yak-ai! Yak-ail Yak-ai!"*

From the wooded sea-shore piccaninnies came running out towards the plain. Presently the painted huntsmen appeared coming from among the tall grasses. Feathers in their hair, blood upon their spears. Arrestingly red bodied in the setting sun. Those of the tribe already returned from the hunt clustered together discussing what the hunters might have won.

Nemarluk was acclaimed the mightiest hunter from the Victoria River to the Daly. Moreover, he was a killer of men; a man among men; the example held up to every young initiate, to every boy; the idol of the lubras, young and old. None of any tribe dare oppose him; although away across on the Little Fitzmaurice a grim band were deliberating challenge.

One, only, dared openly challenge. Bul-bul, the police tracker from Timber Creek, distant outpost of the white man. Henchman of the whites, the dog, but a strong man, ruthless as the crocodile, cunning as the mating snake. May he die like a broken dog and his rotting bones never rest beside his waters!

Both men had sworn to eat the kidney-fat of the other.

But Bul-bul was far away. Nemarluk stalked just ahead of his chosen band, a big kangaroo slung over his shoulder, shovel-nosed spears in his hand, his bronze-red body a picture of muscle and sinew in rippling relief.

Each member of this Red Band was oiled and polished with a mixture of wild-goose oil and that little ant-bed which, when burned, yields a rich brick-red powder. Rubbed into the body, then massaged by warm hands, it makes living bronze. They were called in native tongue, "The Red Band."

Close behind Nemarluk strode Minmara, a 'roo also over his shoulder, and carrying the heavy animal effortlessly. A warrior, Minmara, rugged of face, direct of eye; scars of spear and stone dagger plain upon his body. Behind Minmara came Mankee, with a fat rock python coiled around him (the head knotted to the tail) still alive. Those mottled coils were convulsively swelling around the body of the man. Then came Lin carrying a big old bearded plain turkey and several geese; then Mangul and Marragin carrying a wallaby each.

They threw down their game to grunts of acclamation from the men, a chorus of praise from the women, shrill criticism from the children whose practised fingers were quick to feel the fatness of the game.

But the eyes of Marboo were for Nemarluk alone, liquid black, quick eyes, a smile proudly wreathing her face as her warrior lord came striding into camp. Alone silent among the acclamations of the tribe, that approval still was joy. Bitter indeed would have been her silence had Nemarluk returned crestfallen from the hunt.

Small, well built, and swift was Marboo, youngest of Nemarluk's wives. Living survival of prehistoric woman, her wild young heart beating with the mother love of the ages.

Men seized the 'roos and wallabies, for it is only men who may cook such game. It is the law, and an art, too, requiring the practised skill of the highly trained.

Next morning a ringing *"Yak-ai!"* greeted a distant smoke-signal from Coor-i-ning look out. Far away a "white man" vessel was coming, the sun glinting on its sails. The tribe rushed for a vantage point.

"If only they will sail into our water," shouted Nemarluk, "we will kill them and take all the tobacco they have!"

Quick approval greeted this lust for tobacco – one of the two things the aboriginal wants of the white man, the craving for which keeps them chained to the whites.

Late that afternoon the *Ouida* sailed into Port Keats. No real port this, just a name, a bay in a wild coast, mangrove and plain and hills stretching all around.

The three Japanese aboard stared at the wilderness in some trepidation; the three Melville Island crew boys with misgiving that raised a sympathetic shiver in their kidney-fat.

In that April of 1931 the Northern Territory pearling industry was depressed. So, rather than lie idle in Darwin port, Nagata, Yoshida, and Owashi had rented the *Ouida* and embarked on a shark-fishing cruise, sailing south-west.

Now they needed wood, and, more urgently, fresh water.

The vessel crept cautiously round Point Pearce, then into Treachery Bay, where the anchor-chain rattled down to echo over the water.

When the vessel was securely anchored and sails furled, a canoe shot out from the mangroves. Japanese and crew boys watched closely. There were only three men in the canoe that paddled up alongside.

From the lugger deck the crew boys noted there were no weapons in the bottom of the canoe. Narrowly they scanned the long tangled hair and beards of the three men lest stone or bone dagger be concealed there; manoeuvred to glance behind them, lest a tomahawk be slung at the small of the back in the human-hair belt each warrior wore.

A big aboriginal with smiling eyes leapt uninvited up on to the deck of the *Ouida*. His perfect teeth showed almost startlingly in the black laughing face. A human-hair band, bound round his forehead, kept back the wild locks from his eyes, his powerful body warned of aggressive strength. A dangerous looking savage. Yet there was something contagiously friendly about Nemarluk. His fearlessness, his wild head held proudly above broad squared shoulders, his upright athletic body, forced admiration.

The Melville Islanders understood but imperfectly the language. Nemarluk laughed his replies; Minmara and Lin, now also squatting on deck, obviously unarmed, smiled their explanations.

Yes, there was plenty of fresh water just in from the shore across there, and unlimited wood. And something better, explained Nemarluk: abundance of wild geese in a lagoon a little way in from the shore. The brown men could fill the vessel with ducks and geese if they wanted to, if only they had those shooting irons that kill things!

The Japanese were pleasantly intrigued by this chance of replenishing a depleted larder. Ducks and geese promised a welcome change after weeks of fish.

Nemarluk, from the depths of his hair, pulled out a crab's claw, the wild coastal aboriginal's pipe. He flourished the charred claw with a smile. The Japanese captain gave each man a smoke, half a stick of trade tobacco for each eager hand. Captain Nagata gave them, too, a meal of rice. They slept on board that night; made no offer to go away; just showed a friendly curiosity in the ship and crew. Anyway, the Japanese felt secure. They would watch in turn; they knew their crew boys would hardly sleep at all. Best not offend these men; otherwise they must sail away with empty tanks while the smoke-signals of the tribes would be against their landing anywhere along the coast.

Next morning, even after breakfast, the blacks took their time in departing; time was meaningless to them. They would show the crew boys where the wood and water was easiest to get and, when the vessel was watered, where the geese were. Only when the Japanese gave them tobacco did they haul their canoe alongside.

Meanwhile, laughed Nemarluk from the canoe, there were plenty of lubras ashore – young ones. They were very good at cleaning ducks and geese and were handy aboard a boat. Tobacco and rice and whatever else they would give in payment.

The Japanese hesitated; were lost. The three men canoed ashore and presently returned with five young lubras. Among them were three of Nemarluk's own wives, including young Marboo, the favourite. With a wild woman's well-feigned shyness they climbed aboard. Then Nemarluk and his companions returned ashore and the job of watering the vessel commenced.

Two days passed while wood and watering canoes plied lazily from the shore to the *Ouida*. She was nearly ready to sail. Each day Nemarluk and his friends came aboard seeking an hospitable loaf and smoke on the lugger's deck. And at such times Nemarluk's keen-eyed Marboo reported to him the number of guns aboard; that the Japanese slept keeping one watch each; that the Melville Islanders hardly slept at all and were armed with spear and tomahawk. While all hands were squatting about the deck, working or smoking or eating, she told him these things while, apparently, not speaking at all. She gave an exact description of the ironware, the stores, the tobacco, the loot aboard. And none but their own chattering people realized that they were conversing at all.

For the sign language of the aboriginal at close quarters is perfect; for distant communication he has, besides his smoke-signals, a language of sound by the rapping of sticks or stones, very similar to our Morse code. He can even converse while under water.

Nemarluk asked, as a matter of course, for more tobacco than had been agreed upon, and met with a firm refusal. Each worker was paid one stick of tobacco per day, food, a coloured cloth for waistbelt, and a further present of tobacco when leaving the ship. The people who actually worked were receiving payment agreed on for services rendered; nothing more.

Nemarluk laughed understandingly, seemingly well content.

"We will kill them!" he growled on the evening of the second day. "We will get all the tobacco we want then, and iron and all the other things, too." The firelight played upon their bronzed bodies as the Red Band discussed the coming kill.

It was a simple plan, just the age-long fighting tactics of the aboriginal – surprise. Simple, but thought had gone into it. A willing friendship well kept up had blunted the edge of the Japanese mistrust. The crew boys, timid as the aboriginal always is when away from his own country, would not count should their brown masters be taken by surprise. And now –

Early in the morning of 10 August 1931 the Red Band canoed across to the *Ouida*. They were unarmed, their songs and jokes echoed among the mangrove-trees ashore. Old Alligator and Maru, visiting from the Fitzmaurice River country with several of Nemarluk's tribesmen, were already lounging aboard, idly watching the women salting fish.

Nagata, the Japanese captain, was to be taken to the lagoon and shown where the wild geese fed. Armed with a shot-gun he stepped into a dinghy, a Melville crew boy at the oars. Canoe and dinghy paddled and rowed to shore together. Here the Melville Islander stood by the dinghy while Nagata and the unarmed blacks stepped ashore.

The shooting was exciting, clouds of geese and duck rose whirring and whistling and trumpeting to report after report. Nagata was lured farther and farther in among the waterlogged timbers of the lagoon. And now Nemarluk's crouching form was pushing through the water plants ahead of the Japanese. He turned warningly to point through the reeds at geese, then as Nagata bent forward to aim Lin snatched the gun, fired at Nagata and missed! Nagata stood astonished, then leapt around into the arms of those behind. He slipped away, but Marragin raced behind and stunned him by a blow from an ironwood stick. Nemarluk snatched the gun from Lin, took a cartridge from the fallen man, clumsily loaded the gun, held it to Nagata's chest, and fired. They hid the gun; then, loaded with geese, hurried back to the canoe answering the dumb question of the Melville boy with:

"Nagata told us to bring the geese aboard. He is going to shoot us a kangaroo for ourselves. He will come by and by."

They sped the canoe out towards the *Ouida*, Marragin standing at the bow and holding high the geese. Congratulatory calls came from those on board. But the two Melville Island boys narrowly eyed the canoe and their own dinghy now pulling hesitatingly astern.

"Nagata not there!" frowned Jacky.

The two Japanese, plucking ducks at the stern of the vessel, stood up questioningly. As the canoe drew alongside to the laughing inquiries of the lubras, Marboo, in sign language, rapidly told Nemarluk that the guns were down in the cabin, but that the Melville Island boys had shifted the tomahawks from their usual place near the mainmast and had taken them up forrard near their own quarters. Two were now lying near the anchor chain.

"Where Nagata?" demanded the Japanese as the canoe swung alongside.

"He shootem longa kangaroo belonga boy," one replied, and in broken English explained how Nagata had ordered them return with the geese. As they climbed aboard, the two Melville Island boys edged towards the canoe. Four of the Red Band threw the geese on deck and squatted talking to the lubras who obediently handed over a smoke of tobacco. Nemarluk and Minmara strolled casually forward. As they did so the two Melville boys suddenly slipped into the canoe and pushed straight off.

"Where you go?" demanded Yoshida.

"Go longa shore look longa Nagata."

"Come back quick."

"Arright."

All was quite chatty and normal aboard; the sun shone brightly; a bird called from the shore. The paddles dipped as the canoe drew quietly away. With one more glance around, the Japanese knelt again to their plucking, the feathers floating slowly astern. Their backs were turned to the natives.

Nemarluk and Minmara noiselessly leapt astern, each swinging down a tomahawk upon a bending neck. The heads were almost completely severed. In an instant the bodies were slung overboard, one sank, but the other rolled up and went drifting away after the feathers, sinking slowly as it went.

Canoe and dinghy were now speeding towards one another, the Red Band ran forrard and shouted them to return, that no harm would be done them. But the canoe boys transferred into the dinghy and the three men pulled their hardest towards the open sea.

Nemarluk's men sprang to the windlass, while inexperienced hands in wild excitement unfurled the sails. As the anchor came up, the boom swung out; Nemarluk sprang to the tiller and the chase was on. Hopeless. Inexperienced hands aboard the lugger, expert seamen in the dinghy. They followed the shore edge, thus keeping in shallow water while the lugger had to keep far out. She did run on a sandbank at last.

Nemarluk shook his fist in fury to thus see the kidney-fat of three men slipping away. When the tide refloated the *Ouida,* they sailed her back, ran her aground, and commenced the wonderful job of looting.

It was some months after the *Ouida* left Darwin before the Melville Island boys brought news of the lugger. Then was displayed a curious trait of the aboriginal mind that we do not understand. Whether they were afraid of being accused of complicity in the crime, or of the ultimate vengeance of Nemarluk, is hard to say.

Perhaps some deeply ingrained loyalty of aboriginal to aboriginal held them; probably something altogether different. At all events, in Darwin they told a graphic story of how the lugger foundered in a storm off Quail Island, and how they were saved by clinging to wreckage until they reached the floating dinghy. The story was investigated, the owner going into it thoroughly until even he was satisfied and accepted the *Ouida* as a total loss.

So Nemarluk, the laughing savage, was brought into violent contact with the white law. But what did he care about the law! The Japanese were interlopers, coming unasked to a land in which he was chief, his land and his tribe's land from time immemorial. Why should he, who *was* the law, care about the far-away white man's law? Nemarluk did not know – does not know – that the aboriginal is doomed. The end of his cycle has come. He will vanish.

But I wish I could write in full the story of Nemarluk before he and his become only a memory.

Refloating the "Ouida".

18
THE "BLACK INTELLIGENCE"

MOUNTED-CONSTABLE PRYOR, in charge of the Daly River police district, Northern Territory, in 1931, sat deep in thought. That district with its geographical difficulties and the prehistoric men who roamed its fastnesses would keep any officer's thoughts active. His boundary east caused little worry, being mostly cattle country. But practically all the rest was the wild man's land right south to the Timber Creek police district, which had problems of untamed areas of its own.

The little Daly River police station (one hundred miles south from Darwin) is about sixty miles upriver, where it is barely two hundred yards wide. On rich level soil dotted with paper-bark trees the police landing is on a high bank and backed by splendid trees. One magnificent banyan would easily shelter fifty people. To this landing the little forty-ton motor vessel *Maroubra* brings the stores, then returns to Darwin loaded with peanuts. The river upstream is lined with jungle areas and thickets of giant bamboo. Down-stream towards the coast there are no whites. The river gradually widens through richly-grassed flats and plains with swamps and billabongs swarming with bird life. Mangroves line the muddy stream where, nearly a mile wide, it empties into the sea. From the western bank here, for a hundred and fifty miles south, right across to the Victoria River, Nemarluk reigned as king.

Stretching along the placid Daly for a few miles below the tiny police station is the peanut settlement, about fifty whites all told, all within fifteen miles of the station. The largest farm is only eighty acres. Apart from this group there are only about a dozen stockmen in the district. The only other whites are the usual dozen or so wanderers of fortune.

Those wanderers are the bane of the mounted men's lives. They come trailing along from nowhere looking for gold, or "cattle country," or to study natives, or to write books, or hunting for some new animal, bird, reptile, or bug; often a wandering dingo-poisoner or crocodile-shooter, or just those happy-go-lucky drifters who come with a smile, but not a shilling in the world, to seek their fortune – they do not know where or how. Some elusive attraction always lures these adventurers into the wild lands. And not seldom the Mounteds have to ride out and rescue them, or bury them, or report "No trace."

And headquarters expects that every constable in charge shall keep his district safe!

Pryor's thoughts turned to Herb Watts. Now, this was a different case. An experienced bushman, well used to handling natives, he should have been able to look after himself. Rumour had just come in that he was speared by the blacks out near Hermit Hill, hardly more than a day's ride away.

This was not quite unexpected. The bush natives had sworn to "get him." And when the natives deliberately plan that, it means the white man must leave the country or...

Watts had laughed at warnings. "Just let them try it on!"

Widjullee and his band had crept up to Watts's camp and hurled spears into him, through his mosquito-net. Then had dragged his body to a creek for the crocodiles to feed upon.

The crocodile was Widjullee's totem and he had sworn to feed his spirit protector with the body of white man Watts.

Mounted-Constable McCann with Trackers Nipper and Dick had ridden out to discover whether the rumour was true.

Those elusive rumours spring from goodness knows where. Native news comes, either in dawdling rumours or with a speed that makes the whites blink unbelievingly. Always the news required sifting, for sometimes it seemed deliberately designed to deceive.

The restless tribes down towards the coast made Pryor feel his responsibility. What a job for a policeman; to protect the whites; to protect the half-civilized natives; to protect and rule, and yet not interfere with large bands of wandering, prehistoric men. Stirred occasionally by some restless imp of mischief, a wild bush band would make a woman-stealing raid on the civilized natives around the settlement. That meant trouble, retaliation under the primal law of an "eye for an eye." Pryor never interfered in tribal feuds, except when the aggrieved party were civilized natives who came to the police for protection. So long as the bush natives left the whites alone he worried little over their own private killings.

But here was Watts apparently added to the list.

And Tetlow – how about him? He had a favourite camping-ground somewhere in the Hermit Hill locality. Pryor was worried about Tetlow. An inoffensive old chap, he had been among natives nearly all his life. Was very good to them. That, itself, would not protect him. The blacks had been known to kill their best friends. These "best friends" developed such confidence in the natives that they refrained from taking the most obvious precautions.

Pryor was worried too over another report from the Black Service. It had been whispered him that Nemarluk's men down near Treachery Bay had guns! If so, whom had they plundered and killed?

Very useful, that Black Service of the Northern Mounteds. It often puts the officer in the camp of primitives hundreds of miles away; tells him of raids, of feuds, of killings, of initiation ceremonies, of big corroboree movements. The Black Intelligence can pick up a whisper and follow it for months, if necessary, until a whole grim story is unfolded. Often receive a story on the wings of the wind. Many an aboriginal bewildered within the walls of a "white man" gaol has never realized that it was himself, his best friends, or his tribesmen enemies that caged him there. The miracle to him is how the "white pleece" found out.

Bul-bul, the tracker, was the eyes and ears and cunning brain of the Black Intelligence. Did a native killing occur down on the coast by the Finnis, the Daly, the Moyle, the Fitzmaurice, the Victoria, Bul-bul would probably know. Did the Mulluk-Mulluks slice the kidney-fat out of a man, or the Brinkens throttle a lubra, or the Carn-mahs spear white or black or brown, the news would probably drift through to the police station. Did the men of the farthest ranges, or of the egret swamps, or the lily lagoons or the loneliest plains raid a camp or spear cattle or slaughter some unknown wanderer, a tracker almost certainly would come to know.

Not immediately, perhaps not till after many months. The news might come by whispered words in the night, or by innuendo, or by a straight-out accusation given in malice or triumph or with the desire of vengeance. It might come by sign language. Often the trees, apparently, whispered it, so vague was its coming.

Sometimes Bul-bul found his own news. It might be a footprint on the earth, a footprint that represented a man's signature to the reading eyes of Bulbul. A tracker on patrol two months ago saw a track. He mentions it to Bul-bul. Now Bul-bul knows that man of the track is taboo to that particular area of country. What dire necessity has driven him to cross through it?

Bul-bul makes inquiries. Here he has the whole complicated organization of native life to help him.

The tribes, with their sub-tribes and their groups and hordes. Then the family groups. Each group intensely loyal, but each with its antagonisms, its age-old feuds against other groups. Individual members alive with rivalries and jealousies and sheer hate against individuals of other hordes. Family groups in different hordes at age-old enmity with other families in other hordes. And the traditional enmity of tribe against tribe, tribesman against tribesman. And among them all the ever-present betrayer – jealousy, ambition, love and sex. Bul-bul touched all these nerves to gain the news he sought.

The tracker would know the footprint of the wanderer, probably now an outcast. He would know the man's tribe, his horde, his family group, he would know his enemies. Bul-bul's friends, or those seeking his favour, with native diplomacy, would approach both the man's friends and enemies. It might be days, weeks, months, but eventually he would learn why the footprint of that man had been planted on unaccustomed soil. And thereby a whole grim tragedy might be unfolded.

Through the Black Service each officer in charge has a fair idea of the horde groups in his district; knows any dangerous groups amongst them, the localities in which they roam, according to the wet and dry season, or to the seasons of animal, fish, bird, or vegetable foods. If serious trouble occurs, he can sometimes decipher the cause from his inside knowledge of aboriginal life; can localize the men responsible; can ride fast and straight. Should any wandering whites intend going through an area of country that he knows to be dangerous, he can warn them; if they still persist and do not return in due course, he knows where to search for them. There have been instances where he has told beforehand just where he will bury them.

Each police district, whether administered by two officers or by one, has its "service" – invariably the head tracker. Some stand out above the others. Bulbul of the Daly and Timber Creek is a noted example; Smiler of the country east and west of Darwin is nearly as good; each district has its proved tracker, looked up to but envied by his fellow trackers. The best trackers are always bush aborigines who have been tough customers themselves, and practised all the familiar dodges of putting their enemies and the police off their trail. The more notorious he has been, the more feared by the wild bush native as well as the civilized, the longer he has successfully defied the police-the better tracker he will be. A town-bred or civilized bush native is seldom of use; he has lost his bushcraft.

The mounted man and his head tracker often become attached to one another. Invariably the officer in charge of an outpost station will swear that his head tracker is a better man than the admittedly good head tracker of an adjoining station. Frequently the trackers are jealous of each other: to be the recognized head tracker of any police outfit is an honour they scheme and fight and endure much for.

Bul-bul is a tracker among trackers; cunning, tremendously powerful, ruthless in pursuit, a fully initiated warrior too. The life of the wild, the secret rites of the stone-age men, the hunt, the chase, tribal war and intrigue are as familiar to him as to any of the wild men. He has taken another man's kidney-fat and knows that many have sworn to take his. He may have lost it before these lines see print. Life to Bul-bul is a grim jest, full of expectation.

This aboriginal information cannot always be obtained. For the aboriginal can be intensely secretive. There are some things which happen in aboriginal life that no native, civilized or otherwise, will ever tell to a white man. There are things no tracker will tell.

Mounted-Constable Pryor was troubled over that whisper of guns held by Nemarluk's men. There were no whites down on the coast. Probably some adventurer had landed from the sea. That was how they had got young Renouf at Point Blaze.

Pryor frowned. This Nemarluk; very little was known concerning him, except that he was a warrior, a killer of men as strong as Bul-bul-and as cunning. Even a tracker might be excused for being afraid of him. If this Nemarluk had really started on the killing of whites then he would be a dangerous man.

A converging patrol eventually caught Widjullee, Don from Brock's Creek meeting McCann's patrol west of the Daly. Widjullee had speared Watts right enough. McCann unravelled the deed right to the tracks where Widjullee had dragged the body to the waterhole to feed the crocodiles. With Widjullee they caught Mangul and Lin too! Stiff luck this, that Mangul and Lin should be caught while merely paying a tribal visit! It ranked as the height of injustice that two of the Red Band should be caught so simply when the white police were not seeking them.

Bul-bul laughed his sympathy. It was a hearty laugh, a sympathetic laugh. Too bad that Bul-bul should have heard beforehand about those guns that Nemarluk had down on the coast! Too bad that he should recognize Mangul and Lin during the raid on Widjullee's camp! Yes, he gave them his sympathy. And on the ride back to the Daly Mangul repaid the wiles of the serpent by boasting of the killing of the Japanese at Port Keats by Nemarluk and his Red Band.

Pryor in charge of Daly Waters sent immediate word to headquarters at Darwin. Superintendent Stretton detailed a police party under Constable Koop to sail immediately in the motor vessel *Maroubra* and investigate. They found the *Ouida* beached high and dry at Point Hay, her bloodstained decks bearing testimony to the accuracy of the "black intelligence." She had been stripped of everything except an alarm clock.

Slowly the police organization moved against Nemarluk. He had killed men who, according to our laws, had a perfect right to be where they were. But Mother Nature helped her wild son at the start. She brought down the wet season, which postponed the chase for another four months.

19
UNDER THE MILKWOOD-TREE

IT was a lazy morning. Far away rose hazily the smoke-fires of the Bulluk-Bulluk and the Brinken. But, only some twenty miles behind Bill Tetlow's camp was civilization, the Daly River peanut settlement, with its police station the centre of their little world.

Bill Tetlow was happy there under the milkwood-tree. He hummed an old song as he smoked. He was mending a pack-saddle and making a good job of it, a comfortable job for the old horse's back. This was Tetlow's favourite camp, under the milkwood-tree. It had been their camp for twelve carefree months-his camp and Alice's. She was kneeling there by the fire cooking a damper, humming some girlish lullaby. Her black hair hung down in a fringe over her eyes. A nice little thing Alice, and affectionate. She looked after a man well. Trustworthy too. Why he would trust her with his life! He had picked a winner at last; it takes a lot of patience and luck to pick a woman who really suits a man. With the energy that comes with happy labour Tetlow grunted as he pushed the big packneedle through the tough leather.

Alice, using wire hooks, lifted the camp-oven from its hot hole in the ground, then carefully lifted off the ash-covered lid, peeping anxiously. Then smiled in quiet delight, with practised knuckles rapping the yellow-brown crust. Cooked nicely. A good damper, well risen, light, and done to a turn. Bill would be pleased and would praise her. Appraisingly she sniffed the damper-laden air.

Alice, lubra of the Poonga Poonga country.

Young and slim and strong with pleasing face unmarred by thick nose or lips, Merry face that broke into a smile at a glance, short crisp hair, glossy skin. Secretly, she bathed twice a day because she knew her white man liked it. She liked doing those things he liked. Her big black eyes smiled each time she thought of him.

Back from the camp in a clump of trees, two black men stood. Stockman Jimmy sniffed hungrily the smell of freshly-baked damper. He was anxious to follow his nose. But dared not – yet. Beside him stood Burrar, clad only in a loincloth, ochred bars painted across his chest, a band of white kaolin around his face. Devilish, that grizzled face, glaring out from its circlet of white. Burrar, an Inkata (old man of the tribe) vested with the tribe's authority. And he stood menacingly with war-spears in his hand.

"Kill him!"

"I don't want to."

"Kill him!"

Stockman Jimmy frowned uneasily, a surge of tribal instincts hot with dread and fear warring against his inclinations. At odd times through the years he had enjoyed many happy weeks in the camp of white man Tetlow. A haven of free food, and tea, and tobacco when he craved a spell from station work.

"Alice has been his wife for many moons. He bought her from the tribe. She belongs to him."

"Kill him!"

"Why don't you tell the white man you want the lubra?"

Through the silence there came faintly a little laugh from under the milkwood-tree. Stockman Jimmy moved uneasily.

"Tetlow has been good to me. He never touched me."

"Kill him!"

A very "civilized" boy this Stockman Jimmy, a wonderful rider trained by old Dick Laffan of Queensland racing fame. But now he was on a walkabout in the bush, under the Law of the Wild.

It was oppressively silent there under that clump of trees. From near at hand, as if smothered by reeds and water growth, came the honking of many wild geese. But where the two men stood the silence was pregnant with voices – the ancestral voices of a tribe speaking in the minds of two living men.

"Kill him," growled the Inkata, "or I – kill – you!"

With sullen lip Stockman Jimmy stepped out from the sheltering trees and slouched across the plain to the milkwood-tree.

"Hullo, Jimmy," called Tetlow, "which way you bin come up?"

"Alonga Daly!"

"That way long fella walk. Sit down longa cup of tea."

Alice brought the billy from the fire while Tetlow, now greasing his gun, inquired about peanut growers at The Crossing, not noticing the brooding replies.

A blue-bird whistled cheerily upon the milkwood tree.

"Gib it gun!" said Jimmy suddenly. "I go shootem goose."

He stood up and reached for the gun. Tetlow handed him a cartridge from a saddle-pack. "Don't be long away," he cautioned. "Dinner-time soon. And don't miss him goose."

Jimmy took the gun, he almost snatched the cartridge. "No more miss," he growled as he strode off. "You been greasem gun, him shoot proper feller."

Tetlow sat back lazily against the repaired packsaddle. He refilled his pipe, gazing after the aboriginal.

"Now what is biting *you*?" he mused aloud.

"Jimmy sulky feller, Alice."

"Maybe girl longa him say 'No,'" she laughed.

"Maybe. Perhaps he jealous longa me."

"No more. He uncle belonga me. Me good wife belonga you," she answered softly. She came and knelt beside him, sitting back on her heels, putting her arm around his neck. She laid her head against his; he leaned back, well content. There was silence under the milkwood-tree. Presently her fingers reached out for the pipe between his lips. She laughed as she transferred it to her own.

"You good wife longa me, Alice," he said, smilingly.

By and by Stockman Jimmy came slouching back.

Alice was just lifting the tea billy from the fire; the new-baked damper and the meat were spread upon a clean pack-cover under the tree.

"No luck, Jimmy? Never mind. Come and have dinner. We go and look out goose after dinner."

That meal they enjoyed, for the rough fare was sauced by the appetite of humans living very close to the Wilds. A white butterfly came softly floating to settle palpitating on Alice's coal-black hair. She trembled, for to her this was the soul of a piccaninny. A sharp rustling of speeding wings sounded overhead as a flock of ducks planed straight down upon the billabong. They heard the rippling splash, the whistling and carking and honking as the new arrivals took their places.

"Come on, Jimmy, we go longa billabong get goose," said Tetlow. Handing Jimmy a cartridge, he strode away, pulling out his pipe. Jimmy came after, carrying the gun. When only a few yards away, Jimmy glanced behind. Alice was putting the dinner things away, her back to them, crooning a lullaby. Jimmy slipped the cartridge into the greased gun, raised the weapon, and fired.

A deathly silence over the plain as the report went rolling away. Jimmy stood stupidly. Alice wheeled round, saw Tetlow collapse, and, with a moaning cry, raced on feet that scarce seemed to touch the ground.

She threw herself down beside him, raised his head, and peered into his eyes; she cried hysterical things in her native tongue.

From a gaping hole in Tetlow's back oozed blood, he gasped blood, his eyes that talked into hers were big eyes, questioning, glassy eyes. Jimmy ran back to the milkwood-tree.

"Al-ice!" The choking voice gripped her heart.

In madness she bent to blow her breath down his throat; she tried to hold his head that the blood could run out and he could breathe.

"Tea!" he gasped.

She raced back to the milkwood-tree. Jimmy was there and beside him frowned Burrar, the Inkata. She flew at Jimmy, her fingers hooked like tigress claws.

"Why did you kill my white man? Oh, why –" Her bared teeth snapped at his throat; she wheeled around to the fire, snatched a pannikin, and .with trembling hands filled it with tea. Racing back to Tetlow, she raised his head and put the pannikin to his lips. Her tears fell with the tea he coughed back from his throat.

"I have killed him," mumbled Jimmy.

"Fool!" growled the Inkata.

They stood gazing out at the lubra crying over the fallen man. Tetlow coughed; the tea all came out of his mouth. He was panting; she felt his gurgling breaths deep down , she bent her ear to the command in his eyes.

"You been tell-pleeceman-quickfeller-Jimmy been-shootem me!"

She nodded, and wailed aloud as she helped him turn on his chest. Rapidly he lapsed into unconsciousness. She raised him, rubbing his head, holding open his eyes.

"You leave me," she cried. "Oh, my man, you leave me!" He nodded as his head fell back on her breast. She held him there rocking to and fro, wailing in a misery that culminated in the Death Wail.

By and by she put him down. Slowly she walked to the milkwood-tree and stared around. All was there: the saddles, the pack-bags, the surcingles and bridles hanging up in the branches. The tent-fly was spread there beside his blanket and hers. There was the freshly-cut damper, the pack-cloth. Her gaze rested on Jimmy. She walked up to him.

"Fly like the wild goose," she hissed. "Fly like the duck at night. Fly like the wind spirit – but you will never get away! You will never get away." She turned towards the distant Daly.

The Inkata snatched her wrist. "You go tellem white pleece!" he snarled. She laughed into his bloodshot eyes.

The tribe watched her for days and nights. She got away. Like bloodhounds they tracked her and dragged her back. But one night brought the Wind Fiend screaming through the bush, whipped by driving rain. And she leapt to the ghostly blackness, laughing like a drenched witch as she ran through the night.

The white police came. One day they rode back, and Stockman Jimmy, handcuffed, walked beside them.

20
SEEKING THE TRACKS OF NEMARLUK

IN May 1932 Constables Morey and Mahony, stationed at Timber Creek, received a headquarters' order from Darwin to arrest Nemarluk's men. Alf Martin, manager of the Victoria River Downs cattle station, was expected by car *en route* to Wyndham, the port of the East Kimberleys. The one road from the Northern Territory runs through Timber Creek. Now, Legune Station is near the river-mouth, on the opposite bank to Nemarluk's country. Morey knew that periodically the Port Keats natives came to Legune seeking tobacco from the station natives. Possibly, Nemarluk's men were there now. He decided to travel with Martin, pick up horses at Newry Station on the Western Australian side, and make a surprise raid on Legune. His going to distant Wyndham would be known by bush telegraph, so the bush natives would feel safe.

But *en route* at Carlton Station he mentioned those horses at Newry. The house lubra overhead him with the result that when Morey raided Legune every bush native had crossed back over the Victoria. So much for the "animal" brain of the simple aboriginal.

On his return ride of one hundred and forty miles to Timber Creek, Morey, ruminating on the efficacy of native bush-telegraph, resolved that even he himself would not know where he was going next time.

The Black Service, much less efficient in Bulbul's absence, could only tell Morey that Nemarluk was "travelling," which the police already knew. When Morey and Mahony started from Timber Creek, McCann patrolled from the Daly. Nemarluk's country was in between. But station boys on the Victoria River, and boys working for the peanut growers on the Daly, had kept Nemarluk posted with news of the mustering and outfitting of horses and mules, and the activities of trackers. In their inland strongholds, of sandstone bluff, and coastal hide-outs amongst the vine jungles, the Red Band held council and defiant corroboree. Then in the arrogance of assured confidence Nemarluk doubled back with his horde towards Legune. Apart from bravado, it was a shrewd move.

With Morey's patrol were Trackers Splinter, Bogey, Charlie, and Mick, with horses Tarzan, Tasman, Target, Tramp, Tripod, Trivale, Triangle Trixie, Trumpet, Tekara, Torpedo, Teamster, Turner, Tomcat, Thora, Tailor, Tom, Taxation, Three, and eight mules. Old Taxation would never leave

Morey's horse Tasman. Wherever Tasman went, Taxation followed, a long way behind at such times when Morey had to gallop.

"If those tax men are as hard to shake off as old Taxation." laughed Morey, "I don't envy the poor old taxpayer."

They crossed over into Nemarluk's country and rode down-river through richly grassed plains. On the second night, they prepared to raid the native camp at Bradshaw Station, leaving their horses hidden two miles back.

"These station natives are awake to the usual daylight stunt," said Morey, "so we'll raid towards the middle of the night. By Jove, it's cold! You take Bogey and Charlie and work around the camp from the river side while I come in opposite with Splinter and Mick."

To a howling of dogs they rushed the camp but not one of the Red Band was there nor any of Nemarluk's horde. Among the station blacks as usual were visitors from the Fitzmaurice tribes, but these denied any knowledge of Nemarluk's whereabouts.

The trackers could extract nothing but misleading information from the station boys; and sarcastic glances, sullen looks, or stony silence from the bush natives – until they questioned Jacob, the garden boy.

"You savvy that Port Keats mob?" inquired Morey.

"Yui, me savvy him."

"He been come in here?"

"No more."

"Which way him bin sit down now?"

"All about sit down longa Collareeoo."

"You savvy that camp?"

"Yui, me savvy."

"That good place longa horse?"

"No more, him properly rough place – him big fella stone all away. Horse no can go."

"You come and showem that camp?"

"Yui, me come."

"Think I'll come as far as Coolondong with you," said Harold Cook the manager. "The blacks, not content with spearing the outside cattle have now started on the quiet old milkers. A trip around the run with a police patrol might scare them off a bit."

Bradshaw's Run is famous for its beautiful horses.

One notorious blackfellow called Deven used to spear the horses and cut the tongue out just as a dainty morsel, disdaining the remainder of the carcass. He had been captured, but had escaped from the Darwin gaol and was now roaming in the ranges.

Behind the tree-sheltered homestead runs a range and from its cliff-like wall trickles a crystal-clear spring. Pipes carry its water down to the homestead and its famous garden. On the opposite side or the Victoria River is Auvergne Station, managed by Shadforth, whose wife has lived a life crammed with pioneering adventure.

"Nemarluk has put the wind well up these station boys," said Morey as they saddled up next morning. "Even our trackers are scared."

"Yes," answered Mahony. "And if this Jacob guides us to a hide-out of Nemarluk's, then I'm a Dutchman."

"Well, they're not here, and they're not at Legune. If Jacob proves a failure we'll push straight out east into the big yam country. It is the season and we are sure to find natives hunting out there. Quite evidently they are not going to put the big chief away. So we've simply got to go out and hunt for them. We haven't the best of trackers, and they're scared at the start. All we can thoroughly depend upon is ourselves and our horses while we can nurse them. So there's a long and tough hunt ahead."

"Primitive versus Modern," laughed Mahony.

"No favours, a fair go, and all the world to play hide and seek in."

"Um!" grunted Morey as they swung into the saddles and waved the patrol to start.

They followed the Victoria down past Bradshaw's tomb, from which height a sentinel of Nemarluk's spied down a grandson of the warrior who had speared Bradshaw.

The patrol rode to Kurri jungle with the trackers spread out seeking tracks along the wide valley to Luberie Creek.

"How far Collareeoo from Coolondong?" inquired Morey of Jacob.

"No more long way."

"Which way moon when we catch him Collareeoo?"

Jacob pointed upwards.

"It would take the moon about four hours to get to that position," remarked Morey. "So in distance Collareeoo might be anything between fifteen and twenty miles from Coolondong. We had better camp now; pack up about sundown and go to Coolondong in the night; camp there tomorrow in shelter; then go on foot tomorrow night and surprise Collareeoo. There are too many look outs in this country for day travelling when in the vicinity of a camp."

"Yes, they see you coming from a surprising distance," agreed Cook. "You find that out when you are after the cattle-spearers."

There was a bright moon and they needed it amongst that scrub and fallen timber. It was nearly midnight when the horses pulled up by the ghostly waters of Coolondong Billabong, surrounded by sweet, green feed. It was a very silent camp.

At daybreak they posted the trackers on commanding spurs in the ranges; then at late evening started off on foot, walking into country impassable for horses. Breaking their way through scrub, climbing rough hills, travelling for miles over spinifex-covered boulders, at midnight Morey called for a spell and a smoke.

"Useless country," said Cook, "good only for wallabies and snakes."

"And blacks!" added Morey.

"Yes, and blacks. I don't envy you chaps your hunt after them. Why, if I wanted to hide from anybody, I'll bet it would take more than a regiment of soldiers to dig me out of here."

"You go back now?" inquired tracker Charlie from the shadows.

"Go back? No, we are going on and we are going now," answered Morey decidedly. "Up on your legs, boys!"

"Jacob talk it too much rough place alonga nighttime," protested Charlie.

"Yes? Well sitting here won't make it any smoother! So get a move on now." And Morey set the example.

But soon they found that Charlie had not protested without reason. They crawled through a tangle of jungle, climbed over tumbled boulders, and slid down polished rocks slippery as ice, into a water-washed gorge. In the bitter cold before dawn they reached Collareeoo and looked in vain for a camp.

"Nemarluk has given us our first walk," said Morey grimly. "And I'll bet it won't be the last."

Or the long day's walk back to Coolondong camp, they trudged through Talakinyin Gorge, stepping gingerly along the steep "concrete road" leading into Cab-bie soak-hole. In this savage prank of nature, roaring floods had scoured the rock into an approach like a concrete chute hemmed on either side by shining walls of rock. The hole itself, once started by water, had been pounded out during ages of time by floods that whirled boulders into mill wheels while grinding them into dust.

The following day Harold Cook returned towards Bradshaw homestead while the patrol pushed on seeking any band of wandering hunters, any smokes, any sign of native life. They sought in Bottle Tree Creek too where the weird old boabs, their huge stomachs of trunks carved with the fantastic imagery of stone-age men, line the banks like bloated gnomes; they camped in hidden pockets of forest and scrub, and made no betraying smoke; but they could not hide their tracks.

They divided the patrol at times; Morey with a tracker scouring the country fifty miles away, then circling until he cut the tracks of Mahony travelling with the pack-animals ahead. They searched creeks where the big yams grow, and by devious ways surrounded hidden billabongs. But no lubras were wading for lily-roots; no men were seeking tortoise or water-rat.

A type of the Northern Territory "Mounteds".

21
NEMARLUK'S VISITING-CARD

THEN Nemarluk's men spoke in fire that darkened the sky with rolling columns of smoke.

"Burning out the country, by Caesar!" exclaimed Morey. "Covering their tracks while destroying every blade of grass."

"A shrewd move," frowned Mahony. "We know they're all around us, but still we'll have to ride a hundred miles or more before we've any chance of cutting their tracks. Meanwhile the horses will wander for miles at night, looking for feed. We'll waste half the day searching for them."

So it proved, on numerous days.

Miles apart, they rode far into the Wingate Ranges. Before this patrol ended they were to travel altogether fourteen hundred miles by horse and foot. One morning they abruptly reined in their horses and stared at two policemen carved on a big .old tree. A tall policeman and a smaller one, standing out in fresh relief from the rudely chopped bark.

"Nemarluk!" laughed Morey.

"He's full of beans," smiled Mahony. "They've marked this tree in our line of march. It's taken bushcraft to work that out."

"Dignity and impudence," chuckled Morey.

"Well, they've got the laugh on us anyway."

Typical mounted men these, Morey well over six feet, broad shouldered, with big eyes above a square set jaw. One of the strongest men in the Territory; invariably cheery; a great camp mate. Mahony shorter, but solidly built, direct eyed with a fleeting grimness of face. Fond of horses and dogs; fond of map-drawing while travelling through unmapped areas; a man always ready to carryon. They had ridden into a sandstone pocket and saw the big tree towering majestically from a grassy glade hemmed in by heights of weather-beaten brown rock. In such places well hidden, yet with unsuspected getaways, are the hide-outs of the natives.

Those were moonlit nights when the billabongs reflected dull silver shadowed by the black silhouettes of screw palms; when the castellated sandstones threw coal black shadows into weird pictures of some primal world; when the rustle of a snake in the grass drew instant attention, and the throaty cackle of a nocturnal crane made the skin creep on the trackers' necks. "Spirit birds call at night like that."

"Makes a man wonder just where he came from," said Morey

dreamily, "and where he's going to, and what it's all about."

"H'm," replied Mahony, "we might as well be up in the moon. As it is –"

The howl of a dingo made the trackers' eyes gleam white as they stared towards the black tracery of the trees. Charlie's leg quivered reminiscently. After a waiting silence, that long-drawn howl came again from far away.

"What name?" asked Morey sharply.

"Dingo," mumbled Charlie, and rolled himself again in his blankets.

But it was a sulky, scared reply. Charlie's head was really out from under his blanket and he was looking, listening, and smelling with all his might. So was Bogey, ready to leap to the police for weapons. The police strained their ears but could not quite catch the end of the dingo's note – could not be sure.

When an aboriginal imitates a dingo howling, he does it so perfectly that even a dingo is deceived. But invariably at the conclusion of the long drawn howl, he slightly coughs. And a keen human ear, if the owner knows enough, and is close enough, can detect that coughy ending.

Among certain tribes that howl has preceded the attack on more than one patrol, the stone-age dingoes calling their pack closer and closer around the camp. So once, Charlie and Bogey had awakened to the bite of those dingo fangs – the points of the long war-spears.

By this call, too, the men of Nemarluk signalled warning and their whereabouts to the scattered family groups. And it proved the howl of a Nemarluk pup that signalled "police" that night.

The patrol followed many a trail which led to nothing; they raided camps to find that the wanteds had snaked in the grass past the cordon. They met nomads too, who genuinely did not know Nemarluk's whereabouts, and they could not have read his signals had they wanted to. The signal of horde to horde is intentionally not always decipherable by all the members of either.

Some tribes live in isolation, prepared to defend their country against all others. This isolation, however, is fast being broken down. Over great areas of country differing tribesmen, if strong and game enough, travel to ever widening boundaries.

When the patrol reached the Fitzmaurice River bar they saw across the MacAdam Range to the east, and there, in the upper reaches of the river, the first definite smoke-signals gently rising in the clear blue air. Some of Chugulla's men were signalling the Coolondong look out of Nemarluk's tribal horde.

The trackers looked serious. Reasonably so.

They were out of their country in a notoriously hostile land – especially to trackers.

One day Splinter pointed to fresh tracks of three spearmen in open country. They followed and eventually caught them. The police learned from these frightened men (whose facial expression, all the same, showed satisfaction) that one of McCann's trackers had been killed, and that Bulbul and Tracker Waggin had found the body of Nagata at Nemarluk's Ande-mallee camp and had buried it. But they shook their heads to questions concerning Nemarluk's whereabouts:

"He is far away."

The patrol pushed on persistently seeking the tracks of a Nemarluk man, while ever and anon from some scrubby height a smoke-signal shot up into the air. Chugulla and Nemarluk's men made the signals in this way: a big heap of dried leaves that give "long distance" smoke were piled coneshape and lit. Then a long, broad mat of weaved grass was thrown over it, a bending man grasping each corner. Under the edges of the mat, just sufficient air is allowed in to keep the leaves burning and forming the greatest volume of smoke which slowly rolls over itself under the imprisoning mat. At a grunt from the leader, the mat is sharply withdrawn with a peculiar whirling motion that draws air under the mat and helps to shoot up a puff of smoke. The mat is immediately replaced over the leaves and another puff formed. The blacks signal in puffs, in long thin stems of smoke, in a big or a little cloud, or in distinct spirals. They can form variations; send smokes to different heights, and in varying colour, speed, and density. A still day with clear air is the best for signalling. Then there is no wind to disturb the smoke; it hangs in position longer while aircurrents seem to rise up from the plain to lift it high into the air above the look outs. The visibility too, is such that a column, a "balloon," a cloud, a "mushroom," a spiral can be seen at great distances.

But the aboriginal must hunt to eat. And the patrols are tireless. An aboriginal horde or group when spread over the country, hunting as they go, will travel only six or seven miles a day. A patrol will travel forty if desired.

A lone warrior, knowing the patrol is close behind him will travel a hundred miles in twenty-four hours, and another quick fifty almost immediately afterwards. He may travel swiftly yet another hundred, or until such time as he joins again a tribal group or horde and drops to their daily hunting distance, five, six, or seven miles a day. The patrol has been left far behind, but it comes on; comes on.

They grow careless in hiding or disguising their tracks; count it too much trouble and effort to travel only on such areas of country as are rendered impassable to horses by bog, swamp, jungle and scrub, or are waterless.

The patrols are kept travelling, often for many months. Then horses have to be left behind while the patrol load their own backs with food and press doggedly on by foot. That evens the chase; the horde hunting for their food; the pursuers constantly delayed as they temporarily lose the tracks, and walking under a heavy load. Daily at journey's end horde and patrol have frequently travelled an equal distance. But the chase keeps on and on until the patrol have chased the horde from the broken country and can use their horses again.

Patrols understand much of the aboriginal's life; .when and where he hunts; when he sleeps. They know that when the hunting is good he sleeps often and heavily and travels hardly at all. They know the country he must hunt in according to the season, and can read well the signs of the bush. This knowledge often enables them to cut off many a wearisome journey by foretelling the locality to which the hunted men are making. Patrols, moreover, have a very unpleasant habit of travelling far at night. This travelling the aboriginal universally objects to, though he will travel at night when necessary. The night belongs to the Spirit World. Often, the patrol will at dawn arrive at a camp which went to sleep with easy minds the night before, having received a smoke-signal that the "pleece" were turning into camp forty miles away.

Then the hunted horde become flurried; their defiant corroborees at the campfire change to silence over hardly glowing coals; to uneasy sleep interrupted by many a glance into the dark and many a listening ear. Their mongrel dogs know and sleep with one green eye open. Now, when travelling on the hunt by day it is with many a backward glance. And as they lose confidence so they take less and less care to disguise their tracks. Presently the patrol is at their heels-constantly at their heels.

But the chase after such a consummate warrior of the Wilds as Nemarluk became a great strain. Later, Nemarluk left the lagging horde for considerable periods, travelling alone far and fast, hunting as he travelled, with a cold fury that wasted no time in securing his game, nor in eating it, nor in overlong sleep.

22
CROSSING THE VICTORIA

THE patrol crossed Wa-ta-puk Creek in black night, then at dawn galloped the signallers on Mount Na-ra-lon. These leapt for their hide-outs like mountain goats. The patrol caught one. Too late for a get-away he had leapt into a crevice in the rocks and a tracker saw his toe dirt in the crack. Peering in, he grinned at the man's heel then prodded his hairy back. The frightened one whispered that Nemarluk had gone to Legune Station.

They rode in forced stages back to the river and when near Blunder Bay reined in their horses to admire yet another of Nemarluk's visiting-cards. Among the timber the leaves had been scraped clear from a circle fifty feet in diameter and on the bright red soil was drawn a huge but unmistakable picture.

"Well I'm blessed!" exclaimed Mahony. "That is the *Maroubra* towing the *Ouida* away from Port Keats; there is no mistaking the small wheel-house on top of the superstructure. They must have been watching us salvaging her from the mangroves."

"It is the work of Nemarluk's braves right enough," laughed Morey. "Freshly drawn too. I've never seen such a large aboriginal drawing. A coincidence too, for by now the *Maroubra* must be nearly due from Darwin with stores for Victoria River depot. We'll signal her to take us across river to Legune. I'll go with two of the trackers. You had better stay on this side in case Nemarluk evades capture and crosses back."

When the country became impossibly rough for horses they formed a base camp clear of bush-fires and dingoes; then, carrying a week's food, set out on foot. If hostile natives raided camp or Deven got amongst the horses – well, that was a risk which could not be avoided.

Through rugged country with a scenery peculiarly its own they trudged to Blunder Bay at the mouth of the Victoria, and one misty morning the *Maroubra* appeared. Rifle-shots, fires, shouts, failed to attract attention, and she steamed past into the mists.

"She won't return for a week or ten days," said Morey in exasperation. "We must build a raft and chance it."

They sent the trackers back to the camp for more food, straps, halters, and bags. With these, the axe, and two canvas sheets they set to work, selecting the lightest of driftwood, notching the logs and strapping them securely together. They rammed the bags full of grass and fastened a sheet in waterproof fashion around them. This buoyant "float" they lashed on the logs, then wiped the sweat from their brows as a good day's work was finished.

"The *Hesperus!*" declared Morey with a proud sweep of his arm.

"She *does* look a wreck!" admitted Mahony.

Morey grunted, eyeing Mahony somewhat askance. He had felt rather proud of his handiwork. The trackers said nothing – not aloud.

They launched her and she floated. "There you are!" exclaimed Morey. "She floats!"

"Like a duck – a dead one," answered Mahony. "We'll try her paces anyway."

She proved unwieldy, difficult to control.

"You'll have to conscript your crew," laughed Mahony. "There'll be no volunteers."

Morey glanced at the trackers; they kept looking at the raft.

"Anyone would think it was a life and death job," growled Morey. "There are only a few whirlpools in the river anyway."

"And a few big crocodiles," corrected Mahony. They tied the *Hesperus* to a tree then shifted camp to a long point from which they could watch both the raft and the tides.

"I'll sail in the morning," decided Morey, "when the tide is at its highest or lowest. The currents and whirlpools are not nearly so strong then."

"I'll get the streamers ready," said Mahony.

"What are you looking for?"

"My swag!"

They looked around and discovered that the swag, a rifle, a pair of handcuffs, and Tracker Dick were missing.

"He takem my shirt too!" wailed Splinter. "By cri, he plurry tief that feller!"

Morey was furious. They started out on the tracks immediately. "Why he run away?" shouted Morey.

"He fright longa river," wailed Splinter. "He more fright longa Nemarluk. He stealem my shirt. More better Nemarluk cut 'im kidney-fat longa that feller tief!"

At sundown they found the rifle and handcuffs under a bush, but never saw the swag, or Tracker Dick, or Splinter's shirt again.

The nights were bitterly cold, and Mahony sympathetically lent his ground-sheet to Morey, who mourned his lost swag as a warm friend. He slept between two fires, and each time he woke up with the fires burned down he realized the value the aboriginal puts on a dutiful wife.

They sat down to a delicious breakfast of johnnycakes and jam, the big river singing tremulously with the inrush of a racing tide. Swift little wavelets were tearing around the point before them. Suddenly the *Hesperus* broke her moorings. They leapt to save her, but too late.

"By cri," shouted Bogey, "she fly all a same airyplane!"

"She *is* travelling," agreed Morey, admiration overcoming dismay.

They raced to intercept her at the point, but with a burst of speed she left them lamenting. "Par Lap!" yelled Splinter as the current whisked her outstream.

"So much for the poor brainless aboriginal," said Morey bitterly. "Talking racehorses out here in No Man's Country. Do you know, I feel proud of her," he added as they watched the *Hesperus* bobbing outstream. "Admittedly, distance is kind to her crude lines, but she looks trim and smart and is travelling at an incredible speed. There's some 'sea' on out there too!"

"Don't boast about her strength yet awhile," advised Mahony. "Watch what that whirlpool does to her first." She was heading straight towards a giant funnel spinning in the tortured water, its rims almost iridescent with movement. The whirlpool caught the raft and whisked her round and round like a match-box.

"What a wonderful sea-sickness if a man was only aboard," said Morey. "But then a man would be sucked down the funnel. I wonder how long the whirlpool will hold her, it seems only to be spinning her round its edges."

"Surprising it does not tear her to pieces or swallow her," answered Mahony. "I'd like to see a twenty-foot crocodile in that whirl; he'd spin like a toy lizard."

"Make him lay 'em egg!" laughed Splinter.

"Jack Hayles tells me the whirlpools in this reach sometimes suck the *Maroubra* down over a foot," said Morey. "Look, she's gradually working to the outer edge!"

Suddenly the raft was jerked clear of the whirlpool and sped as if in crazy fear only to be thrown aside by another "whirl" that suddenly "made" before her. Picking herself together, she dodged several other whirls then careered up-stream in the grip of a raging current.

"'Twas the wreck of the *Hesperus* ... Whence all but he had fled," quoted Mahony.

"She sails on her last voyage," sighed Morey.

"And it means about ten pages of foolscap to 'please explain' to the Department why two Government ground-sheets were lost!"

They had to remain and await the return of the *Maroubra*; there were no more straps to make a *Hesperus II*. They piled grass heaps together ready for signalling, and lived patiently on johnnycakes and jam. For some perverse reason fish refused to be caught. The trackers prospered, enjoying their johnny-cakes with snake and goanna. During the days that followed, twice they saw the *Hesperus* sail gaily past with the tide. She was holding together surprisingly.

One sundown Splinter shouted and rushed to the grass heaps with a firestick. Up sped a column of smoke.

As the *Maroubra* came cruising around a distant bend she was swept over towards the northern bank.

"By Jove, those currents are strong!" exclaimed Morey. "Ah! They've spun the wheel hard over!" – as the vessel's nose sheered outstream again to cross the current.

"She appears to be slipping sideways," sail Mahony. "Just like an aeroplane side-slipping from a height!"

"They've seen our smokes. Hurrah!" waved Morey. "See! there is Jack Hayles looking through his glasses."

The vessel sheered across stream at an angle towards them, but boiling currents kept her off and she sped past, rounded a point, and into a little sheltered bay. They heard the mud hook splashing overboard.

Even in shelter, currents were too strong for the vessel to remain at anchor. Provisions were quickly rowed ashore to Mahony, then the *Maroubra* with Morey and Splinter and Bogey aboard sailed for an anchorage several miles down-stream.

Skipper Jack Hayles is a renowned cook, and he had a potato-pie just nicely browned.

Shortly after dawn Morey, Splinter, and Bogey were cautiously put ashore, and the *Maroubra* immediately steamed away into the mists.

Morey found himself among broken ranges whose valleys were blocked by masses of fallen rock overgrown with timber and vine. A sighing came down to them as if of wind around crags and through clefts, whispering around cone-shaped hills and square-capped tablelands. Birds whistled down below there in the timber, rock pigeons hooted in solemn bass up above. But there was neither sound, nor smoke, nor track, nor smell, nor any sign of man. Cautiously, with eyes and ears alert, keeping to the timber or hugging the ramparts of rock they commenced an unbelievably rough walk that in ten miles brought them to the edge of the Legune plain. A wall of range marked one boundary and this they followed around until sundown brought them in sight of the low drab buildings of Legune homestead.

Morey halted under cover. Away out above the grassy plain the dark backs of cattle and horses could be seen. The lovesick call of a bull came rumbling across the plain and the bark of a dog at the homestead. With the dusk, fires began to twinkle from the bush blacks' camp by the ridge behind the homestead, answered by a red glow from the station blacks' camp on top of the ridge, and from a camp farther along. Impossible to raid these camps successfully with only two trackers. Under darkness, they crept closer to the bush blacks' camp. It was quiet; no corroborees; just the chatter of campfire gossip-apparently no strangers in camp. About nine o'clock they were all asleep, then the patrol lay down and slept until half-past three in the morning. Morey woke the trackers and told them he would attend to the camp in front while they scouted around the camp on the ridge. They were to keep hidden, and at dawn answer his whistle by repeated whistles. Only if they saw Nemarluk run from any camp were they to show themselves. The trackers, shivering with cold, crept away while Morey sat there longing for a smoke. Every now and then a lubra would crouch up and scratch the family fire together, then sleepily roll back in the ashes.

At dawn Morey crept forward to a bush within twenty yards of the camp; not even a dog heard him; shivering he stretched his limbs, flexing the cramped muscles. An old black fellow sat up, with a blanket draping bowed shoulders as he crouched over a fire. One by one the folk rose and stretched themselves; dogs stretched and yawned as they were disturbed by the blacks sitting up. There was much yawning and coughing and spitting and blowing of coals into flame. Then one aboriginal called to another and general conversation began.

23
THE TRAP IN NEMARLUK'S CAMP

MOREY waited until it was properly light then whistled softly. It was immediately answered from high up on the ridge, and farther along behind the ridge again and again. Apparently numerous men were watching from there.

Yabbering broke out as Morey stood up and strode swiftly forward. He did not want the usual stampede. Noting an aboriginal in shirt and trousers, he recognized Yarry, a station boy who understood pidgin-English, and called to him to tell the people to sit down quietly; he wanted to "talk-talk longa them." Dogs barked furiously. Morey, almost upon him, stared at a man of a strong Malay type who stared back. As he leapt up Morey was on him and they both rolled over, the aboriginal kicking frantically as Morey slipped the handcuffs around his ankles.

"Mankee!" challenged Morey. The man's startled face showed answer enough.

"Deven up there longa stockboy camp!" volunteered Yarry.

"Where Nemarluk?"

"Down longa river longa timber islan'!"

Morey glanced hastily around but most of the squatting aborigines were known to him. He hurried towards the ridge and Splinter shouted recognition.

"Look out!" called Morey. "Deven up there!"

"He bin run away!"

"Which way him go?"

"He bin run down longa creek!"

"Well why the blazes didn't you catch him!"

"Him too much quick fella."

Morey, a lover of animals, would particularly have liked to lay hands on Deven, the man who cut horses' tongues out.

"Stop those men from calling out," he shouted.

Silence fell where before was warning shouts all along the ridge.

Bob, Dave, and the cook, roused by the commotion, came strolling across from the homestead.

"I'm after Nemarluk, the Port Keats killer. Will you lend me horses?" asked Morey.

"Yes. I'll get the boys to run in some now."

"Good. I've just missed Deven and for a certainty he is running to warn Nemarluk. Yarry tells me Nemarluk has a camp down on the timber island. That must be nearly twelve miles away. With horses I might beat Deven to it."

While the horses were being run in Morey questioned Mankee, who admitted that he helped kill the Japs near Port Keats. Morey quickly realized that the Lezune natives feared Nemarluk but were more fearful still of betraying him. They whispered that Kummungeegut, whom white men called Charcoal, Kerinbo Davey, and Pooneemillar Charlie were in Nemarluk's camp. Charcoal was one of the attackers of the lugger *Pat*; Davey and Charlie were wanted for cattle-spearing. But the Legune natives would not tell of Nemarluk, Minmara, or others of the Red Band.

At last some of the stockboys volunteered to help in the arrest of Nemarluk. They would make no attempt to seize him, they carefully explained, but would "work" on horses. They were mounted men used to mustering cattle and they reasoned that Nemarluk could have no objection to them rounding him up providing they did not get off their horses. They mounted and rode away.

Morey thought rapidly. He knew that "island" of timber down towards the river-mouth. It stood out on a plain, a range enclosed two sides of it while a heavily timbered creek bounded it on the other two. A look out man must notice any approach to that timber. Morey instructed Splinter to take four stockboys and ride right around the creek, keeping its timber between him and that little "island" of timber on the plain, until he got right to the north. From cover, he was to watch towards the timber camp but not to come out on the plain until after dark} unless natives saw him. Bogey was to do the same with four more stockboys on the east side, his party to ride amongst the timber which grew along the foot of the range. They were to turn in towards the camp and meet Splinter in the middle of the plain after it was dark. If Morey did not meet them then they were to ride straight into Nemarluk's camp. But if he wanted them by day he would send up a smoke-signal and they were to gallop the camp.

The parties separated, Morey riding with one stockboy.

In a few miles he came to the edge of all possible cover and reined in. Before him was the plain, yellow-green under grass five feet high; a mile out in front was the dull green "island" of timber, walled by the partly encircling range. The plain extended for miles elsewhere. He thought quickly. Even if they had forestalled Deven, still he could worm his way through the grass and warn Nemarluk before night. Morey rode straight out into the grass, Almost for a certainty he and the stockboy would be seen, but if the trackers were alert they might see Nemarluk break camp and run him down on the horses. .

That grass hid sun-cracks and holes, traps for the stumbling horses. Morey stared at the timber ahead, positive they could not approach unnoticed. But they did! As they neared the edge of the timber he saw a wisp of smoke, as they rode closer still, he saw several black heads moving about, heard the "chop! chop!" of a native chipping at a boomerang in the making. He held himself ready for a gallop, wondering if his horse would break leg or neck in a hole. Then he saw two lubras walking about, and the heads of several bucks. Incredible! But they got within thirty yards of the camp before the black heads looked up at sound of approaching hooves. Morey held up his hand and motioned them to sit down; the Legune stockboy called out reassuringly as Morey's horse plunged into the camp.

Nemarluk was not there, only three lubras and four bucks. Disappointed, Morey glanced swiftly around, meeting blank amazement. His eyes settled on a magnificent specimen of a man well over six feet in height with a huge chest and shoulders and, very unusual for an aboriginal, thick and muscular legs.

Morey dismounted casually, said "Davey!" and immediately slipped handcuffs on his ankles. The giant cattle-spearer just sat there, his hairy face quaintly expressive of bovine astonishment.

Then Morey recognized Sandy, a renegade stockboy of the "cheeky" type who understood "pidgin."

"Where Nemarluk?" demanded Morey.

"He go longa Charcoal, Charlie, look longa kangaroo. Altogether boy been go hunt."

"Where lubra belonga him feller?"

"Altogether lubra been go look longa goanna, lizard, sugar-bag, 'shnake.'"

While the stockboy collected the weapons Morey concealed the horses, then gazed thoughtfully at the scattered fire and sleeping-places. Sandy pointed out where Nemarluk and his four lubras slept on the extreme outside while Charcoal's sleeping-place was in the centre of the camp. Deven did not use this camp, he was a "cave man," pinning his faith to the impassable ranges. Morey, with bushes, built an aboriginal breakwind in such a position that, hidden behind it, he would be able to see every aboriginal in, or approaching the camp, the stockboy building a screen strategically opposite. Then Morey told Sandy to tell the others that when the hunters came returning to camp they were to behave naturally at their tasks, while the boomerang maker was to keep chipping at his boomerang. Sandy nodded and obeyed, loosely enough, as is the way of a civilized boy when translating to "bush niggers."

Time passed. The natives, squatting there, spoke in low tones with an occasional glance under shaggy brows at the stockboy and Morey. Davey, sitting with huge arms folded over his knees, stared amusedly down at the little steel links imprisoning his ankles. A cheeky scrub bird fluttered down and dusted in the ashes, then preened his green and yellow feathers upon the cooking-stones. In the middle afternoon, the head and shoulders of a warrior appeared above the grass away out on the sunlit plain. He approached unconcernedly, feathers in his hair and in the grass bands around his arms. He carried spears and wommera, and four possums. The corroboree paint of a week before was still upon his body. Sandy was chip, chip, chipping at his boomerang. The hunter walked right into camp and to within a yard of Morey. His lower jaw dropped, his eyes slowly bulged. Morey laughed, forgetting fatigue and anxiety and hunger in the ludicrous astonishment of the warrior. Davey laughed reminiscent of the throaty rumbling of a bell, the stockboy laughed, Sandy laughed, the gins shrieked with waving arms and the scrub bird sped indignantly away.

As the good old sun went slowly towards rest, one by one, then in twos and threes, the hunters dawdled into camp. Soon there were a score of them, squatting in the camp with faces expressing the liveliest surprise. Evidently the Legune natives had made not the slightest attempt to warn this horde. A fighting crowd these men, wild bushmen, not loved by the easier living stockboys. Charlie came in to be handcuffed to Davey who roared as at a great joke. The fellow has a neck like a bull.

Toward sunset a mob of black heads appeared in the north, with horsemen around them and Morey knew that hunters or huntresses had wandered on to Splinter and he was now perforce bringing them into camp. Then two horsemen appeared on the opposite side of the plain and Morey's heart leapt; but in the same instant he realized that Nemarluk and Charcoal would not be taken so easily as that.

When Splinter's party arrived some twenty lubras among them carried more than three hundred snakes and lizards, shiny scales and skins gleamed repulsively through the bulging bags of open-work fibre. Morey was surprised at the variety in the reptile kingdom.

Two lanky youths, gawking their surprise, were Old Bogey's capture.

Morey ordered Bogey to return to Legune homestead, riding with all the stockboys in full view across the plain. In the morning he was to return with food. Splinter would remain with Morey.

Perhaps, if Nemarluk and Charcoal saw the men riding back in the sunset, they would conclude that the patrol had left the camp. Perhaps!

24
TWO TRAPS FOR NEMARLUK

THE life of the camp went on, the lubras threw down their dilly-bags, fires sprang up. But Marboo glared in frenzied dismay, side by side with three others of Nemarluk's wives. Splinter collected all the weapons and tied them in one big heap behind Morey's breakwind. Under explicit instructions, Sandy interpreted that the usual night-life of the camp must be carried on. Fire-lights gleamed on the squatting bodies of men, on the bending forms of lubras around their cooking; big-eyed piccaninnies and uneasy dogs stared towards Morey and Splinter. When many fires made many coals, cooking-holes were dug for 'roo and wallaby, while the lubras threw the snakes and lizards on flattened coals and raked coals and ashes on top.

Morey impressed on Splinter that if he dozed for an instant through the night he would awake with shovel-nosed spears through his body. He was to watch from behind his breakwind, seeing but unseen. Should a wanted man enter camp Morey would arrest him while Splinter protected Morey from attack from the rear.

Splinter nodded understandingly, then retired to his breakwind, his nostrils sniffing hungrily. Sandy was then ordered to tell the horde that neither man nor woman must leave camp. All were to sleep in their family places as usual, each fire must be kept burning brightly. If Nemarluk or Charcoal sang out they were to answer and tell them to come in.

Sandy translated in a general silence. The women were raking the blackened coals off the snakes. The blacks would never be certain whether Morey, behind his bush screen, was asleep or awake.

"Thank heavens," he sighed, "I don't snore."

An odour of roasted reptiles filled the air. Morey watched the feasters pulling the cooked things to pieces with their teeth; baby piccanins clawing for pieces from the mothers' mouths; dogs growling amongst them, wolfing skin or bone. Then he gazed out through the smoke wisps into the night. Those sounds of hungry eating reminded him he had not tasted food since leaving the *Maroubra*. He wondered if Jack Hayles had made another potato-pie.

When the dogs were gnawing the 'roo bones, Morey ordered Sandy to play the didgereedoo and start the people singing corroboree. Sandy strolled to his long bamboo blowing-tube and soon the hoarse "didgereedoo-doo-doo" was blasting its monotony across the plain. The women started a chant, the men joined in with a tense silence after each cessation of the chant, eyes staring out into the night. Then the didgereedoo droned again, and again the chant joined in. Morey, listening and staring, wondered whether it was his nerves made the whole scene seem strained and unnatural; he wondered whether Charcoal or Nemarluk would possibly fall for it; uneasily he began to feel that at any moment spears might come hissing out of the darkness. Two hours went by.

In the abrupt silence after a chant, a shrilling scream electrified the camp. Morey felt his hair on end as he stared out to the left; but that animal scream shrieked again directly behind him. He twisted around with levelled revolver. That beastly scream could surely never come from a man!

An old lubra shrilled reply. Did she warn him?

Or did she tell him to come in? Was it Nemarluk? Was it Charcoal? Were the two together? Was Deven there? There was bitter murder in the eyes of Marboo as she glared towards the old woman.

A shadow glided into camp fifteen yards on Morey's right. As it came within the light of a fire the body gleamed strangely. He glided on, propped his spears against a tree, walked to a fire and squatted down. He grunted to the native squatting there and received guttural reply.

Morey glanced swiftly around; there was no following shadow. He darted from the bushes in a line that would keep the fire-light in the aboriginal's eyes. Even so the man glanced up and, leaping backward, clutched his spears as Morey brought the revolver-butt down on his head. As he fell, the handcuffs were slipped on his ankles and Morey wheeled around facing all those glaring eyes.

But not a man moved – except Splinter. He had leapt out, threatening all who squatted there. Morey smiled, and turned to look down at Charcoal. He gazed in admiration at the most handsome and graceful aboriginal he had ever seen. His height over six feet, his shoulders broad with powerful chest, his symmetrical body tapered down to slim hips. Health and strength shone from the muscles and skin of the ochred body. The well-shaped head possessed features with no suggestion of coarseness; the nose was almost Grecian, the lips no thicker than a white man's, the big black eyes were alight with defiance. Morey had been given a good description of this elusive raider, but still he gazed in surprise. The only blemish he could see on this splendid human specimen was a rapidly growing lump on his head.

Charcoal met the gaze with a sore, cheeky stare in reply. In answer to Sandy's questions he growled that he and Nemarluk had gone hunting in the morning but had separated. In the evening he had watched the patrol riding back towards Legune, but being suspicious had waited for night before crossing the plain. No, he did not know where Nemarluk was and, smiling brightly, he did not care. Then, as he squatted up and looked towards the old lubra who had called to him, his handsome face changed to a fiendish glare.

But Nemarluk did not come.

"Too crafty," thought Morey. "He is in some hide-out in the ranges with Deven, where they can overlook the camp." At dawn he ordered Sandy to bathe Charcoal's head. But Charcoal was quite unconcerned and wanted none of it. He accepted a cigarette with a laugh. A young lubra shyly brought him a fat go anna, nicely browned. He wolfed the lot, but he did give her a draw of his cigarette.

Morey again questioned Nemarluk's lubras, and though they told quite freely of the killing of the Japanese, they would give no hint as to the probable movements of Nemarluk. All he could get from Marboo was a defiant flash from black eyes; from the others a sulky shake of the head. Admiring their loyalty he made the horde bring the prisoners all the food they could eat, then waited in a hungry impatience while Splinter enjoyed a hearty breakfast of cold roast goanna. At last came the welcome thud of hooves as Bogey rode up with salt-beef and damper from Legune.

No information of Nemarluk was to be got from any of these people, It was plain, from the glowering looks cast on the stockboys, that there would be a little vengeful blood-letting immediately the patrol was well away. But Morey clung to one faint hope. He had four of Nemarluk's lubras; three were witnesses who told how Nemarluk himself had taken them aboard the *Ouida*. Morey knew that it is a wild man's boast not to lose lubras of value. And here was Marboo, Nemarluk's youngest and favourite, apparently a captive. Marboo, a great digger-out of yams, a keen smeller-out of possums, a tireless traveller with a not too-complaining tongue. And the silent horde waiting to see whether the leader of the Red Band would come and claim his women.

So Morey set his forlorn trap. It is one thing to catch an old bull, quite another to trap a tiger.

He ordered Splinter and Bogey to guard this camp, to see that the horde went about their daily tasks as usual, without straying from sight. If Nemarluk came in the night they were to seize him. Meanwhile, Morey would go to Legune, obtain supplies, and take the prisoners to a native well sometimes used by Nemarluk, eight miles beyond Legune, and wait in ambush there.

Sandy, the runaway stockboy, had also run away with the shirts and trousers of several of his mates. Morey commandeered these clothes and, to the delight of the women, dressed two sheepish looking myall men, topping them with the hats of Splinter and Bogey, much to those worthies' disgust. Then, with the four prisoners walking before him he rode in full view across the plain towards Legune, the two amateur "trackers" clinging to their horses with expressions anticipatory of early disaster.

Morey grinned, then immediately looked stern.

He felt certain that Nemarluk was watching from the frowning heights that girdled the plain here, and he could imagine the hearty laugh of the big leader should a disgusted horse buck a "tracker" and bolt away.

At Legune Morey enjoyed a few hours' much needed sleep; then, provisioned with salt-beef and damper, walked away with the prisoners, in full view during the afternoon. They walked before him with ejaculated warnings at grass-covered cracks and holes.

Morey wondered yet again at that foolish regulation recently brought into force that aboriginal prisoners should be handcuffed and not chained. These men walked in pairs, a handcuff from wrist to wrist. He could not find it in his heart to handcuff the four together even if they could have walked through the bush in this way. If both pairs bolted simultaneously he must lose one pair; he could only hold on to one lot and threaten to shoot the other. If they called his bluff – well, he would have to answer authority for allowing two prisoners to escape.

Whereas, if these men were secured by the usual light police chain around their necks, they could walk one behind the other in comfort; their arms and hands would be free to ward off the bushes and the long grass-seeds that sought their eyes; they could brush away flies and mosquitoes; their hands could reach and protect any part of their body; they could collect their firewood, carry their water, kill by throwing-stick, and carry any tit-bits of game within reach *en route*. They could eat and sleep comfortably; attend to that great necessity of the night, each man his fire; and could also attend to what scanty toilet arrangements were necessary. They could walk with swinging arms; dodge holes and stakes, logs and bushes, vines, boulders, and trees; could ford creeks and rivers easily and naturally.

Morey, a powerful man of six feet two inches, and noted as one of the strongest men in the Territory, admired the splendid physique of these four stone-age men walking before him. Three of them were over six feet, all had broad, deep chests and heavily muscled shoulders, Pavey's great body from hair to toe-nails was the build of a heavy Hercules, and his rugged face matched. Charcoal, dangerous as he was handsome, had come within an ace of knifing Constable Kennett. There were brains behind his flashing eyes, as there was swift cunning behind the Malay-like eyes of Mankee, with the swift agility of the fighting Malay in his smaller, compact body. Morey could not help thinking what a dangerous crowd he would have had if Nemarluk and Deven were there too.

He walked warily behind these four strong backs.

Just one day-dream and he would awake with them on top of him. Despite handcuffs, they could bite and crush a man to death should they once fall upon him. He wondered if their occasional guttural laughs portended what they would do to him should he fall asleep tonight.

25
THE CROCODILES AND THE RAFT

MOREY brought his prisoners to the soak under cover of night. Sternly he promised them that if Nemarluk came and they attempted to warn him or to escape or to help him he would shoot every man of them. He glared at each in turn, the revolver gleaming in the starlight. They glared back silently, but he could not fathom what lay behind their eyes. He handcuffed their ankles while wishing he could have chained them around a tree as usual; they would have enjoyed a far freer and more comfortable night, and he would have been free to tackle Nemarluk or any eventuality.

He watched throughout a night of silence, but only wallabies and some fierce-eyed night bird came to the well to drink. He waited there all next day, wondering how Bogey and Splinter were faring, wondering if Nemarluk had broken their necks or sliced out their kidney-fat as he so often had promised to do.

They had not caught Nemarluk, otherwise a messenger would have come before this. Perhaps the wary aboriginal would return for his lubras to-night.

Night came, with that deathly silence that magnifies a cracking stick to a pistol-shot. Morey started his prisoners back towards Legune, the trackers and he must have sleep. He walked close behind his prisoners with tensed legs ready for the leap back, and when Davey and Charcoal stumbled he stopped instantly until grumblingly they picked themselves up again. Patches of plain under ghostly grass appeared in the starlight, black clumps of timber to right and left, with the shadowed masses of the ranges in the distance.

When half-way to Legune, Morey saw a long black shadow ahead that he knew was a narrow point of timber running from the range edge out on to the plain. He knew that across the plain a wellbeaten cattle-pad followed parallel with the range, pierced this timber, then went right on to Legune homestead. He was pretty certain that the watchful Nemarluk would have come down from the range and walked along that point of sheltering timber until he came to the cattle-pad. He would seek on that easy walking pad for Morey's tracks returning to Legune.

"Might as well keep him guessing!" thought Morey, and ordered his prisoners to make a detour around the timber. This roundabout way took them up on to a timbered ridge from which, through the trees, he noticed the gleam of a small fire. It disappeared, then presently gleamed again. Could it be Nemarluk?

They crept quietly towards the fire, catching a gleam now and then through the trees. The fire soon was plainly to be seen. Suddenly it was blotted out as something passed in front of it, then gleamed again; now they saw two shadows crouching over it; heard the smothering of the lighted sticks in the ashes. Then spears rattled against bushes as two black forms stood up and strode out past them making towards the spring.

"If I attempt to seize them," thought Morey, "the prisoners will escape into the timber. If I call them to halt, they will bolt." He decided to let them walk ahead out on to the plain, then make his prisoners run on a wide detour and get ahead of them.

He did so, with a long swift run, all doubled up.

When he judged he was in a line well ahead of the two men, he made the prisoners lie down and waited, ready to rise up at the feet of the unknown.

But their ears had caught the soft thud of those running feet. He never saw them.

He hurried his men back to the fire. But all that was to be learned there was that two men had waited under cover and cooked a goanna, waiting until night had long descended before venturing out on to the plain.

"Well, they won't find me sleeping at the well!" thought Morey grimly. "Now, were Nemarluk and Deven planning to fill me with spears?"

But the prisoners would not say, they just smiled in that elusively inquiring, uncomprehending way the aboriginal has, and looked pleasantly puzzled. Davey turned his broad, hairy face to the stars, while subdued laughter rumbled from deep down in his throat.

"Laugh," thought Morey, "laugh! Anyway, the joke did not come off!"

And he marched them on through the night, glancing swiftly behind as an uneasy man will.

But Nemarluk was in a towering rage; he rattled his spears and chewed his beard. Before daylight he and Deven had killed a bullock within two miles of Legune homestead and invited all hands to the feast. He added a proviso, that he would take the kidney-fat of any station man who helped the police and roast it with the bullock.

But with Nemarluk and Deven on the run, with Charcoal, Mankee, Davey, and Charlie prisoners, with a patrol here amongst them, the natives felt assured and swiftly brought the news to Morey. He, as swiftly, decided to attend as an unwelcome guest.

But the host fled. He knew that now they had his tracks his case was hopeless. There was only one way to beat them – the big river.

At Legune Morey obtained an empty oil-drum and as much wire as he could find, then hurried away to the "island of timber."

Here, Bogey and Splinter, tired-eyed and nervy, greeted him thankfully. They had kept the horde together, but Nemarluk had not appeared. Marboo smiled, a mocking smile, quickly hidden. The trackers had also found that several lubras were badly in need of medical attention. Morey sighed. Here he was in urgent need of speed, with a long patrol and numerous geographical difficulties before him, and now, in the name of common humanity, he had to turn his patrol into a travelling ambulance.

"Bring them along!" he said gruffly to Splinter, and tried not to see that Bogey was apparently showing signs of a touch of fever.

On foot, they hurried through bush to the river, and near sundown sent up "smokes" to warn Mahony on the opposite bank. At sunset they camped on a point opposite Johnny Cake Point. At dawn Morey started making a raft out of dead pandanus palms, wiring the light wood together and rigging a mast with a camp-sheet as sail.

Unfortunately, the day was calm and the opposite bank a mile away; it looked dangerously farther. After several hours' labour by all hands the raft was launched. Morey ordered the two sick lubras aboard, climbed aboard himself, and secured the oildrum in the centre. In the oil-drum he placed the rifles, revolver, and ammunition. The idea was for all, hands (except the sick) to swim while holding on to the raft, but he was not going to swim himself until the raft was outstream and all hands in their places and working. He looked at the muscular chests above water all around the raft and smiled at those waiting, expectant faces, picturing how Charcoal, Davey and Co. would grab him and hold him under water, if only he gave them the chance.

"Push off!" he nodded and they leaned their weight into it. Slowly she moved, Morey anxiously gazing across stream and hoping he had gauged the tide correctly. Soon they were swimming. Then Morey slipped off into his own strategic position with eyes alert lest a man dive under from the other side, and seize his legs. He kept a watch on those women too, lest they suddenly attempt to throw the firearms overboard, ready to hurl himself aboard and snatch at the weapons.

Each man, with one hand to the raft, swam hard but steadily while pushing. Not a breath of wind moved the sail. Slowly they crept out towards midstream, then Morey noticed Bogey's eyes rolling, his teeth chattering, his limbs trembling. Sharply Morey ordered him aboard, but the prisoner next to him had to lift and push him aboard, and then his legs began to draw up with cramp. The cold water, lack of sleep, and a touch of fever had found Bogey's weakness.

In midstream they were fighting the crosscurrents; it seemed that an unseen hand pushed them slowly up-river, hesitated a while, then slowly pushed them down. The farther out they got the less ahead they seemed to travel; there came one three-quarters of an hour when they fought solely to keep the raft from being swept back. Morey, breathing deeply, encouraged them all he knew, calling in pidgin as to what would happen should the tide start racing and sweep them down into Whirlpool Reach. No need to tell them – they knew! Then a lubra cried out in a low, expressive cry, and with one horror-struck glance around they pushed forward and put all their magnificent strength into it. "Hit 'em oil-drum! hit 'em longa handcuffs quick feller! hard feller!" shouted Morey, and the women seized the cuffs and swung them against the drum chanting the weird, shrill chant that implores the totem spirit which drives away crocodiles. The men fought on with deep breaths; Morey prayed for wind with the agonized thought that if a crocodile came under below and saw all those kicking black legs and only one pair of white ones.

Bogey started to mumble to himself, then in low tones that rose to a high-pitched wailing he began to "sing" the river. Morey's spine crept. He could feel the panic spreading among all those gasping swimmers. If they rushed this clumsy raft with those crocodiles waiting ...

Then with a wild, laughing shriek Bogey flung up his arms and rolled off the raft. Instantly Morey kicked out and his long arm snatched at the submerging hair. Bogey rose up and clutched with clawing arms and shrieked wild laughter as Morey thumped his fist fair on his jaw then turned ready for the fight of his life. But big black arms reached out towards him; frightened black faces stared into his; they could just grasp his wrist and hauled him to the raft. They helped him push the unconscious man aboard; he leapt up and trembled at the quiver in the waterlogged thing ....

My God! if it began to break away now, stick by stick! Swiftly he wired Bogey to the raft, twisting the wire into his flesh, the reverberations from the oil-drum ringing in his ears. He looked behind, then snatched a rifle and aimed steadily. Fifty yards behind were three long snouts, effortlessly following. With the crack of the rifle came a "Smack!" and a snout disappeared as a long serrated tail rose, writhed, smacked the water and swirled away to the crack of the rifle again and the longdrawn "Ahs!" of those gazing behind.

Morey slipped the rifle in the drum and leapt overboard as suddenly the raft surged forward, the tiny sail filled, the rude mast creaked. They laughed their delight, and kicked out and swam and pushed with all their strength to the screaming chant of the lubras.

The breeze held and they ceased their gasping and just hung on, laughing while they drew deep, deep breaths. But only for a few hundred yards; slowly the raft lost momentum, the sail flopped. Doggedly they commenced swimming again. Away across on Johnny Cake Point they could see the little dark figures of Mahony and his trackers watching, not yet realizing the desperate struggle taking place before their eyes. The men's teeth were chattering, the water seemed turning into ice, their eyes began to bulge. Then another breeze helped them and they hung on, getting breath for yet another struggle. A quarter-mile from the bank a strong breeze came and carried them to within shouting distance, but their voices just rumbled away. Then Mahony's trackers caught the crocodile chant of the lubras. Mahony ran to a vantage point, a tracker ran to another, they stood peering away out behind the raft. Then their rifles rose, there came the "Crack! Crack!" with the smoke-puffs, the "Smack! Smack!" of rifle-bullets striking water. The exhausted swimmers sighed in unmeasurable relief. They just hung on, waiting for the tiny puffs of a breeze, Morey in an agony of mind, knowing that the outrushing of the tide must be due. They got nearer the shore and Mahony's trackers swam out and gave them a hand. They could only crawl to the bank. Beside a roaring fire, it took Mahony and his trackers an hour's hard massaging before they could coax a groan from stiff old Bogey.

26
MARBOO

THEY camped a day to give Bogey a chance. There were three sick people now, with the two lubras suffering from V.D. Better try to get them to civilization and a doctor than let the poor devils rot in the bush. But the three sick ones would be a drag on the patrol.

Sick encumbrances have brought failure to mounted patrols from the Kimberleys right through the Territory and northern Queensland to Cape York Peninsula. Meeting V.D. natives and bringing them hundreds of miles through the bush back to civilization for treatment. Sometimes, if the sick are few and can travel at all, a tracker is left behind to follow on with them. Many stricken ones mean the end of a patrol. The patrols are not ordered to do this work, but they do it. Again and again a mounted man, when almost in touch with his quarry has ridden on to a scene of dismal misery. A family – father, mother and children squatting hopelessly in the bush, awaiting slow death. The mounted man silently chooses. Leave these poor devils to rot while he hastens on, possibly to a capture that may lead to promotion, or give up all hope of capturing his men and turn back with the unfortunates for medical treatment? That the majority of the native patients sent in for treatment to the Government Native Hospitals are brought in from the bush by the police, is proof of the choice of the mounted patrols. That is the real tragedy of the aboriginal, V.D. If the white man would only conscientiously and scientifically eradicate it, he would do the aborigines the one great service we can do them.

The patrol decided to cut straight east through bush to the big Fitzmaurice River camps, Tal-a-kinyin, Coo-larry-co, Mudg-i-lindi, and Wack-itch. If Nemarluk's horde had not sped back to this prolific hunting-ground, they would probably make all haste for the coast at An-de-mallee camp, where the Japanese had been killed.

They started out for Tal-a-kin-yin with the trackers uneasy. This was the wild man's land indeed.

But Marboo's wild eyes shone with unholy delight; she was all eyes and ears and limbs twitching for action. Every step took her into country of which she knew every little hill and creek and waterhole, every claypan and hollow, almost every tree and rock. It was the country which had mothered her and given her her spirit child, the child of Nemarluk. The patrol hurried, horses and mules standing up to the strenuous task when battling over the trackless areas of the rougher country. On a broken sandstone divide, between Laberie and Paperbark creeks, they lost. Marboo. She was beside Morey as he led his horse, but the next instant had vanished. Morey's long legs were powerless to overtake her; though he leapt from rock to rock he did not even see her again.

"Here's a go!" he shouted to Mahony. "She'll go straight and warn Nemarluk. Let's get down off this divide and into open country. Then we'll have to leave the packs and try to beat her to it."

As well try to beat the wind! Horses against a lubra in a distance of a hundred and fifty miles through the wild bush that gave her birth! No chance. She laughed as she ran and the bush laughed with her; the sun shone and the birds sang and there was a scent of sweet grass in the air. She was travelling for her life – for Nemarluk!

The patrol pushed on for thirty-six hours, until animals and men could only stumble on. Through broken sandstone country well grassed into a maze of sandstone hills, gullies, and steep jump-ups; past Kib-ah-leing spring into rugged country of quartzite and ironstone; through a saucer-shaped country thickly timbered with woolly butt and bloodwood and rimmed completely by sandstone ranges. Then they came out on to the plain country. They ate and slept; left the packhorses and witnesses and sick with two trackers; mounted their horses and rode for it.

But Marboo paused neither to eat nor sleep; through day and night she sped straight as the flight of a bird.

She gasped into camp in the dead of night and flung herself across Nemarluk. She could not speak. He leapt up, rattling his spears, chewing his beard. One glance and he knew exactly which way to go – straight for the Fitzmaurice River. Marboo, her dark passionate face alight with longing as she snatched one look at her cub in the arms of another of Nemarluk's wives, turned and sped after her lord; and followed him into the cold dark river and swam beside him. I would not swim one of those crocodile-infested rivers, even in daytime, for all the money in the world.

Wild excitement in the camp! Minmara fled miles down-stream for a canoe. The others of the Red Band had scattered days before, but these of the tribal horde boasted they had plenty of time, the white police were like piccaninnies at travelling.

Yet they did not have quite so much time.

Shortly after daylight the dogs rose snarling – Yes! the dull thud of galloping hooves.

They fled.

It was a day later before the two trackers arrived with the pack-animals. The patrol enjoyed a rest under the trees, the sick ones just sprawled down and never moved for a day and a night. That sickness is torture; the white folk should help them. Then the chase was continued. There was no shortage of tracks in this country of the big camps, for trails led across bush from camp to camp; trails to the hunting-grounds; to the lagoons for the lilyroots, and the turtle and the Johnstone River crocodile; trails over the sandhills to the coast with its fish and crabs and oysters.

They located and searched camp after camp deserted. Just the ashes of burnt-out fires; gnawed bones of 'roo, wallaby, and possum; the blackened carapaces of tortoise and turtle; husks of roasted pandanus seed, and heaps of broken shells of wild fruits. All beside the scratched-out sleeping-holes where the family groups had dug shelter from the winds of night.

"This is the flying-fox season," suggested Tracker Splinter. "They will separate into groups searching for flying foxes."

Yes, this was the season of the white-gum flowers, when the orange scent of their sweet white flowers filled the air and invited the bats in screeching hosts to the feast.

So they turned their horses' heads towards the flying-fox country, and the floundering of the animals in a bog left tracks which will be plain after many a wet season. But never a sign of Nemarluk. Wily chief! As he strode from camp after camp, men, women, and children walked directly behind him and the tramp of their feet blotted out his tracks. The patrol left their horses and the sick ones under a tracker's guard and walked across the boggy country into the mangroves. There they searched the slimy salt arms of the sea, bamboo-banked watercourses, and sub-tropical lagoons – all the localities that the trackers knew or instinct told them might shelter a flying-fox colony.

One day the trackers "Hished!" and stood listening to a screeching that slowly grew deafening. They emerged from the trees and there across a little grassy plain above a dark line of timber that fringed a creek was a black cloud of foxes; the sound of their wings was like wind in the trees. The patrol hurried towards that deafening screeching, but arrived just too late. The cloud screeched away up-stream, leaving their sour smell, and underneath the trees the tracks of men and women who had been hurling their throwing-sticks. It was not until the patrol was quite close to the coast near Treachery Bay that their stern patience bore fruit. Here at Lad-dan-te-din waterhole they just missed Minmara and Marragin who had been flying-fox hunting with others of the horde.

"Marragin!" pointed Bogey. And there were fresh tracks. The trackers followed swiftly where the tracks led up from the waterhole and away through the grass, making across country.

"He go longa Ill-lin-ee camp!" pointed Bogey in excited voice.

"We'll try and reach the camp before them!" said Morey. "They are sure to dawdle on the way. Mahony, you take two trackers and make straight for the camp while I travel at the double and try to get around behind."

Mahony and his trackers had just got hidden in the camp when the hunting-party came singing home. Men rose from the very feet of Marragin. He was seized with the hunting-song wet upon his lips.

"Good!" said Morey. "That leaves only Nemarluk and Minmara. I'd love to know just where *they* are!"

As if in answer, Nemarluk left his visiting-card.

Next morning they stared at a tree on which was a freshly carved drawing of the lugger *Ouida*.

Yet again, the wild chief's insolence came within an ace of costing him his liberty.

"He is at An-de-mallee camp where he killed the Japanese if I know my man," said Morey grimly. "He is laughing fit to kill himself. Let us be in on the joke before he has time to sober up."

With a tracker following, and bringing along the pack-animals and sick people, prisoners and witnesses, the patrol rode fast until they floundered through the treacherous crust of a saltpan that spread far to right and left amongst coarse-tufted grasses and scraggly timber. Here they took a risk and left their riding-horses tied among a clump of trees, then walked gingerly across the bog towards where, behind the timber, rose the red and white crowns of sandhills fringing the coast. Between these were little grassy areas growing patches of grey scrub trees, and darker green clumps of vine jungle.

Lizards scurried before their feet into burrows in the sand; big plain turkeys solemnly watched them; the hot sun made them long to lie down and sleep under any shady bush.

Nearing Port Keats they kept close to the timber belts and ran across each open place lest the eyes of stray hunters or fishers or lily-root seeking lubras detect them. By sundown they were getting close to Ver-di, Nemarluk's camp. Here Bogey stopped with arm upheld, his face questioning the gentle breeze while he sniffed, sniffed for the smoke of Nemarluk's fire. He smelt it a mile away, nodded and grinned to Morey.

"Big feller camp; plenty feller fire; cook 'em pish, yam, lily-root!"

They waited under cover until dark, hearing occasionally the yelp of a dog, the voice of some screeching lubra. Several hours after sundown they crept carefully forward among the shadows that sometimes seemed to move. They drew fairly close to one shadow that looked like a black cloud pressed upon the ground. They listened. Now and again· the voice of a warrior and the shrill chatter of a lubra, all muffled within that belt of dense vine jungle, reached their ears. They crept forward, ready to "freeze" on the instant should some prowling dog appear. Though the trackers whispered of a fire, the whites had to crawl much closer before they could distinguish the dull glow.

They waited, talking seldom, then only in whispers, praying that no light breeze would carry scent of white men to dog or warrior. The shivery hours came. Pitch darkness all round. The heavens, a cold blue dusted with gold of stars.

At dawn they spread out and crept cautiously into the pitch-dark jungle. Each man came to a dull glow of coals, and each hesitated. The problem was to know whether these were decoy fires or not. If so, then they would make their rush too soon. Yet if they crept into the undergrowth to prove the decoy, the sleepers beyond or the dogs would hear.

They rushed the camp at dawn. Those *were* decoy fires spread two hundred feet from the real camp. By the time they passed the decoys the dogs were already howling, the horde snatching spears while glaring themselves awake. Nemarluk and Minmara were already running. Two trackers barred their way but the warriors leapt straight on them with upraised spears and the trackers leapt aside. As the thin cordon crashed through into the real camp most of the horde were running.

A few were caught, dumbfounded by sleep and the suddenness. Among them was Oo-la-gin-ee, one of Nemarluk's wives, clutching his cub to her breast. She was a witness, but Morey let her be.

They did, however, bring along a piccaninny, a little half-caste Japanese.

"It is hard to know what to do," said Mahony. "Leave the child here to take its chance of being killed or grow up a savage, or take it to Darwin where it will grow up a half-caste."

"We'll take it to Darwin and let the fates decide. They were responsible in the first place, and may have something better in store for it than the life of a savage out here."

They camped until the trackers brought the horses up, then Marragin and Mankee and witness after witness took them to the scene of the murder and showed them everything in pantomimic detail.

Nemarluk had again taken to the water. At first, his tracks headed towards the Moyle country, but he twisted back into the water. There he had rivers and coast, bog and salt arms of the sea, to wade along and through. He might come out anywhere and double back.

"We'll go to the Moyle," decided Morey. "We may cut his tracks or hear of him. If we stay here he can lead us to and from water for months and laugh. The sooner we go the sooner he will seek dry land."

They turned inland towards the Moyle and came out on Did-ee plain, which runs north and south farther than the eye can reach, and is some ten miles across. Its big swamps teem with game. A tabletop hill, Yan-jar-roo rising from its centre proved an excellent landmark for the patrol. The trackers did not know the Moyle country. They travelled on. Dancing in the sunlight were long lines of brolgas, bowing and prancing in the quaintest of quadrilles. Occasionally a slate-grey buffalo stared curiously. Grass and bushes and odd clumps of trees appeared alive with birds. The Moyle meandered through the plain almost lost to view in the long grass, its waters lying stagnant on a black muddy bottom. Far away noisy, black-grey clouds of ducks and geese rose protesting at marauding aborigines robbing their nests. As the patrol splashed across the Moyle, birds screeched agitatedly, and two spearmen suddenly appeared to see what had caused the alarm. They turned to fly-too late, for Morey on Tasman galloped from the grass behind them and they were prisoners.

Here was an unexpected capture. These men knew of the robbery at Nugget Huggins's store on the Daly River several months ago. The aboriginal finds modern life full of surprises. He makes a raid on a lonely store and escapes far away back to the Wilds. Yet the "white pleece" spring on him from out the very grass.

The main offenders were camped at Lar-la-ar camp and a raid was planned. Perhaps Nemarluk would be there too – perhaps. The patrol continued on to a Bar-ram-lone water hole, picturesque amongst tangled scrub and stunted timber in from the edge of the plain. From this water hole Morey with two trackers rode away on a fifty-mile trip along the Moyle. When night fell Charlie was standing by a small tree, staring into the gathering dark.

"More better you sleep," advised Mahony.

"No fear! Can't sleep here!"

He pointed to several trees that still showed the scars of spear-marks. They had pitched camp right on Hemmings's old camp. Charlie stood by that tree all night. He remembered that night of two years ago and dreaded a repetition. And it would have come. Just before dawn he stealthily awoke the party. They snatched their rifles and knelt behind trees as ochred figures came creeping up. Charlie had smelt them. They noted the alarm and hovered in the darkness, but vanished with the daylight.

It gave Charlie supreme satisfaction to point out their tracks, showing how closely they had surrounded the camp.

But the patrol never caught Nemarluk. They followed him until their food-supply was exhausted. Then slow moving and encumbered with prisoners, witnesses, and sick, made for Daly River police station. From there, they started on the ride back into Darwin.

The Black Service brought word to Daly River police station that Nemarluk and Minmara were camped in the Moyle country. A party was quickly organized which resulted in the capture of Minmara, Nemarluk again escaping.

The Red Band chief now roamed alone.

Nemarluk's drawing of the Ouida being towed away by theMaroubra.

27
THE BOADICEA OF ARNHEM LAND

JUST to understand a little how the prehistoric man's life, his hates and loves and ambitions, his laws and ceremonies and councils of the old men, his daily routine, sometimes cause disaster to white and brown and black alike, we will live a moment out in the frontiers and watch fate manoeuvring all together.

A Boadicea (as the *Sydney Morning Herald* so aptly calls her) queens it in Arnhem Land-the half-caste Clara. How a woman comes to rule a fighting tribe like the Balamoomoos, is an intriguing puzzle for anthropology. Although the fact has precedent here and there in the history of savage peoples.

Clara is a somewhat shadowy figure. For years past any questioning of natives by wandering patrols as to what she is and where she is, has been met by direct lies or an uncomprehending silence. In the big Arnhem Land patrol of 1929 Sergeant Bridgeland, Constables Abbott, Heathcote, and Langdon endeavoured to unravel the mystery. Except that she was the organizer of enticing parties to bring ashore sea roamers, they learned little more than what is already known.

At the head of her braves she has harried tribes antagonistic to her wild ambitions, while to individual tribesmen who opposed her she made life just one quick thing after another. Among other islands she has harried Groote Eylandt with disastrous results to the Yeti-bah tribe. A few years ago, when the missionaries settled on Groote Eylandt it was touch and go with them several times. As the mission became more firmly established, Clara's bargaining instincts, sharpened by youthful memories among the whites in the far inland Gulf country, overcame her belligerency. Canoeing across from the mainland she would leave her savage tribesmen hidden close by while she advanced on the mission demanding, in fair pidgin, tobacco, blankets, iron, flour, and sundry other perquisites.

In the early war years Clara's aboriginal husband (she was then a little half-caste girl), and several other aborigines, were engaged as crew by a white man owning a small cutter. From the small township of Borroloola, apparently, they sailed down the McArthur River into the Gulf of Carpentaria searching for trepang. The natives attacked them and killed the white man and those of his crew they could catch. Clara, taking a liking to her savage captor, became his as the spoils of war.

In 1917 Nemesis fell on the killers. Clara as a witness was being taken to Darwin but she leapt overboard in the night and swam to the Arnhem Land coast.

Gradually her experience as a half-caste allied to her shrewd native wit gained her ascendancy over horde after horde of the Balamoomoos until for some years past she has been leader of the combined tribe. If inquiries were deeply enough persevered with, most of the intrigue, numbers of the killings, and the inter-tribal feuds could be traced directly or indirectly to the inspiration of the elusive Clara. Woe betide the native whom she discovers has betrayed her least secret.

But the book of Clara's life is written in the destiny of the whites, in the councils of prehistoric men, in a life and land as savagely primitive today as in the ages gone by. The life of Clara, the Boadicea of Arnhem Land, will be a grimly fascinating book for the one with the knowledge and vision to write it.

Now, one tribal horde of the Balamoomoos was led by old King Wongo. It is believed in various quarters that aboriginal tribes have no chief or king. Such is generally the case; the Council of the Old Men represents the unquestioned authority in every tribe. But in almost every tribe there is a noted hunter or fighter who is tacitly accepted as the leader, and who, occasionally, even among wild tribes is spoken of to any white man as "king."

Old Wongo was and is a king. More of him anon. Among his men was a warrior stripling, a promising lad, Clara's son. He was ambushed, and fell under savage spears.

The horde of Tuckiar and Merara were blamed. Grim warriors these, who would kill Clara's son! A demon was let loose in nativeland when swift tidings came to Clara. Her instant message to Wongo was "Kill! Kill! Kill!"

Tuckiar's horde, numerically weaker than Wongo's, fled the mainland to Woodah Island, a long, narrow, heavily wooded island a few miles off the Arnhem Land coast. Its waters teeming with fish, its shores with yams, its little jungles a rampart in native warfare, it was a favourite rendezvous of Tuckiar's. Here the warrior proceeded to "dig in." On the mainland opposite, the enraged Wongo awaited him to be driven out, while farther down the coast the tribesmen on Bickerton Island (ten miles from Groote Eylandt) at the command of Clara were getting ready their canoes to do the driving. It looked like extermination for Tuckiar's horde.

But annoyingly embarrassing, to say the least, for old King Wongo. For among his subjects was Noming, husband of Clara. And this liege was loud in his outcry against the slayers of his son, full of the moral support of the distant Clara. Was ever a king more harassed. A tribal vengeance to be wiped out, the shadow of this vicious woman over him, her husband a spy here whom he dare not touch, a tough fight with Tuckiar's horde looming ahead, war on two of his boundaries!

Incidentally, the old king eventually squeezed out of divers of his troubles, one such being Noming, it is believed by strangling.

Unaware of all this turmoil, two luggers, the *Myrtle Olga* and *The Raff*, were sailing towards Blue Mud Bay. And far west at Port Darwin two wanderers, Traynor and Fagan, were patching up a tiny cutter preparatory to a venturesome cruise.

As fate with a light breeze will presently bring these various craft slowly along those hundreds of miles of lonely coast we will glance a moment at another interesting character in Arnhem's native land – old "Baldy Bill."

That was his "secret number"; his police name, it identified him perfectly while betraying nothing. His native (not his *secret* tribal name) is Ar-umbar-ma-roo. Baldy Bill is possibly unique in aboriginaldom. Not a tracker: never has been, never will be, never wants to be. Under an aboriginal skin he was born with the mind and ambition of a secret service man; he is as much a secret service agent as any X pigeon-holed in the secret archives of the Great Powers.

The work is his mania, his delight, his elixir in life. And he runs probably a shade more risk than his confreres of Europe. For aboriginaldom knows no "peace time" for the spy. Old Baldy Bill takes his life in his hands in visits to hostile tribes; he cultivates the old council men, the killers, the mischief-makers of the hordes among differing tribes. To him, warriors as well known in the aboriginal world as Tuckiar have boasted of their killings. A wise old man Baldy Bill; in a land of violence recognizing the power of mind over matter. Baldy's mind shields him from the ambush and the strangler. He is a high priest of the Nara ceremonies, with a comprehensive knowledge of the Muraian, the jealously guarded spiritual life of these prehistoric people. His inner knowledge of their totemic life is Baldy's passport among numerous hordes of people.

In the Muraian reside the spirits of their ancestors, and Baldy has seen the totem Muraian of various hordes. This gives him great power.

Baldy Bill, in his fishing excursions, his hunting trips, his visits, his slow wandering from horde to horde, with his wonderful memory, his ever listening ears, his suave tongue, his harmless, ingratiating personality, his cast-iron cheek and cool daring, collects the violent deeds of native life. Then from island to island, along the coast, wandering into the interior he finally returns to Bickerton, or Groote Eylandt, or some other. Sooner or later white police will come. Some deed of exceptional violence which necessitates white law will surely bring them. They will not directly seek Baldy Bill; possibly he will not seek them; but in their own way they will meet.

But the day was fast coming when Baldy Bill would know *too* much; when he would flee for his life by night in a canoe to the white police who then would be at Groote Eylandt. As a day was to come, too, when even Tuckiar's people, the killers, would implore white police aid from Wongo's men on the coast and the Bickerton Island people close by.

Fate manipulates strange happenings. Just as now she had brought the *Myrtle Olga* and *The Raff*; just as, later, she would bring Traynor and Fagan; just as fast coming events would ultimately bring Morey's police patrol.

Constable Morey (right) with trackers.

28
KING WONGO'S SPEARMEN

SEPTEMBER, 1932. Sunlight sparkling on the waters of Caledon Bay. Vessels anchored there, the pearling luggers *Myrtle Olga* and *The Raff*, far from the pearling-grounds, and from civilization. This Arnhem Land coastline is one of the most lonely and dangerous in all Australia.

Between the luggers and the shore were four dinghies and a number of canoes dotted upon the shallow water. A black figure sat in each, while from the water a black head occasionally bobbed up to blow like a grampus, then with lazy arm and kick of leg shoot to dinghy or canoe and drop into it some long, ugly slugs of the sea.

This was a trepang, a *bêche-de-mer* fishers' camp and the work of the day was well commenced. On the shore wispy smoke drifted above a smoke-house, just a few sheets of iron, bark, and bushes. Men were slowly moving about this centre of operations. Nearby, on the open beach, were two iron boiling tanks with the fire under them. A little figure was busy placing the treated slugs on the wire tray in the smoke-house; another little figure, near the boiler, was busy with a knife opening up the slugs; a third was bending over the ground as he pegged down the opened trepang with tiny wooden pegs. Yet another little figure was busy among the few pots and pans at the kitchen, a rough bough shed by the beach with its table and tools enclosed by a high, wire netted yard as protection from a sudden raid. To these small brown figures larger black figures walked carrying things.

A dinghy with the little brown figure of Kinjo astern would come rowing inshore to a snatch of aboriginal song. A native would step out and effortlessly carry a bag of the slugs from the dinghy across to Higasaki who was washing and gutting the slimy things. From Higasaki a native would carry the cleaned slugs to Tinaka who would see them emptied into the boiler, while yet another carried the boiled, soddy things to the pegging shed, where Shibasaki pegged each slit slug wide apart ready for Kimishima to put on the wire-netting trays in the smoke-house to be smoke-dried and cured. Inamora was cook at the tiny kitchen. To him would come, from the thick fringe of trees back from the shore, a native carrying firewood. Presently two more would appear walking down the beach with a load of wood on their shoulders, one to Kimishima at the smoke-house with the mangrove wood that smokes so well, and one to Tanaka at the boilers with the mangrove wood that burns so well.

So the Japanese worked, always within sight and call of one another.

Among these shoreward figures, but aloof, stood a giant of a man with a gorilla's chest, a big beard and a black scowl. No-one seemed to take any notice of him or to have anything to do with him. Erect by the smoke-house, gnarled hands clasped loosely behind his back, his grim gaze roved over the toiling Japanese, the wood carriers, and out across the bay at the dinghies and canoes. He glanced often and long at the boilers – at one in particular. Of flat sheet-iron, it would when cut up make the blades of many spears. It was priceless. It would arm his horde with iron spears in a way that no Caledon Bay horde had ever been armed before. But the little tree that stood near the smoke-house appeared to fascinate him. That tree was just behind the centre of operations. Stacked at its butt were the guns and rifles, and higher up, the revolvers, hung upon nails driven into the tree. Weapons ready for instant use. Leaning against the tree were the dinghy paddles.

For the Japanese were not going to be cut off from the luggers should the natives rush the dinghy that always rested ready at the water's edge. Such a mistake would mean a swim for it; helpless targets for spears. They did not anticipate attack, but if that came they expected it from the trees inland. Then they would leap for the oars, run to the dinghy: and row out to their forts, the luggers.

So every morning, when coming to work on the beach, they carried the oars and rifles to the tree that grew near the smoke-house.

And the big, old, bearded man came every day, seemingly not knowing what to do with himself. Nobody took any notice of him – yet.

Few would have noticed the guarded watchfulness over everyone in this camp and those working upon the water near by. Here were really two distinct camps though apparently one, working well in team work. The Japanese covertly watched and were watched by the boys working near them; while out in the canoes and dinghies where the fishers so leisurely dived, the surveillance was savagely acute.

The Caledon aborigines were powerful men who, sometimes, before they dived or when they arose to clamber back into a canoe would growl some significant remark directed towards the blacks working from the dinghies. More often they conveyed their thoughts in sign language, while ever and anon their fierce gaze would roam towards the two anchored luggers and from there dwell on the brown figures now toiling on shore. They worked too, most lackadaisically, securing much less fish than the men in the dinghies.

The dinghy men were aboriginal seamen, signed on men from Melville and Goulburn islands; twelve of them had sailed with their

Japanese employers from Darwin. They covertly watched while working, uneasy at being watched. Far better than the Japanese they understood the danger. They were foreigners to the local blacks and as such liable to be killed, according to immemorial tribal law. And they were in Caledon Bay! The country of the Balamoomoos. Fierce groups of untamed tribes obeying only the Laws of the Wild.

The Japanese had been warned before leaving Darwin. Even here. Not three miles from their camp was that of Fred Gray, the one white trepanger on that long strip of coast. He had warned them to be very, very careful. They hardly needed such warning. Well they knew of savage fights, of luggers looted and burned to the water's edge in the seasons gone by.

But pearl-shell was low in price; trepang was marketable; and this was the best bêche-de-mer ground on the coast; they were well equipped, well armed, and – very careful.

In late afternoon the canoes and dinghies would row ashore with their final load. All hands then crowded around the cookhouse for now was payment time; rice and tobacco and tea were issued out. Tanaka was just finishing work by the boiler, his trepang knife lying on the sand. Surreptitiously Noming's black hand reached out. Quick as thought Tanaka scooped a handful of trepang refuse full into the aboriginal's face. Then retrieved the knife and stood glaring down at the astonished man.

Instant silence from the cookhouse. All eyes turned towards Noming crouching for the spring. But no signal came from the old warrior standing near. Four of the Japanese now stood near the tree.

The incident passed oft. As had several previous incidents. The Japanese paid their casual labourers, then with their crew boys rowed out to the luggers. They always took care to be snug aboard by sundown.

Half a mile farther along the coast was the aboriginal camp. And there reigned the old man who only stood and watched the trepangers. All looked up to him; bowed to his every word, his gesture. For this was Wongo, king and father, patriarch of the tribe.

Wongo ruled and rules as the wild bull rules the herd. He has many wives, and is jealous of every one of them. And would increase his troubles if he could. But his little band comprises hardly more than a hundred souls. And the majority of the women and grown girls are Wongo's wives; the majority of men are his sons. One will eventually kill the old bull and annex his harem, but that day has not dawned yet.

Wongo's little strip of the earth comprises barely thirty miles of the coastline. Beyond his inland boundary live populous bands of the Balamoomoo tribe. But on either side of him live hostile people with whom he was at "war." To increase his diplomatic difficulties, he was anxious to cut Tuckiar's liver out. He had a wholesome dread of Clara now holding him feudally responsible for the death of her son if he did not wipe out Tuckiar's band. Her son, according to the complications of tribal law and birth, had been one of his own horde. Wongo would rather have lost one of his own sons than Clara's. He had just succeeded in suspending hostilities with his fightable neighbours and was ready to raid Woodah Island and exterminate Tuckiar and his band, when these Japanese vessels had come along.

And now his best laid plans were all awry. He had decided to withhold his vengeance until opportunity showed him how to deal with these new arrivals – the Japanese trepang fishers.

His first thought had been to hurry his women into the bush. But the energies of the Japanese were concentrated on harvesting the slugs of the sea. So Wongo had allowed his harem to drift back, while he sought what tribute he could from the industrious brown men. Born traders, these Arnhem Land coastal aborigines. Made shrewd by centuries of haggling and bargaining with the Malays who sailed their proas to this coast seeking pearl-shell and trepang. From those agile sea-roamers, numbers of them have inherited Malay blood, which probably has improved their physique and quickened their minds.

But the Japanese stood aloof. They wanted no assistance from Wongo, nor Wongo's men. Particularly not from Wongo, whom they distrusted because he was king. Now, had the Japanese only understood, they might have saved much trouble. For Wongo, as did aboriginal law, regarded all things on and in the earth, all things in the air above and in the waters below, that lived within his tribal borders, as his. Thus all trepang along this strip of coast was his.

Wongo did not want that trepang , his people never ate it; had no earthly use for it. But he claimed tribute: demanded tobacco, tomahawks, and what else he could imagine. The Japanese had scornfully refused. They offered to pay in tobacco and food for any trepang that King Wongo's men actually brought in. They did not want labour; they had sufficient boys of their own; but if Wongo's men wanted tobacco or rice, they could earn it.

And so matters stood.

Each day in their own good time a number of Wongo's men launched their canoes and paddled up to the Japanese day-time camp for what they could earn, or steal should opportunity occur. All who only pried about the camp had from the first day been warned off. Even the king had been warned to keep away. The brown men feared his obvious authority might harbour mischief. He had even offered to work – he, Wongo! They had refused his offer. But still he came daily. They did not enforce his retirement as they so sternly did other spiers from his camp; they simply ignored him. And so day by day he stood among them aloof, and ignored – he, Wongo, king and owner of everything in this his country.

King Wongo glowered at the campfire, a grudge in his heart. His sullen face reflected deep thoughts. Around him squatted his wives and quite a litter of babies and piccaninnies of all ages and sizes. Some wives were girls not quite fourteen years, others were worn old dames whose cunning and tongue had been tempered by wommera, fighting-stick, and claw. These old girls indulged in a low-toned conversation that reached every ear, and their plaint was of the cruelty of the Japanese, of their robbing the sea of the rights of Wongo; of their insulting high-handedness in this land where Wongo only was king. Particularly they dwelt on the two big ships out in the bay and. the tobacco and tomahawks and foods and many desirable things they must contain. All those things ought to be Wongo's! Did they not sail upon the water that was his? All could be Wongo's if the young men were only men such as their fathers were!

The young men scowled, squatting there around their fires a little distance away, and the young lubras tittered. Wongo silenced the now derisive cackling of the old lubras, the shrugs and smiles of the young ones. He was thinking. How could he separate those iron fire weapons from the little brown men? Those weapons were always against the little tree, the little men worked just out in front of the tree, but an alarm only meant a few leaps back and they would be at the tree. How could they possibly be struck and yet not be given time to reach their weapons?

29
THE ATTACK ON THE JAPANESE

DAY dawned bright and clear; the water unruffled; for wind seldom disturbs the serenity of sea or land at this time of the year. Work went as usual until midday rice. Although there were no outward signs of uneasiness, the crew boys sensed danger; instinctively realizing that events were brewing for a storm they drew closer together. At midday ricetime Woolaware very nearly started the trouble. He stole the cook's tomahawk. Kimishimi happened to note the warning glance of a crew boy; his quick eyes saw the tomahawk was missing.

"Give it me!" he ordered with outstretched hand.

Woolaware in apparent innocence was sitting on the tomahawk, his hands clasped over his knees. He stared in well feigned stupidity at Kimishimi's repeated command. With one lightning spring Kimishimi spun him clear of the ground. He fell on his ear and grunted. Instantly he was crouching, his arms held low and slightly forward with fingers like talons. Springing sideways he bounded straight at Kimishimi who dropped at his feet and sent him flying through the air. Wongo's men, on their toes for the rush, gazed spellbound as their tribesman struck the ground.

The Australian aboriginal is an "all-in" wrestler, with wild man tactics of brute strength, tooth and claw that never varies. This startling exhibition of jujitsu clothed the little Japanese with an undreamt of strength.

Kimishimi stood calmly waiting. Ears and eyes were attuned to Wongo's signal but he stood motionless by the cookhouse. Shibasaki and Tanaka stood over by the boiler but the other four Japs were grouped near the guns by the tree. The crew boys stood ready to run or fight according to how this turn went.

Again the incident passed off. After the midday rice the Japanese lit cigarettes.

"The guns want cleaning," said Tanaka; "the sea air rusts them quickly."

"Bad for us should we need them in a hurry and they prove unserviceable!" added Inamora.

"We will fire them off," decided Shibasaki, "a few shots each when we go aboard at sundown. That will help clean the barrels while the shooting will remind these savages that we are well armed. We will shoot at a floating target and give them a warning exhibition."

They did so, and the bay reverberated to gun-fire.

It was an exhibition warranted to produce a quietening effect: six well-armed men against spears and tomahawks. There would be eighteen in the Japanese party all told, for if cornered the crew boys would fight with their own weapons.

Wongo hardly considered the crew, he did not intend to corner them, they could be disposed of later. As his warriors watched the shooting, his eyes roved from the boiler, the cookhouse, and the smokehouse, to that little tree twenty yards nearer the beach; then to that little sandbank some twenty yards to the side but running behind the tree. That ridge of sand was hardly much higher than a man's head. But lots of men could creep up behind it. If they did so, then just before them would be the tree and the guns and the dinghy oars, and before these would be the boiler and cookhouse and smokehouse where the Japanese would be working.

Wongo turned thoughtfully and with kingly mien walked over the sandbank and disappeared apparently in the direction of his camp.

The 17 September 1932 dawned bright and clear. Japanese and crew on board the *Myrtle Olga* and *The Raff* were already sipping morning coffee. Dawn had hardly lifted the shadows from the shore edge when the dinghies were manned and rowed out for the early fishing. At about eight o'clock Inamora ordered his dinghy ashore. At the cookhouse he lit the fire and prepared breakfast. To his hail, the dinghies came ashore. Some Caledon men were already working; others now came strolling along, hungrily sniffing the curried fish. All hands squatted down to breakfast, after which the work of the day commenced in earnest. Dinghies and canoes rowed and paddled from shore back to the fishing. Murgoo, a crew boy, walked towards the timber for wood for the smoke-house while Sambo started carrying trepang from the beach to the boiler. Woong-i-in, Melville Island crew boy, was stoking the boiler while each Japanese was busy at his separate job. Meanwhile King Wongo, in his camp half a mile away, ordered four lubras to gather oysters. They picked up their network bags and obeyed in a general silence. Now the oyster-ground was behind a point of land and invisible from the Japanese camp. The lubras were visible, however, to some of the men diving from the dinghies out from shore. Then the women disappeared.

All were busy at the Japanese camp. Suddenly a hoarse, long-drawn bellow echoed over sea and land. Instantly action ceased, every ear listened, though the Japanese merely gazed around inquiringly. Again that bellow as if from an enraged bull calling his herd. Every vessel manned by Caledon tribesmen forged straight to shore at an angle away from the Japanese camp. In short minutes they had beached their canoes and disappeared.

The Japanese shrugged and carried on with their work. What was troubling these savages now was beyond their comprehension, some tribal fight away in the native camp probably.

But the crew boys ashore glanced meaningly around, as covertly edging nearer one another the dinghies out from shore began to draw closer together while drifting nearer inshore, towards that little tree. The busy Japanese did not notice this ominous precaution: the trepang catch was very good and they were toiling while it lasted; toiling at the boilers; at the smoke-house and the cookhouse, all a few yards out from the little tree.

King Wongo stood in a towering rage, his big arms thrust above his head, his eyes rolling. He bellowed like a bull insulted on his own stamping ground. A crowd of women shrieked and chattered around him; young men ran into camp while he roared and foamed. Swift runners came, their eyes staring with the excitement that spreads so swiftly amongst the Australian aborigines. Spears were rattled, warriors chewed their beards-sure sign of fighting passion. Natchelma, Mow, Narkaya came running; Chalmer, Marawata, Noming, Wuninya; then Mowembowie, Wool aware, Kipaboo, Nikolo, Namjin , sons and near sons all came running to forge around the towering old man. Dogs barked; piccaninnies squealed.

"The Japanese have my women," roared Wongo. "They have taken four of my wives; one has not returned. Kill them!"

"Yes, kill them," cried Natchelma. "If they shoot at us with guns we can't see the shot, we can't dodge as we dodge a spear. Kill them swift before they kill us."

"Kill!" cried Mow.

"Kill!" cried Narkaya.

"Kill!" cried Wuninya.

"Better we tell white man Gray," ventured Woolaware uneasily.

"Yes," seconded Mowembowie. "Perhaps better that we travel even to the mission station and tell them. If we kill, the white police might come!"

But this caution was drowned in angry dissent by the men, shrieking vituperation by the old lubras whose screechings suddenly rose in the war-cry. Wongo instantly quietened that ominous yell.

A rush for spears, for tomahawks, and men were speeding towards the Japanese camp, eyes gleaming to the blood lust.

It came suddenly. A painted native sprang up from the sandbank and bounded towards Inamora bending at the cookhouse. At Inamora's piercing scream painted figures leapt up and over the sandbank, and with one paralysing yell bounded down upon the Japanese. Kinjo and Kimishimi stared towards Inamora, then jumped towards the tree. Too late! Howling warriors were already leaping past it, others paused and snatching up the unaccustomed weapons fired them, only to throw them disdainfully aside and snatch their spears again. Three were already upon Tanaka who dodged, then screamed, pierced by Narkaya's spear.

He staggered up and fell, pierced yet twice again as his countrymen swerved back towards the dinghy. But striking men closed around them and Kimishimi crashed down with a spear-blade, piercing straight out through his chest. A stone hurled by Miniowie grazed Kinjo's head, who reeled but raced desperately on. The short legs of the Japanese were outsped by the aborigines who reached the dinghy and wheeled around laughing as they flung their spears. Kinjo leapt aside and they all turned and tried hopelessly to break through and run towards Gray's camp, but they were wheeled back to the water. Higasaki reached it as a spear ripped his arm but he plunged in, swimming hopelessly towards the luggers. Shibasaki fell pierced at the water's edge. Noming swam out after Higasaki and tomahawked him. Kinjo as he swam saw Mow running from the little tree carrying the dinghy oars so he turned and swam desperately along the shore, gained the beach and ran as he had never run before. Laughing shouts sped his heels with the terror of death. A pillar of rocks stood out on the beach, he just reached them, and clambered up to crouch panting on top. Three of Wongo's men laughed as piccanins would laugh at treeing a lizard. They disdained to throw spears; they collected sticks, and these whizzed up faster and faster with the dodging man staggering from blow following blow. Only a matter of moments before he should be knocked back and over.

Distant shouts drew the aborigines' attention, canoes and dinghies were speeding for the luggers. Loot! With one accord the three men sped back, to track and kill Kinjo would be pastime after the looting was done.

Kinjo dropped down and, half-dazed and bleeding, ran as best he could up along the shore. He met one of his Melville Island crew boys, also running for his life, then met five others. These stuck to him all through that nightmare chase, all the way through wild bush to far away Milingimbi mission station, carrying him much of the way after his feet had been cut to shreds.

30
TIGER

TIGER stared at the canoe. His were cold unwavering eyes that saw all things. He saw the motor vessel *Maroubra*; but he was not interested in her nor the passengers embarking, nor in the little crowd of bushmen all busy with laughing farewells.

The Victoria River Depot race-meeting was over; a happy-go-lucky picnic meeting in one of the most isolated spots in Australia. Eighty miles up-stream from the mouth of the Victoria River is the Depot to which supplies come for the big cattle stations inland. Here, too, is Timber Creek police station, from which patrols go out into the dangerous lands.

Bush people come every year for hundreds of miles to this little Depot race-meeting. There is just the one long track which runs through the Depot, coming all the way from Darwin to go on to Western Australia where one branch ends at Wyndham, while the other meanders down inland into the East Kimberleys. Along this bush track from inland stations the scattered visitors came, even from Hall's Creek goldfield, three hundred miles away. This year the *Maroubra* had brought a few visitors from Darwin. In these Tiger was not interested, nor in the crowd, of station and bush boys who chatted while they watched on the river-bank by the landing. It was the canoe he was interested in, and in the two white men putting it aboard the *Maroubra*, and particularly in the stores they owned.

Stephens and Cook were smilingly proud of the canoe they had built. Of the paper-bark tree, it was so buoyant that a man could paddle it along hour after hour with little exertion. The paddle was a long-handled shovel, the blade flattened and well shaped. Tiger noted that shovel-blade. He knew wild warriors who would value it far above its weight in gold.

The builders had sawn the canoe in halves and rejoined it with boards, thus widening its centre and ensuring more stability with greater carrying capacity. Jim Malony, the one and only bookmaker, ventured that it might break apart in rough weather, but Stephens laughed good humouredly.

Stephens was an arresting type of man: considerate to others and self-reliant. Six feet one inch in height and proportionately built he could pick up a three hundred-pound anvil with ease. Good looking, a widely travelled man and a conversationalist, he spoke fluently English, French,

German, and Spanish. A cheerful man, well-liked.

Cook, short, thickly built and strong, was of a more stolid disposition; a good worker and quiet. He had served five years in the French Foreign Legion. They were going to prospect the Fitzmaurice River country for tin – an adventurous voyage. Mounted-Constable Fitzer, now in charge of Timber Creek police station, for the last time warned them against the venture. They would be far away from any white man; the country they proposed going to was the least known, the wildest, and held the most treacherous and bloodthirsty natives south-east of Darwin. He assured them that their chance of returning was remote.

Stephens thanked him while he laughed. Cook shrugged while loading their stores into the *Maroubra*. Jack Hayles, the skipper, had offered to take them down to the mouth of the river. Stephens reminded Fitzer that he was a fair bushman; that he had an extensive knowledge of the aborigines and felt assured that he and Cook could well look after themselves.

It was Fitzer's turn to shrug.

To rousing cheers the little vessel unmoored and steamed outstream, the hum of her engines soon diminishing. And now came the general dispersal: to Wyndham, to Hall's Creek, down the Territory to Wave Hill – even to the Katherine.

In a few hours Victoria River Depot would home only half a dozen isolated whites until the great race-day next year.

Tiger turned to the wild lands. A fast walker Tiger; tireless too; his lithe tread creepily suggestive of the ruthless animal whose name he bore. He stopped once only in fifty miles. Soon after leaving the Depot he shed his clothes and hid them in a cranny in the rocks. None dare touch the clothes of Tiger. He scowled towards the distant Depot, picked up his spears, turned, and strode on. Tiger had gone back to the Wilds.

He had always carried the Wilds in his heart: gardener boy at Bradshaw Station, or rouseabout for a musterer's cook, he was Tiger all the time. An interesting study, a Jekyll and Hyde among aborigines. A warrior among warriors where the test of a man is the taking of another's kidney-fat, yet he worked for the whites; came in from the Wilds again and again,

"The dingo crawls to lick the white dog's paws!" once sneered an enemy. But that enemy was dead before the next season came and his hands went to feed the dog of Tiger. None among the wild coastal tribes, only warriors of the Nemarluk class and, yes, Bul-bul, the accursed tracker, dared stand against him. But Tiger was the most dangerous of all.

"I have been among natives all my life," declared the manager of

Bradshaw Station, "and I have only met one aboriginal with brains – Tiger. And he knows how to use them."

Tiger had been warned off Bradshaw Station, lest he bring about tragedy. Because she did not bring him the tobacco he had sent her for, he split the skull of his woman, then savagely kicked her. The Chinese cook had run out shouting:

"Wha' for? Wha' for?"

Tiger let drive with his spears and the cook fled for the kitchen.

So Tiger had been warned off the run. He was very cruel to his woman. He only had one at a time, and he thrashed her unmercifully until he took another. To ill-treat a wife and take another ... yes, that is recognized. But to cast off his woman altogether, in sight of the other, to hunt her from him as a thing accursed – that is baiting fate. Numbers of warriors, fallen foul of the white law, would probably never have lost their liberty had it not been for the bitter jealousy of a discarded lubra. But now Tiger was on business bent and his smoke signals rose up behind him:

"Meet me at Wack-itch camp. Have big news." He was in the Fitzmaurice River country before the canoe reached the river-mouth. And the fighting men of his band were there to meet him. Chugulla the king, a wild-looking but physically perfect specimen of young manhood; old Walung, an Inkata of the Council; Wadawarry of medium height, thick set, with a heavy frowning face; old Alligator, a thin six-foot specimen of a grizzled old bad man of the Wilds (he with Maru were on the *Ouida* when Nemarluk attacked the Japanese); Walung, an Inkata too, with cold eyes set in a quiet frowning face; Chalmer, a warrior of six-foot-three with a ready laugh; Chin-arnon, and others. But those mentioned were Tiger's chosen band, though Chugulla the king was actually leader, standing to gain all credit or blame from the results of Tiger's scheming.

When the formal ceremonies obligatory to such a meeting were gravely gone through, Tiger spoke simply:

"Two white men are coming. In a canoe loaded with tobacco and food. We will kill them."

When the mopoke croaked that night they squatted around the council fire and gravely talked. And it was agreed.

Stephens and Cook were doomed even before they saw the Fitzmaurice River.

Some three days after leaving the Depot, the *Maroubra* steamed out from the mouth of the Victoria. Stephens and Cook were busy loading their supplies on to the canoe. Aboard the *Maroubra* were several Darwin solicitors who had come on the trip to see the Depot and its races. One of these kept a diary and had entered:

Off Indian Head. Stephens and Cook preparing their canoe, loading six kerosene-tins of water, flour, sugar, a sail cloth, a few nails, hammer, axe, folding kit, rope, etc., two guns, they have to live on these. At ten-thirty the winch slung the canoe overboard off the near point of Quoin Island. We all shook hands and to three cheers off they went on their great adventure. They will land on Quoin Island today to dig for water, camping the night. Tomorrow they will paddle on, *en route* to the Fitzmaurice River to seek tin. I feel anxious for them on account of the native tribes known to be both fierce and treacherous.

Smoke-signals were thinly rising long before the two adventurers paddled up the gloomy Fitzmaurice. They did not go far, some tree-lined ridges inland from the river attracted their attention. Those hills looked like granite, and granite is often the mother rock of minerals. On the Little Fitzmaurice one afternoon, they landed near Mutdjack Hill, a native name for a prominent ridge that runs parallel with the river. They secured their canoe, made a bucket out of a kerosene-tin, put the billy on, then cut and drove in mosquito-net pegs. Very quiet it was that night, each man under his net listening to the eerie night noises of the Wild. Next morning they unloaded a few things, intending to return here and camp a few days, then paddled off and entered Neinara Creek, which ran closer in towards the hill.

They landed, tied their canoe to a mangrove-tree, unloaded a little tucker and their prospecting tools. Suddenly natives appeared right amongst them. Naked, glowering natives, each armed with shovelbladed spears; their ribs, shoulders, thighs, and faces painted with bars of white and yellow ochre.

The prospectors' sudden alarm was quickly eased when one spoke in good pidgin:

"Good day. You look longa gold?"

"Yes," answered Stephens, "or tin. What boy you?"

"Me Tiger. You savvy me longa Depot." Stephens looked hard, then laughed in relief. In this naked, ochre-daubed savage so obviously trying to be friendly he would never have recognized the clothed rouseabout of Bradshaw Station. Everything was all right then. Civilized boys.

"This one Chugulla," introduced Tiger with a wave of his hand. "Him king!" The tall young aboriginal pointed to smiled quite pleasingly with a flash of perfect teeth. "This one Alligator. This one Pat, piccanin boy belonga Alligator." Tiger laughed and beckoned to a lad possibly nine years old. The boy came, shyly gazing up at the big white man. Stephens smilingly patted the boy's head.

The others of the band could not muster six words of English amongst them. Stephens and Cook were further relieved to see lubras peeping from amongst the trees.

They carried their tools across to the big hill. "We must carryon," said Stephens. "Do not show the least concern. I don't think there is cause for alarm, though I wish there were four of us here now, two to guard the canoe."

After several hours desultory prospecting, feeling somehow chilled, they returned to the canoe and boiled the billy ashore, their new-found friends squatting singly and in twos all around them, smoking a gift of tobacco. More natives began to drift from the timber to the group upon the river-bank.

Stephens grew alarmed. Tiger, talking to him, suddenly snatched up his spear and hurled it straight at Stephens's chest; at the same instant Wadawarry threw his spear at Cook. Stephens thumped straight back at the piercing impact, but Cook jumped up and ran as spears came hurtling from all sides. With a yell the warriors closed in and hacked the writhing men with the shovel-bladed weapons. Little Pat ran screaming into the stabbing mob and snatching a spear plunged it into Stephens. A roar of delight greeted the prowess of this son of old Alligator, whose grizzled face beamed with pride. They stood gazing at their handiwork while the lubras came running, screaming, "Kill! Kill!" Quean, youngest wife of Wallang, rushed to the loot, snatching the calico sheet. With a snarl Tiger stopped her; with claws outstretched for the loot they crouched back from the menace in his eyes.

"These white men will never see the sun again," said Tiger grimly.

He walked to the canoe and took from it the axe he had seen put aboard at Victoria River Depot far away.

"We will chop them up," he said craftily, "and put them aboard their canoe. Then, if policeman come, he will not find their rotting bones."

They unloaded the canoe, then chopped the men up and threw the pieces aboard. Tiger chopped the mooring rope; chopped a few small holes in the bottom of the canoe; then pushed the vessel outstream. The running tide caught it and sped it out towards the river.

"They came," pointed Tiger; "they sail away again."

"Into the bellies of crocodiles," laughed Alligator as the canoe began slowly to sink. "How will the white police find them now!"

"Not even Bul-bul will find them!" snarled Tiger. After eating and smoking, the blacks systematically divided the spoil. Tiger took a blanket, Wadawarry the tent-fly; each had something he could take away. The paddle was the most prized, for that would go to make shovel-nosed spears. Then Tiger broke the two guns and threw them far out into the water.

"Guns put Bul-bul on the scent after Nemarluk killed the Jap men!" he explained grimly. The others grunted approval.

When all the business was over they scattered in twos and threes. Several started for high up the Fitzmaurice; some made down towards the coast; others set out for Nemarluk's country; Tiger turned back towards Bradshaw Station.

Months later vague whisperings of the fate of Stephens and Cook trickled into Timber Creek police station.

The smoke-house where five Japanese were killed by King Wongo's men.

31
THE CAPTURE OF NEMARLUK

MOUNTED-CONSTABLE FITZER, in charge of Timber Creek police station, was worried. This Nemarluk, grown overconfident by repeated escapes, was now a distinct menace. Probably his example would be emulated by bucks anxious for native hero worship. And the Fitzmaurice River country mothered material for a dozen Nemarluks. How to catch this elusive firebrand before he set the tribes alight?

Fitzer walked out on to the police station veranda and gazed at the rocky hills. Close by was Timber Creek, meandering along to the Victoria River one and a half miles away. The river there was one quarter of a mile wide but shallow and tidal, and there was The Crossing. Three miles below The Crossing, and eighty miles from the river's mouth, is Victoria River Depot, where the *Maroubra* brings the stores for the cattle and police stations. The Victoria widens as it flows through rich grassy flats and picturesque ranges, and between flat-topped hills to Blunder Bay and the sea. There it is a mile wide. Torn by furious currents, with ever shifting mud and sandbanks, and swift tidal eddies and whirlpools, it is very treacherous. A beautiful river, but hard to understand, like the country through which it flows. A big river and a big country, they support the largest cattle station in the world, Victoria River Downs, covering thirteen thousand square miles.

On Nemarluk's side of the country there was only one cattle station, Bradshaw's, with the tree-sheltered homestead on a high knoll close to the river Shaw, running into the Victoria.

Timber Creek police station is one of the most isolated police outposts in the Northern Territory, and because of its geographical position one of the most important. This police outpost is merely of four rooms with a veranda all round, a detached kitchen, store, harness room and stockyard. Fitzer stood watching his baby toddler, as usual when apparently unobserved making on chubby legs to the nearest water hole. Baby's inseparable companion "Beris" walked gravely beside him, his big shoulder gently urging the youngster to explore in some other direction. But the toddler was determined, so the big Alsatian, despite energetic protests, simply shouldered him right away from the danger.

Fitzer smiled. Great dog that, the best nursemaid ever. Would not let a native go near the baby either; would tear a bush native to pieces if he dared to come within a hundred yards of the child. And wouldn't let a clothed native come much closer either. Even warned off the trackers, and he knew them well enough. That dog – on patrol in hostile country was worth half a dozen trackers when it came to sentry duty on a dark night.

With his mind full of Nemarluk, Fitzer walked to the harness store. He unlocked the door and walked down between the big heavy rails with their neat arrays of riding- and pack-saddles for horse and mule, their saddle-cloths and bridles and halters. The usual accoutrement store of any northern Australian mounted police station. Everything in place with military precision, all ready for immediate patrol.

Hobbles, bells, shoeing tools, spare horseshoes, shoeing nails, dandy brush, spare girths and surcingles, repairing outfit, awls, needles, thread, wax, copper, rivets, punches, etc. Chain, half-cuffs, handcuffs, padlocks.

Tent-flies, swags of Birkmyre, ground-sheet, rugs, mosquito-net, valise with change of clothing, towels and shaving-gear, holdall, needles, thread, and buttons. Trackers' swags and contents all complete and ready. Rations for a three months' patrol: flour, tea, sugar, coffee, carbonate of soda, cream of tartar, salt, dried fruits, potatoes and onions (preserved), tobacco, matches, soap; and pouch containing knives, forks, spoons and tin-opener; butcher knives and steel, camp-oven, dishes, billy-can, small shovel, half axe, salt meat. Waterproof satchel to hold official correspondence.

Fitzer locked up the store and strolled back to his tiny office. How to catch Nemarluk? His primitive but efficient spy system operated from the Victoria to the Daly. Patrols might chase him for months – had done so.

Against horses and mules this King of the Wilds could dodge amongst swamps, jungle areas, mangroves, salt arms of the sea, pandanus, palm marshes, rivers, rock-bound gorges. The difficulties of this unmapped area made it a fairly safe refuge. With such a leader it was surprising that the patrols had caught the others of the Red Band so quickly. Now the lone dingo would lead the hounds a chase indeed, and woe betide any unwary white man who crossed his trail.

"Set a Greek to catch a Greek!"

Fitzer sent for Bul-bul. The big tracker's eyes gleamed; he was laughing silently. Only that morning he had received another message from Nemarluk to the effect that he was going to get Bul-bul's kidney-fat.

Preparations were made for patrol, with a whispered leakage that Fitzer with Trackers Bul-bul, Splinter and Sydney intended to raid Legune Station. The information was promptly smoke-signalled to Nemarluk. He really was on the outskirts of Legune. But then Legune was on the opposite side of the river. The patrol must ride down-river a hundred and forty miles, and when it arrived Nemarluk would have ample time to slip back across the river and leisurely make his escape, while the patrol must ride all the way back up-river before they could cross. Regaled with food and ample tobacco by the hero-worshipping station blacks, Nemarluk sneered at the fools of "white pleece"; boasted what a dance he would again lead them, and how he would spear any who pursued too closely.

The patrol was all ready to start when the *Maroubra* from Darwin steamed up to the Depot with stores. She unloaded, and when about to cast off on her return trip Fitzer quietly smuggled Bul-bul and Splinter aboard. The understanding was that the vessel would land them somewhere on the Legune side.

But Fitzer, as the vessel was casting off, told Bul-bul that it would steam into Blunder Bay and land them on the river-bank opposite the Legune side. They were to lie in wait for Nemarluk when he crossed the river as he would when the patrol came riding down the Legune side. Bul-bul laughed. So, for the first time, information of importance failed to reach Nemarluk.

As the *Maroubra* steamed down-river Fitzer's patrol started on the meandering ride to Legune. Smoke-signals wirelessed its progress.

Fitzer's patrol ultimately raided Legune native camp. But Nemarluk, astride a log, had crossed the river some hours before. A big old-man crocodile came nosing under below but Nemarluk disdainfully poked a twelve-foot spear down towards its snout. A jab in the eye from that was more than any crocodile wanted.

Nemarluk strode up the bank, the sun glistening on the water drops sliding from his wonderful body. Fierce-eyed, his big black beard hiding the snarl now growing at the corners of his mouth, he was the epitome of all wild men on the earth. With long, springy strides he walked leisurely into the bush. He had plenty of time; more than two hundred miles start already and all he had done was to swim a river, He gazed around at the wild free bush and laughed. Less than two hours later Bul-bul was gazing in delight at the tracks of his enemy. And Splinter too, although he felt an uneasy shiver at this silent witness of a man whom all aborigines feared. And Bul-bul's friend was there; a totem brother, a link in Bul-bul's black service, a link who had shown the way to the spot where Nemarluk invariably crossed.

They fell on him while he slept. In a moment there was a snarling fury of writhing bodies, snap of teeth, pant and gasp, tearing grass, deep grunts of struggling men. They slipped a cuff upon his wrist but he snapped at Splinter's throat and upending Bul-bul kicked the totem brother flat. But Bul-bul clung to the other cuff while snatching Nemarluk's ankles, and they bore him to earth again as dogs swarm the under-dog. They jammed his head under a leaning root, levered his arm behind his back and snapped on the remaining cuff. Then sprawled upon him, spitting blood, panting.

Mounted-Constable Langdon, fresh from leave, reported to his station at Timber Creek. Fitzer was on patrol towards Legune seeking Nemarluk, so Langdon rode down-river and met him at Bradshaw Station. And Nemarluk was with him. And with Nemarluk wag Pundck captured by Bul-bul as he returned with his prisoner. Langdon looked once and the recognition was mutual. For not long since the lugger *Pat* was anchored in Blunder Bay. Aboard was Constable Kennett, old Ah Mat, and a Japanese *en route* to Turkey Creek, in the East Kimberleys. The wild men attacked from canoes at night. Kennett was asleep but awoke with a split second to spare. The tomahawk chopped his fingers instead of his head.

"You try kill him policeman!" accused Langdon. "No more kill him!" protested Pundck. "Me been chop it head but hittem pillow!"

Two lubras and scared little Sandy, a piccanin of twelve years, were also following Nemarluk into exile.

Fitzer asked Bul-bul if he had learned any news of the two white men who with their canoe had gone to the Fitzmaurice many moons ago.

"I think that two feller white men he dead," answered Bul-bul confidently. "Tiger savvy." And Bul-bul brought forward yet another "link" in his service. This man told Fitzer that it was "big talk" in the camps that Tiger's band had killed Stephens and Cook. This might be only native rumour. However, Tiger was hanging about Bradshaw Station again. Fitzer sent for him.

"You savvy that two white man been go down longa Fitzmaurice?"

"No more! I no savvy longa that man!"

"You liar! You savvy!"

He was confronted and accused by the native who had informed Bul-bul. Tiger scowled at the man.

"Well," demanded Fitzer, "you savvy now?"

"I only bin see canoe longa tree and track belonga man!"

"You must been follow those tracks!"

"I bin follow him longa camp longa kerosene-tins. I been losem there."

"What's the matter you been losem him?"

"Big rain come, washem out track."

"What's the matter you no more look about, pick him up again?"

"I want to see brother belonga me, longa Bradshaw, get him tobacco."

"You been have plenty time to tell him policeman before! Why you no come up?"

"Oh, I wait about, that's all!" And Tiger's expression told it was useless to question him further.

Late that day, Langdon learned from a half-caste that with tales of plentiful dingoes Tiger had tried to entice Fisher the dingo-shooter down into the Fitzmaurice country.

Little Fisher the wanderer, with his big moustache and blue eyes known from Borroloola to Bradshaw's run. He had shrugged with a wink at the half-caste's warning.

Fitzer became increasingly anxious for the safety of Stephens and Cook. He tried a little bluff to learn the truth or otherwise of the rumour. Through the interpreter, he accused Nemarluk.

"I reckon you been killem these two man!"

But Nemarluk laughed. "You ask Tiger!" he laughed again.

"You will have to come to Timber Creek police station with me!" Fitzer cautioned Tiger.

After that twenty-eight-mile ride they asked Sandy. He was afraid to talk; but when alone came to whisper, his eyes big with fright and news.

The two men had been killed near Mutdjack Hill near the Little Fitzmaurice.

"Who been tell him you?"

"Ununyah" had told all the hordes at a big corroboree at Legune and showed in the dance how Tiger, Wadawary, Walung, Coonbook, Maru, Anglaitchie and Chin-amon had killed the white men.

They planted the boy behind a curtain in the police store, then Bul-bul brought in Tiger. They accused him of the details. Sullenly he denied. They confronted him with the boy but one glance at Tiger and Sandy almost fainted. He could only whisper that Nemarluk had told.

Tiger glared unbelievingly; then suddenly he turned to the police with almost a smile. He explained that he too had heard that the men were killed but was afraid of tribal vengeance should he admit so. However, if the police would promise to protect him now and afterwards, he would willingly enough guide them to the locality of the alleged murder.

They had to be content. Meanwhile, it was Langdon's duty to escort Nemarluk on the long trip back to Darwin. There at headquarters he would report the alleged killing and return with orders. Fitzer had work to attend to meanwhile. Tiger was given a job about the place to hold him in the vicinity. So away rode Langdon, and Nemarluk walked beside him.

32
THE SEA WANDERERS

A TINY craft bobbed alone in a lonely sea. Safe enough in a river, this cutter barely eighteen feet long and half decked over, but she looked like suicide out here, creeping along the coast. She bore evidence of much repair, despite her covering of red and white paint. Her two tiny sails enlivened her general air of battling resignedly on. At the least squall she might go to pieces plank by plank. None but superoptimists or highly inexperienced men would venture to sea in such a craft.

Traynor and Fagan were a mixture of the two.

They should have had better sense, for each had had experience of a sort. But both had an overflowing share of that bane of the sea-roamer:

"We'll chance to luck."

Their fortunes were at that low ebb when beggars cannot be choosers.

"We may as well chance the sea," growled Traynor, "as stay in Darwin and go on the dole."

So they had sailed. Traynor was a strong, stockily-built man, a little over medium height. Somewhat grumpy at times, otherwise of that stolid disposition that makes up its mind and then plods ahead.

Fagan was tall, with a loosely built frame that suited his rather long face and prominent jaw. That jaw, picked up many months later on a beach by missionaries Dyer and Warren, was to tell of his fate. Fagan was careless of things in general; quicker to smile than Traynor though not so stubbornly patient. A pair of beachcombers in need of a lot of stubbornness, a lot of cheerfulness, a lot of luck: Luck often rules the destiny of such men. Until now, luck had been with them; right until they changed their minds and their course for Borroloola. They had done the wrong thing; taken the wrong turning. They had left Darwin with the intention of creeping north-east along the coast through Clarence Strait until they rounded Danger Point, then hug the coast east to Cape Wilberforce. Here, weather being favourable, they would make a dash across the great gulf to Cape York. From there to Thursday Island would be easy. In those warm coral seas they hoped to win a living from pearl-shell, trochus, *bêche-de-mer*, and tortoiseshell.

A little cruise of a thousand miles, more if they hugged the coast all the way, no civilization bar several isolated mission stations, the coast notoriously unsafe, But sea nomads often carry out such trips in the north.

En route they had called in to Milingimbi mission station to effect very necessary repairs. There they met Fred Gray, trepanger. He towed them via Elcho Island to Arnhem Bay, in which dangerous locality they stayed three days, unarmed; then sailed north-east out through the Malay Road on their voyage again – for Borroloola. They changed their course and crossed their luck.

Borroloola is a tiny place about sixty miles up from the mouth of the McArthur River; a depot to which stores are brought for cattle stations back inland in the Gulf country.

Traynor sat with his thick arm held loosely on the tiller, smoking. He was sitting bent slightly forward to the rise and fall of the boat, frowning thoughtfully. Fagan sat beside him gazing out over the bows at the long low form of Woodah Island looming ahead. To a fair breeze, the little craft was sailing almost merrily.

"It's a case of necessity almost," growled Traynor.

"We've only a couple of bags of flour aboard, a little tobacco, a few tins of meat, a little tea and sugar. If we call in at Borroloola we'll probably pick up work that will pay for fresh stores. Then we can sail for Thursday Island."

"It's the sensible thing to do," agreed Fagan.

"Anyway, time doesn't matter."

"No," replied Traynor thoughtfully. "Time is neither here nor there, it is luck that counts."

"The devil looks after his own."

"Yes. But we are between the devil and the deep sea."

"What odds! If we get there we get there; if we don't we don't."

"That old saying of yours has worked out many a time."

"Why not now?"

"I don't know. Remember me telling them at Milingimbi that if we changed our minds, we'd change our luck?"

"Yes."

"Well, I've got that queer hunch still."

"The old saying will work out true for all that," insisted Fagan cheerfully. "If we get there we get there; if we don't we don't."

Traynor stared grumpily towards Woodah Island. One among other islands that men know little about.

"We'd better make it an anchorage," suggested Fagan. "Sun will be going down soon."

Traynor nodded. The breeze was dying out. Shaggy men from Woodah Island watched the tiny craft drawing slowly closer. She crept closer still in a red sunset that turned her into a bobbing black log with a rosy sail. One gull above her stick of mast was snow white. These warriors stood on a jutting point, a sloping beach before them, green jungle behind. There were warriors amongst these men, looked up to by the huntsmen of the tribe and praised by the women as shining examples of what a man should be. Tuckiar the killer, Merara the fierce, Mondugal the planner, young Jimbarrion the ambitious, and others of Tuckiar's horde.

With them were wild-eyed lubras, wondering how their lords would greet these strangers, hoping that the white men would be encouraged to anchor. Craftily then they made allusion to tobacco and things to eat, and things of iron that the vessel would surely hold. Piccaninnies shook reed spears at the craft as it drew surely closer.

At sundown the cutter cast anchor in a miniature bay. As the sails came creaking down, Merara turned to stare at Tuckiar, a mirthless smile creasing the corners of his mouth.

Tuckiar only grunted, gazing at the shore shadows creeping out towards the cutter. A gleam of fire, then a wisp of smoke rose from the galley-box aft.

A fierce savage, this Tuckiar, with thick body and limbs, broad chest and deep. Slow-thinking, but cunning; ferocious when he struck.

Silently, Mondugal the leader watched these two best killers of the horde. Jimbarrion, the young brave lusting for a kill, eagerly did the same.

Morning dawned peacefully; not a ripple on the sea.

"And that's that!" said Traynor. "We're euchred; not a breath of wind."

"But a great chance to stretch our legs," yawned Fagan. "And we might lay in a store of salt fish and perhaps trade for turtle-shell. There's sure to be niggers about."

"They're coming now," nodded Traynor as a canoe shot out from the beach.

It was a picture. Tuckiar, Merara, and Jimbarrion paddling that long canoe so easily, so swiftly, three strokes to this side, then the flash of the paddleblades as they dipped three strokes to that side, each movement as one in rhythm, the canoe as one with the men.

"Their canoe is as long as our boat," said Fagan.

"Yes, and more seaworthy."

"That leading paddler would draw crowds in a wild man show."

"Hmm. I'll bet he eats his meat raw."

As the canoe skimmed up beside the cutter black arms reached out and black hands grasped the gunwale.

"Good day," nodded Traynor.

The blacks grunted. They had one universal word between them, hardly a word more.

"Tabac!"

"Make them bring some wood for it," said Fagan. "Then we can arrange for fish if they are willing to work."

Traynor nodded, and reaching towards their tiny galley, held up a stick of firewood. Tuckiar nodded. Traynor showed two sticks of trade tobacco as promised payment.

From their tangled hair Tuckiar and Merara both produced a crab's claw pipe, holding the blackened things mutely out. Traynor pinched a smoke of tobacco from a stick of trade, and pointed to the galley fire. Eagerly they stuffed their pipes, reached to the galley and picked up a glowing coal with bare fingers. They smoked as a famished opium smoker might smoke.

"They haven't had a draw for a very long time," growled Traynor, "look at the young fellow's eyes nearly sticking out of his head."

"H'm," answered Fagan. "They haven't had a bath for a long time either. Don't smell too sweet."

"Plour!" suddenly grunted Merara.

"Why they're civilized!" laughed Fagan, and Traynor nodded acquiescence. He handed them a couple of tomahawks with which to cut the firewood. The eyes of the black men gleamed as they reached for the iron weapons. Tuckiar smiled at the balanced weight of this thing in his hand; as he eyed the keen blade the feel of the thing seemed to talk to him. They sped the canoe towards the shore. Then fate spoke through Fagan:

"What if we stretch our legs ashore? We can be back before they return with the wood."

They rowed ashore and walked leisurely along the beach. Not far. They should never have left the vessel at all. But then they had often done foolish things and got away with it.

"Luck favours the brainless," as Fagan used to say.

On the sand, in the shade of drooping trees, they spied a little crowd of natives and knew instantly they were meant to see them, for women were squatting there. They walked across and tried to open up a conversation. Some of the women were young and well formed; their teeth flashed and their eyes laughed to the white men's unintelligible words; then with bowed head one would look sideways at a sister, and at the quick guttural joke both would throw back their heads and laugh. Piccaninnies peeped timidly from back in among the trees.

Jurparrie was slim and swift with faultless eyes and ears. She supplied the wit to the arm of Tuckiar. His other two wives Newgar and Burramool were there too, and one a startling replica of a young Japanese woman, while yet another had the colouring, features, and physique of a lass of

Macassar.

The men squatting there with arm held loosely across a knee watched the whites from under shaggy brows. Lying on the ground within reach of each man's hand were shovel-nosed spears.

The white men walked away at an angle, not so foolish as to leave their backs exposed. They returned to the cutter. When the woodmen returned two hours later they stood in the canoe and unloaded the wood leisurely into the cockpit of the cutter. Their keen eyes searched every corner of the vessel but saw no fire-arms; still, weapons might be hidden under the blankets in that tiny stuffy cabin leading forrard from the cockpit.

Several days and nights went by. No wind came.

But the last night did. The cutter lay motionless under the starlight, the water a dull mirror, star reflecting and faintly rosy because of the hurricane lamp shining from the little dark boat. On shore, invisible among the tree-shadows squatted the Unguraripa warriors. Occasionally with the quick lift of their brows or when a star beam fell on them through the foliage, those eyes would glow like a cat's at night. They had decided to kill the two white men for the sake of the loot the boat might contain. As the one man who could speak English explained later, "We proper hungry feller."

Just before dawn a canoe crept out from the shore, making no more sound than a shadow, and drifted down beside the vessel. Black hands reached out and cushioned the vessels apart, black arms reached down and clutched tomahawks.

The canoe men leaned over the cutter's side, peering down into the cockpit. Black luck! it was empty, the white men must be in the cabin. Tuckiar swung his leg over into the cockpit, silent as a cat.

Stealthily he lifted his other leg into the cutter and squatted there to glare into the cabin forrard. Noiselessly Merara stepped beside him. Uneasily Traynor stirred. No human noise had awakened him, but his eyes opened. He realized that the little cabin opening was black whereas it should show the faint blue of the sky.

With bowed head he leapt out into the cockpit and Merara's tomahawk caught him only a glancing blow. His outspread arms closed around Merara's body and they tumbled back over Tuckiar. Traynor was instantly erect swinging a lump of firewood straight down on Merara's neck. He grunted hugely and clasped Traynor's legs who slung his arms around his middle and threw him clean overboard. Fagan sprang at Tuckiar's upraised arm and both men thumped back upon Traynor, who was upended yet again by the two wrestling men while Merara, bleeding at the nose was hauled aboard the canoe by the excited Jimbarrion. Traynor was on his feet glaring around for other enemies as Merara's clawing hand fell on Jimbarrion's tomahawk; he threw it swiftly, and the weapon struck Traynor on the back of the neck. His arms shot up, he toppled backwards over the cockpit and fell into the sea. He struck out, choking, dazed and blinded. Tuckiar and Fagan were locked in a death-grip. They fell, Fagan beneath, his head striking the edge of the cockpit. Tuckiar immediately threw him overboard. He sank like a stone. Tuckiar stood panting, his hair torn allover his triumph-lit eyes. All stared out over the lighting waters towards Traynor's head, swimming blindly as they sped the canoe out in pursuit. He sank.

All the treasure the raiders found in the little cutter was two bags of flour, several pounds of tobacco, four worn blankets, a few threadbare odds and ends, and a few pieces of iron.

Shovel-nosed spears: The "Assagai" of the North.

33
THE DEATH OF McCOLL

A TOUGH proposition awaited police headquarters, Darwin, in the capturing of the killers of the Japanese at Caledon Bay-part of the real unmapped Arnhem Land, uninhabited by whites, the least known of any area in the Northern Territory. None but police patrols, or a very occasional wanderer of the old Dr Bloomfield type, a bushman, or a missionary has ever been through its inland areas. Added to this, the coast has its island system; and the Balamoomoos and other tribes were strong enough to make islands or mainland their huntinggrounds as they chose. A patrol, to stand a chance of success, must be capable of operating by sea as well as land.

Arrangements were eventually made with Groote Eylandt mission to supply a lugger to meet the patrol at Roper River police station, and, as required, a launch for the patrol to operate along the coast.

The patrol assembled at the Roper River, approximately three hundred and sixty miles on the overland route from Darwin, the most easterly police outpost, near the border of Arnhem Land. The Roper empties into the Gulf of Carpentaria approximately seventy miles south of Groote Eylandt and is navigable up to the bar for about sixty miles by small craft. The patrol comprised Constables Morey, Hall, Mahony, and McColl with their trackers, a strong plant of horses and mules and two inseparable dogs. The land party – Morey, Mahony, and trackers with horses and mules were to travel overland towards Blue Mud Bay, approximately two hundred and forty miles east of north by the route they must necessarily take, and at an agreed-on spot meet Hall and McColl on their return from Groote Eylandt with the launch. The land party would travel through Balamoomoo country as it neared the coast, while the launch would keep an eye on the islands as it came to the rendezvous. By the time sea and land parties met they would probably have learned the whereabouts of the wanted men.

Of the sea party – Hall and McColl, with trackers – Hall is a six-foot Australian of a quiet disposition, emphasized probably by long association with the lonely places. Still, on patrol, he would surprise the party by suddenly bursting into song, generally operatic songs. He is, too, a water colourist, quick to catch the beauty of rugged rock or moonlit lagoon; an interesting companion; a good bushman. McColl, shorter and of broad build, was a very quiet man with a keen sense of humour. His quiet jokes often lightened an arduous march. Used to the Central Australian silences he had sometimes to be dragged out of them.

The trackers, too, were interesting individuals.

Big Paddy, the cheerful one, always willing and game to scout alone at night. Tommy, a good boy, but inclined to be sulky and jealous of head tracker Paddy. Alas, this jealousy was to have fatal consequences to the patrol. As for the two dogs, well, they were the patrol in their own opinions.

At the Roper busy days were spent in handling and shoeing horses and getting the stores down to the river landing. When the mission lugger *Holly* arrived Hall and McColl with Trackers Dick and Reuben embarked for Groote Eylandt. Morey and Mahony with Trackers Paddy, Tommy, Lock and Lorry, twenty horses and six mules, started on their over land ride to the coastal rendezvous.

The patrol was to cover over a thousand miles before returning to Darwin.

After a boggy trip by land and a rough trip by sea both parties met as agreed on, Hall and McColl having secured the tiny mission launch *Hope.*

From a tangle of scrub on the coast they watched smoke-fires from Round Hill Island a few miles out to sea, answered by signals from Woodah Island. At night in the launch they ran across to Round Hill Island, and after unsuccessfully scouring the island, made it a base from which they scouted the nearest extremity of Woodah Island, proving there was a large horde of natives about twenty miles farther along towards its southern extremity. .

Hall and McColl steamed back to the big hill on Round Hill Island, thinking that the tribesmen might put to sea in their canoes. But in the night a heavy south-easterly blew up and it was four days before the tiny launch could battle its way back to Woodah.

After breakfast next morning Morey instructed Trackers Lorry and Reuben to remain on the launch and guard it carefully, not to go ashore except to cook and feed the dogs which would be tied ashore as sentinels at night.

The four white police with Trackers Paddy, Lock, Tommy, and Dick, then packed supplies to last three days and walked on down the island coast, keeping a sharp look out particularly for beached or hidden canoes. If only the canoes could be located the horde would be marooned on the island.

It was twenty miles to the southern end of the island, but a glorious day with a cool breeze made walking a pleasure; the little beaches were invitingly firm to the tread. Stunted scrub interspersed with billowing sand over which trailed broad-leafed creepers among tufts of tall coarse grass, grew on hillocky mounds just back from the beaches. Farther inland were long patches of sombre jungle. The men walked with senses keenly alert; their one hope of surprise lay in hearing first and seeing first. The trackers scouted on ahead, Paddy with a forced gameness as obvious as the uneasiness of his mates.

They fully realized that if disaster overtook these policemen or the launch, their plight would be serious indeed.

After midday the patrol edged from the beaches in among the sheltering clumps of timbered underbrush growing out from the scrub edges. With increased caution they neared the southern end of the island and the hidden camp Mungarrabarramutchee, a quarter of a mile inland from the coast on the edge of jungle. From a mound sheltered by prickly bush they stared at the dull wall of timber. But no smoke-wisp rose from its edge, no shrill voice of lubra, or laugh of piccaninny, no call of man, no sign of gunyah or bark wind-shelter. Out from the dull green of jungle stood the ghostly trunks of paper-barks above the still, yellow water of a gloomy swamp. Spreading out to vantage points the police hid, watching towards the camp, while the trackers scouted out around the flanks to suddenly appear behind it. It was deserted.

But Paddy pointed to fresh tracks leading from the camp into the jungle. Here, undiscernible except to a searcher, was a native path vanishing into greenery. In single file they disappeared into the silence. Treading softly on fallen leaves, edging aside from vines and drooping branches whose twigs but gently swished back, Paddy with eyes, ears, and nose alert, led the way along this faint pad that snaked through the jungle into sunlit glades and on again into further scrub. But there came no hushed sound, no distant yell that might betray a hidden camp. Half a mile in they came to a mossy spring. Morey put down his pack and nodded back along the line. "We eat," he said in a low voice.

Paddy and Lock were stationed ahead. They melted down into the foliage, the eyes and ears of the patrol.

The men sat around the spring, and spoke in whispers as they commenced a hungry meal.

Quietness hemmed them in, emphasized just once by the low sweet call of a bird. Vision was limited to yards, all in a soft twilight. They had just finished lunch when Paddy's head popped up, his hand and eyes signalling.

"Natives close!"

Alert on the instant, they crept up to the watchmen who pointed straight into the jungle. Presently, to Paddy's warning gesture, they heard soft blows as if of pointed sticks digging into earth. Then a woman's voice, low and lazy, answered by some chuckling reply.

Paddy crept on, followed by the others until he knelt 10 cautiously part the bushes. Four lubras were digging yams in a tiny open glade brightened by sunlight. Squatting there they scooped and dug while they gossiped, their lithe figures perfectly built to stand any emergency of the Wilds. None but black trackers could ever have taken such women by surprise.

They surrounded them with a sudden rush. The lubras gazed in astonishment. Men-white men, standing among them!

"Quick!" ordered Morey, "while they're dumbfounded. Paddy, tell them we are police and mean them no harm, only want to 'talk-talk.' Ask where their main camp is, and where their canoes are?"

To Paddy's question a lubra slowly raised her arm and pointed, adding from trembling lips:

"Only little way."

"What tribe?"

"Balamoomoo!" she replied and her eyes gleamed proudly. She threw back her head and the jungle rang to a long, wailing cry.

"Leave her alone," cried Morey to Paddy's alarm.

"Ask her how many men are in the camp. Quickly now!"

She answered several other questions, and offered to show them where the canoes were hidden. Then again she wailed, the low, long-drawn cry that penetrates through foliage and jungle.

"We can't stop them calling. I hope to goodness the tribe are out of earshot," said Morey urgently. "Put the cuffs on for the time being or they'll slip us in a twinkling; their eyes are roaming. We'll have to detain them awhile and try to induce them to show us where the canoes are."

They handcuffed each separately then Morey with Paddy took a lubra out of earshot but not out of sight of the others.

"Ask her who killed the Japanese at Caledon Bay? Quick Paddy."

"Wongo the king," she replied, "Natchelma, Woolaware, Moowembowie, Narkaya, Noming, Marrawatta, Mow." She gave other names too. She was led back to her friends who quickly, were similarly questioned. To Morey's delight each gave the same names; and they corresponded with names given by the Rose River tribe on the mainland. But they would not tell where those men were.

"We know our men now," said Morey. "If only we can locate and catch them!"

Now one of these lubras was Jurparrie, favourite wife of Tuckiar. Her wild eyes were roaming, her feet itching; her ears were hearing the pecking of a bird's bill upon a tree, the sigh of a breeze in the leaves overhead, the whispering insects that the ears of white men would never hear. Then she heard the call of a bird, low and sweet; and her eyes shone.

She had picked up her yam-stick and merely glanced at a fellow lubra who stooped to pick up hers. As she straightened up, Jurparrie's loosely held stick accidentally touched the other's to several tiny sounds. Such natural little sounds, the accidental touching of sticks, sounds unnoticed by the police debating their next move and what they should do with the women.

"We must detain them awhile," said Morey, "until they show us where the canoes are. They seem perfectly willing anyway. Now, Paddy, you listen carefully!" And Morey instructed him to tell the lubras that when they arrived at the camp they were to call out that the party were police, they were not to run away but to sit down, that the police were not going to harm them but only wished to speak. Paddy was to call out likewise.

Even while they talked that stick of Jurparrie's occasionally clicked out faint sounds that answered faint clickings from the nearby jungle. Not a white soul would have dreamt it as the four lubras huddled close together, staring up at the big white men debating so seriously.

But a tracker stationed on watch near by, stared round suspiciously then attuned his ears to pierce the deeper silence.

"We'll take the cuffs off," decided Morey, "and order them to take us straight to their camp. If they slip away into the jungle, well – we can't help it. We'll follow them. They're almost sure to make straight back for their camp, the trackers may be able to keep them in sight. And Paddy you remember to call out to the people immediately you see or hear them."

They had just taken the cuffs off when Paddy saw two black heads peering from the creepers. As he signalled alarm, the tracker who had listened for the clicking of sticks reported the creeping of natives in the jungle behind. As Paddy called out his message in "tribal," the party rushed straight on after him, the lubras directing the way to a camp which opened out almost immediately before them. It proved a dummy camp, the real camp they found hidden close by in the heart of the jungle. Here was the stronghold of Tuckiar, a warren-like maze of tiny camps, a tribute to the bushcraft, the strategic cunning of the Australian aboriginal. Had Tuckiar's primitives been possessed of the grit against white men that they have against their own colour, not one of the police party, trackers or whites, would have emerged from that jungle. As it was, if Tuckiar had only been granted a few more moments in which to muster his men, the party would have suffered disaster.

As they broke into this camp leaves rustled swiftly as black shadows vanished to sounds of thrashing foliage, as if startled animals were breaking away. To Paddy's repeated shouts suggesting a "talk-talk" they gave no heed.

"After them," ordered Morey. "Quick! You, McColl, follow on with Tommy and Dick and bring the lubras if they will come, then wait for us out in the open."

The three whites dived into the jungle following Paddy and Lock to find themselves puzzled amongst that maze of vines. And close behind them came Tommy and Dick, Tommy who was jealous of Paddy, Dick who like Tommy was afraid and deliberately deserted McColl encumbered with the lubras.

All was silence now except their own noise as they pushed through the foliage. They stumbled upon little circular spaces hewn out of the vegetation. These were individual camps, each just large enough for a family to camp in at night, cleared of just enough undergrowth to enable a warrior to stand erect and throw his spear, seeing while not yet seen. The path entrance leading from camp to camp was always disguised by a veil of creepers. In places they were forced to drop to their knees to crawl through the vines, and so became scattered. Meanwhile McColl, now realizing the trackers' desertion was pushing on as hurriedly as possible. But in a moment he was alone with Jurparrie. He snatched her arm and gazed quickly around. The other lubras had vanished. Jurparrie stood there, her eyes blazing with triumph, as close by she heard the low call of a bird. Her stick tapped out:

"I'm here. One white man is with me."

"Bring him to me!" clicked a stick.

Jurparrie turned urgently to McColl, yabbering excitedly, pointing vehemently. He urged her forward while straining to hear some sound of his vanished mates. She protested as they pushed through the bushes, urging him with pointing arm and rolling eyes and uncouth words in another direction. He hesitated, then motioned her to lead the way. Eagerly she pushed ahead, glancing over her shoulder now and again to nod reassuringly. She chose the easiest walking, he pressing on closely behind. He could not see her face but presently he glanced up at the lightening among the leaves and guessed they must be close to a clearing or else the jungle edge. He keyed himself up to surprise a camp or perhaps be shown to the rear of the men who had run away.

But Jurparrie's eyes were shining like crystal quartz, her ears shut to every sound but the faintest signals of a man. Before she emerged from the jungle she saw him, the big spear ready fitted to the wommera pointing straight out from that wild head crouching above the grass. In finger-talk he signalled:

"Give me room!"

She stepped from the jungle, McColl a step behind her. She vanished as if swallowed by the earth; then McColl felt his chest split in halves as he leapt back with a choking cry. Staggering among the vines he whipped out the revolver while wrenching the spear from his chest. He fired twice as he fell face down, his clenched fingers pulling the trigger again as he struck the ground.

A terrible weapon is the shovel-nosed spear.

McColl was dead in the shortest of minutes.

*The fourth man from the left is McColl.
Taken the morning he was speared.*

34
THE LAW OF THE ASSAGAI

MEANWHILE the police party had worked their way out to the more open country fronting the sea-beach. Here clumps of stunted scrub and grassy hillocks were dotted over the sand. The party hurried along the coast, the trackers spread out searching for tracks. Paddy called attention to three warriors running out on to a rocky point ahead and calling to four men in a canoe paddling around the point. The police broke into a run though fully expecting the landsmen to leap into the canoe and escape. Instead, the canoe turned shoreward, the paddleblades gleaming as swiftly she beached at the point. The tribesmen leapt out snatching their spears and all seven ran towards the covering timber, beating the police to it. These found themselves then among clumps of stunted vegetation overlooking a bare circular saltpan partly surrounded by scrub. Natives were giving a high-pitched signal call that was answered from deep within the jungle and farther down on the beach. Suddenly the calling ceased.

Down sloping sand-mounds they hurried to the open saltpan, but no tracks led across it. Morey and Hall with Tracker Lock hurried west along the rising ground seeking to cut any tracks leading from the jungle. Mahony and Tracker Paddy scouted well around the claypan and farther along the beach, searching the little clumps of bush that made such perfect hide-outs. All worked speedily for sunset was coming. Mahony and Paddy searched for half an hour. Then Mahony noticed the others returning. Thinking they saw him, he continued his search around a patch of scrub. He came out near the salt pan, and wondered at no sign of Morey and Hall; even Tracker Paddy had disappeared. He stared around, for the shadows were lengthening and things were losing distinctness. Above tall grass he saw four woolly heads moving in line along the edge of the scrub across the saltpan.

"The trackers," thought Mahony. "Morey and Hall and McColl must be walking ahead of them, all hands must have joined up. I'd better join up too."

He hurried across the pan and on, up a sloping sandbank tufted with grass; ahead the wall of jungle was gloomy with the afternoon shadows. He made haste to catch his comrades then paused staring at a black head rising from the tussocks, two gleaming eyes and an arm that gripped a poised shovel-bladed spear.

"Drop it!" he yelled, and leapt aside and fired high at the same instant that the spear whizzed past his thigh. He heard to right and left a rustling where other natives were creeping to surround him.

He fired at the crouching figure fitting another spear to the wommera and – missed.

He leapt around and ran, coo-ee-ing while erratically running. As he leapt down into the claypan an iron-bladed spear caught him a glancing blow on the head. He ran into the open claypan and wheeled around with upraised revolver, shouting as the thought that Ted and the others might have been ambushed and killed shook him. Up on the bank appeared the head and shoulders of a savage, and Mahony pulled the trigger three times vainly. The cartridges were defective! He sought to reload, ramming bullets into the revolver cylinder. They jammed.

A native stepped on the saltpan edge, but in the act of raising his spear he looked keenly to his left, then stepped straight back among the trees. Mahony yelled in wildest hope, facing again that savage who had never moved. With an answering hail Morey, Hall, and Paddy came crashing out through the jungle, but every native had disappeared.

"A bullet is a clean thing to die by," sighed Mahony as he wiped his brow. "It would be awful to die by a rusty spear."

"What have you done to your hat?" asked Hall.

Mahony took it off. The pugaree on the left side was cut clean through.

"The felt is cut through too," said Hall. "That was what you might call a close go."

"Have you seen McColl?" asked Morey sharply.

"No! Isn't he with you?"

"No. Let us hurry back to where we left him."

At the jungle edge they were surprised to find Trackers Tommy and Dick.

"Where is McColl?" demanded Morey.

"Don't know," answered Tommy sullenly.

"Why don't you know?"

"We bin follow on behind when you been chasem blackfellow. When you come back we been sit down here."

Each constable looked at the others, then plunged into the jungle. It was almost dark. With torches they searched far into the night, firing an occasional shot. A lubra started crying deep in the jungle; they listened questioningly. Plain in the silence, not far away, a native woman crying brokenheartedly. They shrugged, turning their torches to the leaf-cluttered ground. I t would take a more cunning decoy than a wailing woman to lure these tired men into a death-trap. Once, they emerged on the jungle edge and stared at the gleam of a fire on a beach down the coast several miles away.

"A trap!" growled Morey.

It was, for next day they investigated and found that to reach that beach they would have had to pass in single file under a cliff. Stones from above in the dark would have settled them.

Excitement and lurking danger kept them going until exhaustion would not be denied; they had walked over thirty miles that day. Coming out on the beach near the point they found a bitterly cold south-easter blowing, but a full moon in an almost cloudless sky lit up the tree-clumps and beaches and frothy, foamy wavelets. Seeing the big canoe still on the beach, they stripped it of paddles.

"If the natives seize the launch we'll have the canoe," said Morey.

Camp was made on a cliff overlooking the beach with a wide strip of open ground between them and the scrub. After a silent meal they took it in turns to watch.

All were sitting over a small fire before daylight, bitterly cold and gloomily speculating on the fate of McColl. Breakfast as soon as it was light, then into the jungle to search again.

They found his tracks; then found McColl.

As they carried him out into the clearing a lubra called from the jungle. Digging a hole with sticks and their hands, they buried him. Mahony stood on watch while Morey and Hall held a simple burial service. With their hands they filled the grave in; stood there silently a while, then with one last look turned towards the beach.

"We must get back to the launch as quickly as possible," said Morey. "If they attack it will be in a bad way."

The launch was there. Dead tired, all sighed their relief. Events that immediately followed this tragedy, too long for inclusion in this already long book, led to the formation of the Missionary Peace Expedition.

35
THE ESCAPE OF NEMARLUK

NEMARLUK'S dread of the white man's gaol soon changed to pleased surprise. He was greeted as a hero by a crowd of fellow prisoners who squatted around him in the sunlit yard all eyes and ears for his proud stories of the killing of the Japanese; of his outwitting the trackers; of his clashes with the police; of the realistically detailed method by which he was going to slice out Bul-bul's kidney-fat on that longed-for day when he should catch him alone. During their light work in the gaol yard he chatted with numerous kindred spirits, men of tribes whom otherwise he would never have met; men whom if he had caught in his country he would have slaughtered as they would have him in their country; men from Arnhem Land east down the coast; men from the Northern Territory inlands – men from the Centre; strange men from the desert lands far away. A fine bunch of dangerous men who enlarged Nemarluk's world beyond belief, much as a country lad's mind would be enlarged by a trip around the world. While each man still held his tribal prejudices he chummed up with Nemarluk and one another as a mob of lions might in a common cage.

Nemarluk listened with quickened interest to Oo-mu-tell, whom white men called Longlegs, happy when he spoke of Point Blaze, for this was in Nemarluk's land. But Longlegs, the thin, sleek Roper River man, whose walk was like a cat's, lived far from Nemarluk's country. Kalomy and Longlegs had recently been caught for the killing of James Nichols, mate of young Renouf killed at Point Blaze. Nichols had been killed, far to the east near Mainerou Station on the fringe of Arnhem Land. Longlegs, whose eyes never wavered in his smiling face, told how he and Kalomy had gone horsehunting with Nichols; how they had thrown a spear from behind; then chased the unarmed white man while the lubras had climbed trees to watch the killing. How they had brought him to earth and knocked him on the head with a fighting-stick; how they had cut his throat with a shovel-bladed spear. And Nemarluk laughed at memory of the running Tanaka and of Minmara felling him with that ironwood stick.

Nemarluk yarned often with Longlegs, telling him about Point Blaze and Treachery Bay and the wonderful hunting-grounds along the Moyle. And Longlegs cemented the friendship, having a dim idea that he might make use of this man later on.

Nemarluk learned more of other tribesmen's ways, much more of the white man's ways, but particularly of the methods of the police and the trackers. This was a favourite topic of conversation among all hands-how to outwit those tireless patrols. Nemarluk's education progressed rapidly. He was to visit as a forced guest Fanny Bay gaol yet once again, and in it was again to be greeted as king by as fine a bunch of native killers as the famous old gaol ever housed. As he gazed up at the big walls that shut out all the earth he grimly thought that if ever he got out all the police the white man had would never bring him back again.

Nemarluk learned to have a bath regularly, even to cut and comb his shaggy locks. He snuggled into a warm bed under shelter such as he had never dreamed of. He lost his hunted look, his leanness vanished under rolls of flesh. In his wildest dreams he had never imagined such a life, such meals, such content, such untroubled sleep. Even his dreams of the happy hunting-grounds of the spirit folk had never risen to the reality of this. Why the white man went to all the trouble of capturing him to treat him like this simply for killing a few brown men, was utterly beyond his comprehension. He had expected death, and would have met it according to his own irrevocable tribal law of "a life for a life!" He could not understand this.

Nearly four happy months went by; then they whispered: "Escape!"

Nemarluk held his breath; he gazed up to the big walls; his eyes widened. He drew a deep breath:

"Freedom!" the one thing he craved. From beyond those walls came to him a breath from the bush, sunlight gleaming on a lagoon, the snout of a crocodile rising between the mangroves, the thud of a wallaby's tail on the sod, the harsh, wild screech of a black cockatoo as it winged past grey cliffs far above.

He turned to those awaiting and his eyes grew cunning as theirs, his glance as furtive towards the unconscious gaoler.

They pointed out to him the gate at the back of the gaol exercise-yard. Every morning this gate was opened and the garbage-tins carried out to the waiting motor truck. One gaoler only supervised this every morning job. How simple it would be for the mob to rush the gaoler – and away! Beyond the gate was only a five-foot fence to leap, then cleared ground for two hundred yards, then the sheltering strip of semi-tropical jungle leading to the harbour edge. Once in the shelter of those trees – once the gaoler was down so that he could not shoot while they raced across the open . . . They only wanted a leader!

Nemarluk was the leader.

A morning came when the gate creaked open. Bird voices streamed in with the sunlight. The crowd of prisoners at their differing jobs edged imperceptibly closer to the gate. The lone gaoler was busy supervising the carrying out of the garbage-tins. Suddenly the weight of a horse struck him and he was bowled over and over, instinctively drawing his revolver as he rolled. From his knees he fired at Nemarluk leaping the fence, then wheeled around with revolver threatening the crowd pouring out of the gate. To his shouts and ominous weapon they stood to a man, rows of glaring eyes, legs bent at the knees tensed for the spring.

But they really had wanted a second leader.

Other gaolers came running. Sullenly they were forced back into the yard.

Nemarluk got clear away. Once among that subtropical growth his quickened feet made no sound; above all left no tracks on the carpet of leaves. And near him was his old friend the water!

Strenuous efforts were made to recapture Nemarluk. Two of his favourite lubras were in the Kahlin Aboriginal Compound and it was thought he would venture to entice them away at night. But Nemarluk had learned many things, and this was a trap he foresaw.

Yet he did not make straight for the Wilds. He walked bush right around Darwin harbour, eighty miles, and came out opposite the town at an aboriginal camp near Talc Head. From here, natives often canoe across the six miles of water to the town.

Nemarluk gazed across day by day. He took spears and wommera as by right, and the familiar touch of the weapons made him feel again a man.

But he overestimated the fear of his name among these civilized aborigines. He knew there could be no loyalty; these people were foreign to him. Yet he did not realize that here he was not Nemarluk, King of the Wilds, but a foreign tribesman, a very dangerous one, a man with a great spear-throwing reputation and thus not to be tampered with, a man to be put away by less dangerous means immediately the opportunity occurred. From the cliffs at Talc Head they could see the white roofs of police headquarters among the palms on Darwin's headlands, and yet it was a full fortnight before the Black Service whispered word through.

Superintendent Stretton acted promptly. That night Constable Don and Trackers Smiler and Gilby sailed quietly across the harbour. Smiler is among the best and gamest of trackers in a highly efficient force. San Fezo is his correct name; his father a Sinhalese, his mother an aboriginal woman: A tall man but slimmer than Nemarluk , inclined to be taciturn, dogged. A quiet man, his Sinhalese blood blending thought with the bushcraft from his mother's side.

They landed on a tiny beach near the ghostly whiteness of Talc Head.

The shore is lined with vine entangled scrub upon the shelly beaches. Silently a tribesman pointed them out the black patch among the bamboos where Nemarluk was lying, then the Black Service vanished. They crawled into the darkness, but at the sight of glowing coals waited for the first grey of dawn. They rushed the fire, but Nemarluk was not there. He had reverted to his old bush caution of shamming sleep where all could see him, then, when all were asleep, crawling away elsewhere.

Don whispered the trackers to hurry away and search. "Quick! Before sunrise." Ready for action he stooped into the lightening shadows amongst the bamboo thickets.

Smiler searched quickly and silently amongst all likely hiding-places where instinct told him a hunted man might lie. Day was breaking when he came to a steep, scrub-lined embankment, almost a cliff.

He gazed up at the dark trees above. Up there, a man might sleep safely. He commenced to climb. As he reached the top, Nemarluk stood erect twenty feet before him, spears in his hand. Each man advanced straight at the other. "Stand! Stand!" called Smiler with pointed revolver. Nemarluk threw as Smiler fired, holding the revolver as a sword to parry the spear. It ripped his singlet on the left side. He fired again as Nemarluk threw and parried again the spear which ripped his singlet on the right side. They closed with heavy impact and struggled back, the brute strength of Nemarluk pushing the lighter man back and yet back. Smiler raised the revolver and brought the butt down on Nemarluk's head. At the splitting shock Nemarluk heaved forward and both men toppled over, crashing down through the bushes, thudding through the grass tufts.

Nemarluk was up in an instant and ran, ran for his own country far away.

By this time the distant Daly River police had received word of his escape. Thinking he would immediately make back to his own country, they made an instant raid on the Daly River camp through which he would possibly pass.

Nemarluk arrived the very night of the raid, dead beat, hungry, savage. But he was a bundle of suspicion, keyed to action, every sense alert. He escaped, with seconds to spare, and sped through the night towards Treachery Bay.

36
BUL-BUL MISTRUSTS CHUGULLA

Now Tiger the cunning had his friends and his own espionage system, and understood perfectly that at present he was not held in durance vile. In the aboriginal way he sent a message through bush to his Fitzmaurice horde. King Chugulla received the message and saw that it spread to the white man's outpost at Daly River. So when Langdon came riding back from Darwin, via the Daly, six weeks later he heard that Stephens and Cook had been seen down on the coast. No one knew where exactly, but there was definite news that they had reappeared.

Natives who had recently come in from the bush had seen and talked with them.

When Tiger knew his message had got through, he quietly slipped down-river to Bradshaw Station. Later, on being signalled that Langdon was almost back at Timber Creek, he disappeared towards the Fitzmaurice.

Now Chugulla used to make a much rarer and much more fleeting trip to Bradshaw's run. He came as the wild man comes, like a shadow in the night. Leaving his lubras planted in the bush he would sneak into the station natives' camp, demand his lien of tobacco, then vanish back to the Wilds. But the web of fate embraces all, and her tiniest strand is exceedingly strong.

When Fitzer and Langdon debated the possibilities at Timber Creek they felt sceptical of the rumour concerning the safety of Stephens and Cook, for Bul-bul had been whispered it was Chugulla who spread the story of their reappearance. And Chugulla is king of Tiger's tribe! said the big tracker with a laugh.

"We must investigate," decided Fitzer. "If it is a quick patrol I can travel with you throughout. If not, you must carry on alone."

Harold Cook, manager of Bradshaw's, came purring up the Victoria in a launch. A chance visit, but what an opportunity! Langdon took his trackers aboard at night, then sped down-stream to raid Bradshaw's before daylight. No chance of news travelling ahead through the night. With luck, they might catch some Fitzmaurice natives there fresh in from the bush. Meanwhile Fitzer would pack up six weeks' provisions, cross the river, and bring the horses overland to Bradshaw's run.

Disaster almost came that night for the launch party. Two crocodiles, shoulder to shoulder, came slithering down the bank and just grazed the swerving launch as they plunged into the water. Their combined weight would have sunk it.

The raid proved an unexpected success for Chugulla was caught in its toils. Stricken with dismay the big warrior trembled like any trapped animal. Through an interpreter he was immediately asked;

"Why did you tell the Daly River people that the two white men were safe?"

"Tiger make me talk that way."

"Ah! then you helped in the killing!"

"No, no." Then in his fright he admitted the names of those implicated while denying action himself.

"You will guide us to the place!" ordered Langdon.

The big aboriginal stared silently with one glance at Uninya his captive tribesman beside him.

Langdon was delighted. At one stroke he had confirmed the killing and, moreover, learned the names of the killers. The job remained to catch them. At daylight he found five others added to the ration strength of the patrol: Chugulla's five wives, defiant lubras of varying ages carrying their master's weapons, determined on following his fortunes.

When Fitzer arrived, the patrol started east towards the Moyle country where now was the season of the big corroborees. There might be trouble under such circumstances of tribal excitement and large gatherings. But there could hardly be a surprise, for Charlie and Bogey were with the patrol, a very wide-awake and scared pair of trackers, not to mention Beris, the big Alsatian dog.

For a week they wound in and out among ranges; then camped by the three billabongs on the rich flat that forms Meewaa swamp, in season alive with waterfowl, turtle, and fish.

While; the pack-animals enjoyed these green pastures the patrol packed enough food to operate on foot for a week, Chugulla declaring that Und camp was near. Und, during the season of goose eggs, was a large meeting-camp, and Chugulla stated there was "mobs" of water around it. It was believed to be a haunt of the Fitzmaurice men. That October was exceptionally hot. The patrol became thirsty after fifteen miles' walking, and disgusted when they came to a native soak and found the stagnant water putrid from dead snakes.

"Where that blackfellow camp?" demanded Fitzer of the interpreter.

"No more long way. Close up now," was Chugulla's interpreted reply as he stared into the grim, accusing face of Bul-bul.

They pushed on into the ranges. And step by step as Chugulla lifted his feet, the big feet of Bulbul were planted upon the imprint, his legs ready for the pounce, his long arms for the grasp. Doggedly Chugulla pushed on, choosing the roughest country. Presently Tracker Tommy turned sulky:

"That feller Chugulla he no good," he growled. "He tell um lie all a time. He savvy who bin kill that white feller man all right. He savvy where he bin sit down. He want plant him murderer; he no more show us where him bin sit down!"

After sundown, all hands pressed closer together, fearing spears from the night. Their skin-barked legs seemed to be finding every log in the bush. At one in the morning Fitzer called a halt.

"The swine is leading us a dance!"

"Yes," replied Langdon, "the stumbling foxtrot!"

"The only way to make him take us to water is to load him up with swags."

The trackers did so, thankfully.

"Now," said Fitzer to the interpreter, "tell him that the sooner he shows us water the sooner he will drink!"

But Chugulla did not show them water. Like Atlas under the load of the world he pushed on through scrub and forest, among rocky spurs and down into the pitch dark of gullies. When the steel grey of coming dawn brought tree shapes into life the party was still doggedly following him, when the dawn shadows spread upon the grass and birds began to twitter they followed still. They pushed on into the new day that with its heat brought renewed thirst. Chugulla turned at last, gazing around bewildered. He mumbled that he was lost.

A low, sarcastic growl welled from Bul-bul's throat. Menacingly he raised his arm and pointed straight ahead. The two big aboriginals stared into one another's eyes. A grim, determined scowl creased Chugulla's face. He turned and strode on, making for a tangle of broken country. And step by step the feet of Bul-bul were planted in his tracks.

37
THE ARREST OF TIGER

THEY struggled on until all but Langdon and Bulbul were beaten by thirst and exhaustion. Langdon, carrying a revolver only, started back to the camp, travelling in the cool of night which also was protection against the tribesmen they knew were dogging their tracks. He succeeded and returned with horses and water. They rode back to Meewaa swamp on an altogether different route to the way Chugulla had brought them.

After recovery, Langdon decided that the swamp water did not look healthy so he put Chugulla and Uninya on a light chain and, in charge of Tracker Tommy, ordered them away to seek clearer water. Tommy was in a sulky mood. As they walked into the bush Langdon shouted to him to follow farther behind lest the prisoners leap around and attack him. Bul-bul stood gazing after the men, then picked up a spear and leisurely followed on their tracks. Fortunately, it was a crocodile-spear, headed with a round iron spike, no barbs. The prisoners had gone some distance when they suddenly wheeled around and, throwing Tommy to the ground, snatched the rifle. In vain Chugulla tried to work the bolt while Tommy clawed at the rifle and bit the throttling hand of Uninya. Chugulla snatched up a rock but leapt with a yell, then Uninya screamed and plunged at the second stab of Bul-bul's spear.

Langdon syringed out the wounds with Condy's.

Here was a nice mess! But in a few days Chugulla was able to limp; Uninya's case looked hopeless. The patrol had to keep moving. Langdon left Tracker Lightning behind with stores to tend the wounded man; Lightning did not like the duty, but Langdon left him armed, promising to return in a few days. Then, on foot again, they set out. This time Chugulla guided them to Und camp. They snaked their way out of the hills at night, hearing a wild corroboree song, the rhythmic beating of *kylies*, the drumming of the lubras, the rise and fall of the wild women's song.

Across a creek-bank fires leapt up throwing into relief shadow forms painted vividly in white ochre like demons dancing around the flames. The patrol waited until the small hours, then the fires died down and the dancers quietened in sleep. Langdon and Bul-bul scouted around the camp, seeking the "getaways."

The tribe were sleeping in the form of a large outer circle and a smaller inner one. In the outer circle were huddled the dark shapes of family groups with their dogs cuddled among them, in the inner the motionless shadows of single men.

Noiselessly each man snaked his way around the camp to a vantage point. Orders were for all hands to creep close in just before brightening dawn, then at the first scuffle all were to rush while Chugulla must shout: "Sit still, police. No man will be hurt, but if any men run the police will shoot!"

The tribe slept the deep sleep of corroboree exhaustion, not even the whimper of a piccanin, whinge of a dog. Steely shadows presently made plainer the huddled figures, the tree-trunks. All hands crept forward, tense for the rush. Then, right in front of Langdon appeared an apparition, another rose from the depths behind it. Langdon stared at the hunchback, the hunchback gaped, his weird jaw drooping. "Drop that spear!" hissed Langdon. But the dwarf raised the weapon, his brave little arm shaking with terror. Behind him glared a witch risen from the fires below. The poor lubra had been burned out of all shape. A scuffle sounded and instantly Langdon leapt past the dwarf into the camp. Wild shouts then screams, Chugulla's reassuring bellow above the howling of dogs, wails of piccanins, the trackers' shouts of "Stand! We hurt no one!" in different tribal dialects.

Hardly a man escaped, they stood there shaking, the lubras crouched there glaring up with the piccaninnies arms about their necks. They lined the men up, the trackers scanned them quickly. There was not a wanted man there.

"It's all in the game," shrugged Fitzer. "We'd better get breakfast." To the interpreter he said: "Tell Chugulla to tell them everything is all right, we don't want any of them. But tell them not to leave the camp for a while, we want to ask them questions." He handed out a little tobacco and what food they could spare.

Then at breakfast the Black Service proved the raid was not in vain; they brought along Tiger's lubra. An uneasy frown creased Chugulla's face. That lubra came with vindictive eyes gleaming from a shock of tangled hair; her teeth chattered, she wanted to tell so much so quickly. She was Tiger's wife; she *hated* Tiger; he beat her! She showed her scarred body, her broken arm, the deep weals across her skull beneath the clotted hair. Far worse than that, Tiger had cast her off; made her an outcast woman; she was no man's wife now! She could talk pidgin-English, the only lubra of all these women that could. Tiger had often taken her into Bradshaw Station and made her work, and taken all she earned and thrashed her and made her go back and earn more. Finally he had taken a younger lubra and cast her off altogether.

Tiger had planned to murder the two white men; he helped to spear them. Tiger and Wadawarry had been in this very camp only two days before but had cleared out because Chugulla by message-stick had warned them; a tribesman had crept to him in the night while the patrol slept. Tiger was going straight to Daly River now, to the peanut settlement. He thought the "white pleece" would not think of him there. She gave names of the killers; place where it happened; all details. She gave the same names as Ununyah had sung at the corroboree, as Chugulla had given. But she accused Chugulla also. And the eyes of the big roan widened still more.

"So that's that!" said Fitzer. "It gives a man an appetite for breakfast."

Langdon was curious about the dwarf who had startled him. It appears that the little man had planned an early morning fishing-trip, hoping to return loaded before breakfast and receive the acclamations of the warriors. His faithful companion, the burnt old lubra, was to have gone with him and helped him. She had awakened him; he took his fish-spear and stood up to stare straight at Langdon.

They sent two trackers back to Meewaa swamp for the horses, meanwhile attempting to keep the tribe together. Sent the lubras out fishing, and collecting vegetable foods. All the lubras had beautifully woven loop nets made of black grass that looked like plaited hair. In this country are big yams and native onions in plenty; bird life was prolific up and down the creek and on the plain to either side. Being out of beef the whites ate flying foxes; this kept the tribesmen competitively busy for tobacco with their throwing-sticks. Flying-fox flesh tastes like chicken, but there is very little of it. Langdon got busy with the gun among the geese and ducks; this also held the tribesmen's attention.

The police motive was to delay any warning that might be sent to Tiger. This tribe, however, appeared to take very little interest in the fate of Tiger. But all hands, warriors, women and piccaninnies took an awed interest in the trackers, a frightened interest in the whites. Above all, they idolized that huge dog Beris. From a respectful distance they stood, all eyes and deep grunts of intense admiration. To which adoration Beris took only a bored interest.

"They don't appear to be connected in any way with Chugulla's or Nemarluk's crowd," said Fitzer. "Some quite independent tribe or sub-tribe."

"So much the better," answered Langdon, "if we meet them again they'll be friendly and won't be above putting the other crowd away if they happen to be in the vicinity."

Their flour became ropey and they had to boundary-ride the dampers, toasting the crust, an operation in which the piccaninnies took an interest.

It took the two absent trackers several days to find a way around the hills for the horses. They reported that Lightning and the wounded man Uninya had vanished. The patrol packed up and struck straight for the Daly, a week later coming out unnoticed within four miles of Pang Quee's peanut farm. That night the didgereedoos were hoarsely blowing, eighty natives were gathered for corroboree. In the heat of it the dance was raided, Bul-bul throwing himself upon Tiger who, clad in his pelt and painted to resemble a skeleton, glared a fiendish surprise. Wadawarry was caught too; his powerful, thickset body crouched hesitating to spring, his frowning face glaring surprise and anger. When the wild confusion had subsided a blanket was found wrapped around Tiger's hunting possessions, a tent-fly around Wadawarry's.

"Where you get that blanket?" demanded the police.

"I bin get him longa Fitzmaurice where I bin see canoe where two white men bin come up!"

"Where you get that fly?" was demanded of Wadawarry.

"Alligator bin gib it harp!"

"Where Alligator been get him?"

"From two feller dead men longa Fitzmaurice."

"What Alligator been do longa that other half?"

"He been burn him longa fire."

"You been killem that man!"

"No more! All about Walung mob bin kill him!" And with rolling eyes Wadawarry protested his innocence.

"Can you show us where those blackfellows are who killed the white men?"

"Yes, me show. That feller Ununyah he been kill him too."

"That's the chap who told the crowd at the Legune corroboree," said Langdon. "He told young Sandy too."

Fitzer nodded.

"We'll soon have the whole lot with a little more luck," he said. "I'll ride down-river to the police station; get more stores; then we'll ride straight out again. By Jove, how these three fellows glare at one another! If they were facing each other in the bush now, they'd just about tear one another to pieces. Each must believe one of the others has put him away."

"I would not like to be Tiger's wife," said Langdon grimly, "if ever he gets out of this."

But Litchie smiled with laughter in her eyes; she suddenly seemed to have grown younger. She was not much to look at, although she displayed six toes on each foot. Her father, so the others proudly said, had six fingers on each hand and six toes on each foot! She was very glad the white police had caught Wadawarry. He was her husband, but then he used to beat her. Cheerfully she joined the patrol. Wadingie joined too, also cheerfully. She also was a wife of Wadawarry. She was young and strong but she too was glad the white police had caught the wife-beater.

Fitzer returned in a hurry.

"Here are the stores. But you will have to carry on alone. That horse-stealing gang have organized a big raid and I'll have the ride of my life. They've got away with one of the biggest mobs in the Territory. There is Nemarluk news for you too; he has broken out of gaol and native rumour has it that he is making back towards the Moyle to join in the corroborees at the Big Ring Corroboree Camp. He will figure as the leading star you may be sure. You may run up against him so keep a sharp look out. If I can round up my gang quickly I'll bring provisions for your outfit to Meewaa swamp. Good luck."

Langdon secured the loan of two boys from old Pang Ouee. One, Barney, was invaluable; a lively, wicked old reprobate who knew every native language between the Daly and the Victoria.

Langdon's patrol set out for the Moyle country; there were no white men, except those in their graves between Pang Quee's and the Victoria. Langdon felt a bit of a thrill, he was setting out on a dangerous patrol alone. A young Australian this officer; not tall, but well built, keen eyed, intelligent, and with plenty of grit. He held court, and questioned Tiger again. Tiger answered resentfully, sullenly, then fiercely.

Point after point was put to him implicating him deeper and deeper. He soon became convinced that his friends had betrayed him. And he grew savage. He was handcuffed to Barney the interpreter who was taking a keen interest. Langdon sat under a tree before them, watching the eyes of Tiger growing bloodshot and beginning to roll.

"You killed him all right!" said Langdon confidently and he had intended to say nothing further.

"No!"

"Yes. That one Ununyah been tell me!"

Tiger quivered with rage. "That Ununyah-liar!" he shouted. "He been killem himself!"

"All right!" replied Langdon. "I bring him Ununyah talk front longa you."

Tiger sprang straight at Langdon who rolled backward hunching his leg in the flying mare and Tiger shot straight over him, dragging Barney in a grunting heap. Clawing Barney in his fury, Tiger shouted:

"Chalmer kill him too!"

38
THE LONE PATROL

LANGDON had hardly left the Daly River when the Fitzmaurice men, out in the Wilds, knew of the arrest of Tiger and Wadawarry; knew that Fitzer was returning in a hurry for Timber Creek; knew also that, alone, Langdon was coming after them; knew that Tiger had very nearly told! And around the council fires they voiced harsh resentment with a defiance of the police.

Langdon travelled rapidly towards the Moyle, seeking the corroboree grounds now being heavily stamped at this period of the year. Now was the season when the sub-tribes and tribes crowded together on the common ancestral grounds and put the youths through the dread initiation ceremonies; settled new and old scores by tribal fighting; and indulged in the big ceremonial corroborees.

In quick succession Langdon raided six camps without success but in his first rush on the Moyle secured Chalmer, all done up in war-paint and feathers. The startled aboriginal did not understand one word of English, and to Barney's questions denied implication in the murder. When asked of others implicated he shook his head in a smiling silence. Six-feet-three of brawn and muscle, broadly built and wild as a March hare, he stood staring in bewildered indecision as the cuffs were slipped on his wrists. That such flimsy things could hold his powerful arms he could not believe.

Langdon travelled swiftly down the Moyle then across country again towards Meewaa swamp, seeking Alligator, Walung, Chin-amon, and Maru.

No big gathering of the tribes was there, however, though numerous hunting-smokes revealed their vicinity. The smokes rose in country in which the natives could laugh at horsemen. Langdon left several trackers in charge of the horses and struck out on foot. Crossing a sandy ravine they picked up the first tracks and Tiger grunted vengefully, "Walung! Chin-amon! Maru!" Over hills, along valleys, even down the long rocky slopes of spurs they followed those tracks for thirty miles. Slow work.

Then the tracks came out on to more open country, and Langdon immediately sent back for the horses to be brought around the hills. Again they followed the tracks, faster now even though walking and leading the horses where riding was impossible. They rode out on to dried ground covered with decayed rushes that not long since had been a marsh.

Patches were dug up, showing where several days previously the wanted men had dug mussels from the now hard baked ground. Farther on, by a screw-palm billabong they had been eating lilyroots, and had roasted tortoise and water rats. They paused then, the trackers gesticulating at a queer looking track three days old, a track that was all "heels," the track of a man with no toes. Tiger snarled at that track. "When we come longa fresh track," he growled, "we leavem horses and walk, quick feller!"

For Tiger was on the scent, positive that his friends had betrayed him. With head bent towards the ground he followed those tracks hour after hour, hour after patient hour.

Next day they saw a freshly scarred tree where rude tomahawks had chopped out a sugar-bag. Tiger glared around; they all looked around seeking a hiding-place for their horses lest the animals be seen from the hills. As they looked a lone watcher rose upon a small hill isolated from the rest. They were galloping before he had time to disappear. He was too late, they were around the hill before he could gain shelter of the frowning crests farther back. He was skinny old Alligator, quaking "Nemarluk! Nemarluk!" as they galloped up.

Swiftly Langdon took advantage of the misunderstanding; if Alligator imagined they were after Nemarluk the capture of the Fitzmaurice men would be easier. Nemarluk then, the big prize, must be very close. Alligator swore earnestly that he was; he agreed to guide them to Nemarluk's camp. Barney warned Tiger not to "sign-talk" Alligator of the misunderstanding lest the men who had betrayed him get away.

Langdon raided the camp at sunset, afraid to delay lest the tribesmen become suspicious of Alligator's absence. But keen nostrils had smelt their sweating horses. They rushed an abandoned camp spread ready for the feast. Silence waited among those smouldering fires; nicely done fish lay there freshly taken from the cooking-stones; goose eggs showed in plenty with the hot ashes partly scraped off them; roasted berries smelt appetisingly. But the only life was in mongrel dogs snarling from the thickets.

After a while, Langdon withdrew his men, but in the night silence doubled back, hiding in the camp.

Hours later, there came a low, wailing cry.

Langdon tried to force the prowling dogs to return to their masters' call, but the dogs were too cunning. While they did not return the tribesmen would know there was danger in the camp. It was Tiger who eventually forced Alligator to call out that the "pleece" had gone. Cautiously, four shadows came creeping into camp. The hidden patrol rose at their feet.

One was Alligator's girl wife Toycan, very startled. A perfectly made little lubra, thin lips, almost pointed nose. Straight as a reed, swift as a hare was Toycan. And with her was Pat, Alligator's little son.

No others came. When Toycan did not return they knew!

Next morning, the patrol looked around the camp for the tale the tracks would tell. There were many tracks, split in every direction, the tracks of the Fitzmaurice men. Tiger pointed to Walung's big track, to Chin-amon's, and Maru's, "Now, how to catch these three-already intensely alert?" pondered Langdon. Among these tracks was prominent that of Nemarluk, hurrying away from all the rest, and a lubra's track following.

Langdon set out hot-foot on Nemarluk's tracks, knowing that hidden eyes were watching his every move. He followed those tracks until sunset then lit his campfire. With much chatter his prisoners and their women lit theirs. After the evening meal when the fires glowed low they all huddled down to sleep.

Long after the mopokes croaked Langdon woke his people and started back through the night straight for the camp he had raided the night before. At dawn his trackers fell on Chin-amon, Walung, and Maru, They were asleep and tired, for they had followed Langdon until late afternoon, then satisfied he was really after Nemarluk doubled back to their camp.

Walung's three wives were with him. Old Jardar, an abrupt old lubra holding tight to a squealing baby girl; and Quean – she who had rushed in first at the killing and seized the calico.

Langdon felt the thrill of a hard job well done.

He had every man who had buried a spear either in Cook or Stephens. He looked at his wild crowd of prisoners with a benign eye. They looked back; several with a frown, others with a half smile. Still daubed with the grease and ochres and feathers of tribal war, the chase and corroboree, they smelt rather strongly. But Langdon did not mind. He ran his eye over the lubras. A wild-looking crowd, they returned his glance with definitely more defiance than the men; old Jardar, clinging to her skinny legged daughter, seemed inclined to poke out her tongue. Langdon's job now was to get absolute proof of the killing. After which, he had to get prisoners and witnesses straight through the bush for hundreds of miles back to civilization. Several of his horses were now weak from privation. They had been two months on a fast job over a trackless country of swamp and range and bush. Uneasily he glanced at the hot, bright sky; the early storms of the wet season were due. If he was caught there with the rivers and creeks in flood, with every billabong a lake, with every plain a bog, his would be a forlorn case indeed. Meanwhile, he was right out of food. He started for Meewaa swamp where two trackers were still guarding the food-supply.

At Meewaa swamp he accused Chin-amon of complicity.

"You been killem two feller white man!"

"No more me!" answered Chin-amon in alarm. "Tiger he kill 'em; chop 'em up longa axe. I show you."

Langdon's heart leapt. Here was coming proof of the murder, swift and sure. But *en route* to the axe Langdon nearly lost the prisoners. With rolling thunder and vivid lightning came the first storm. The lubras hurriedly cut bark and that night under rude shelters the prisoners were lying, water running on the ground around them. Langdon dared not sleep. He peered through the tent-fly and in the lightning flashes could see the gleaming bodies of the aboriginals. He strained his ears; faintly above the swish of the rain he thought he heard a "tap, tap," just now and again. He watched Beris. When the wet bristles rose and he growled Langdon dashed out into the rain and flashed a torch on the prisoners. They lay huddled under their bark shelters, sound asleep. Especially was old Alligator asleep, all curled up with his wrists between his legs. Langdon dragged out those wrists and carefully examined each link of the handcuffs. Ah! A link almost chopped in halves. Just a "tap! tap! tap!" of a stone on a link while thunder and rain drowned all sound.

Each night after this, Langdon ordered the trackers light a big fire behind the prisoners. Thus, by leaning now and again on his elbow he could watch them in its glow. And he kept that glow glowing.

It was a long ride, but Chin-amon took them to the axe, buried under a candlemint-tree. The handle was nearly eaten away by white ants. This was the axe, so Chin-amon explained, with which Tiger had chopped up the bodies of the two white men before throwing the pieces into the canoe.

Langdon found something else – Uninya. He stared unbelievingly when Bul-bul, with a grin that stretched from ear to ear, came and told that he had found the tracks of the wounded man left behind at Meewaa swamp. Bul-bul showed him the track and rather boastfully pointed out that Uninya walked now with a limp. To prove it Langdon followed up the tracks and surprised Uninya digging out a water-rat. He told how tracker Lightning had got frightened at being left alone and bolted.

Lightning has not been seen since.

When almost out of food Langdon forced his patrol far west almost to the Victoria River, to Kurri Jungle. There Fitzer met him with fresh supplies – in a hurry. He had to return immediately to Timber Creek, and worse still he wanted all the trackers.

"This gang have planned their latest coup perfectly," he explained. "Covered up all their tracks, apparently thought out every detail beforehand. I've spotted every man in the gang though; the difficulty is to find their hide-out. I want every decent tracker I can lay hands on."

He left Langdon with Barney the interpreter, and Tiger as tracker, who could not be bettered while in his present vengeful mood. But he might turn at any moment. He eased Langdon's mind considerably however by saying:

"We kill him alright, I no more lie now, I show you that place where we been kill him that feller white man."

Langdon started his patrol off immediately towards the Fitzmaurice River, choosing his camp each night to guard against surprise. On the very first evening he listened to his prisoners chanting corroboree songs. Old Alligator leading each high pitched chant, the squatting women shrilly accompanying with the clicking of wommeras. Langdon listened grimly while waiting for the howl of a dingo or screech of a night hawk – watching the dog above all.

When Beris rose growling and crouched out into the night, Langdon leapt up and abruptly stopped the singing. He harshly forbade it on any other night.

They were singing to their tribesmen who were creeping around the camp. As the dog rushed out these would-be rescuers leapt from the grass and vanished.

Tiger took them straight to Mutdjack Hill. He showed them the mosquito-pegs still standing and two rusty kerosene-tins; pointed to a pair of old khaki trousers hanging in a paper-bark tree. "Trousers belonga long feller man."

"Where canoe he bin tie up?"

"More further."

He guided the patrol along Nemara Creek to more mosquito-pegs, and pointed out the ashes of a fire. In front of them all he described the details of the killing. Langdon had his eight main prisoners secured in fours, a light chain around the neck of each of the four men. He ordered them to sit down on the creek-bank. Then asked the witnesses to point out where each witness and each killer stood at the killing. They did so, showing where the canoe was tied up, where the white men sat when they were killed, where the prisoners sat and how the white men were killed. While this was going on a low toned mutual recrimination broke out among the prisoners. Tiger's eyes flashed as he learned he was a betrayer as much as anyone else.

A swift plan was as swiftly carried into execution.

At a sudden "patter patter" Langdon wheeled around to see his prisoners racing down to the mangroves. With a yell Barney ran after one lot, Langdon raced after the other. As the leading four plunged into the mangroves one man ran past the wrong side of a tree. In a second they were down, the chain nearly choking them, a mass of struggling arms and legs and entangled heads. Langdon's four with marvellous precision were leaping in and out among the mangrove trees. Langdon whipped out his revolver and shouted:

"Stop, I fire!"

They sped on and he fired, Chugulla pitching headlong. They had him up in an instant, but Langdon fired again and Chalmer fell pulling the others down on top of him. Howls from the watching lubras registered the accuracy of the shooting. As Langdon ran up, to his relieved surprise all four prisoners clambered to their feet, facing him.

"What for you fall down," he panted. "No more shot!"

"By cri!" laughed Tiger, "bullet been go close up longa earhole! I savvy policeman! he can't shoot me! he only want stop me!"

The four were breathing heavily, their eyes protruding from their sockets as they came stealthily forward.

"What for you run away?" demanded Langdon. "That feller Alligator been make us run away!" insinuated Tiger craftily. Langdon stepped back, a wary tingle rising to the roots of his hair. He stared into Tiger's eyes while stepping back as the four; men came on. As Tiger sprang he leapt back, snatched up a stick and brought it heavily down on Tiger's skull. Tiger collapsed to his knees, glaring up with his fingers working like claws. But the other three crouched there, handicapped by the chain, their teeth in a snarl, just not quite game enough to spring. Langdon could hear the thumping of his heart.

"I shoot next time, I shoot to kill!" he almost whispered.

With the story complete, with every prisoner, with every witness, Langdon started on the return journey to Timber Creek, abandoning two of his worn-out horses. He still had to fight, he had to guard his prisoners and witnesses and yet beat the wet season. He beat it to Timber Creek, then hurried on the last stage to the Katherine, with rain already falling and forcing a detour. That last stage by way of Coonbook Station, Victoria River Downs, Delamere, Willeroo, Katherine took a month-a thousand miles in eleven weeks. In wet clothes, eating sodden food, blankets and saddlecloths fly-blown, snatching sleep in the rain, swimming flooded river, ploughing through bogs. He got his prisoners to the Katherine and they nearly died of fright at sight of their first train.

Imagine what those prehistoric witnesses thought of their first picture-show in Darwin when the proud Barney escorted them there!

Mangul and Lin, at Daly River Police Station. Inset is Nemarluk, fresh from a shave and haircut.

39
THE FLIGHT OF NEMARLUK

WHEN Nemarluk escaped from the Daly River patrol he fled with maddened haste in headlong flight that stopped only when exhaustion brought him to his knees. By then, he was a hundred miles from the Daly. With sleep he recovered, realizing a raging hunger.

He pressed on towards the smoke of a grass-fire, a spear fitted to his wommera, his wrist shivering with the urge to throw, his eyes glaring. He smelt a wallaby in bushes two hundred yards ahead. He crouched into position where the advancing flames must drive the animal toward him, and when it came his spear shot out and the animal bounded with a gasping cough and thrashed the ground with its body a pivot to the rattling haft of the spear. He seized it and ran out past the edge of the fire trailing blazing bark behind him. He threw the wallaby on the flames, singed it and tore it to pieces, then walking along ate as a famished animal eats. He carried a firestick and set the grass alight, grinning as he wolfed and walked. Now the tracks of Nemarluk were lost.

Behind him was fire burning out his tracks; a cloud of kites wheeled in the smoke above, seizing the blinded flying things. Ahead he chose the country covered with long dry grass, grass that turned into flames minutes after his tracks were pressed upon it.

The original fire had been lit by a hunting party a day's walk away. Nemarluk signalled his coming; they answered. He met them and rested while the men watched and hunted. Several days later Nemarluk left camp, but left no tracks, for in line behind him walked five lubras and each woman's tracks went down upon Nemarluk's and blotted them out. The others of the band hunted their way back towards Ande-mall-ee camp there to expect a police patrol and put it on a false scent; also to send false news away to the white man's police outpost on the Daly.

Constable Fitzer worked with his head, in swift patrols designed eventually to drive Nemarluk into the arms of Bul-bul. The thoughts of the big aboriginal would be on the police patrol; his activities would be concentrated on eluding and misleading it, on receiving news of its movements. He would not think of Bul-bul operating against him independently of the patrol. Fitzer planned to keep the fugitive constantly on the move until sooner or later he would run into some one of Bul-bul's traps.

Nemarluk made well-planned movement his main safeguard,

travelling fast when he did travel and over country difficult for horses to follow; dodging any scattered band of whose trustworthiness he was not certain; never staying long with hunting-party, horde, or tribe. When he did camp with others he always slept beyond the radius where a cordon could be drawn around the camp, and he always slept beside a steep ravine, or watercourse, or jungle patch, or tumbled mass of boulders, where he could instantly disappear. For long, he avoided his favourite haunts and laughed harshly whenever smoke-signal warned him that some such locality was being "smelled" out. He prowled among the thickets and mangrove shrouded arms of the sea fringing the lowlying coast, ready to speed inland and zigzag across the country between the Daly and the Victoria. When he heard of a patrol riding towards the Moyle he doubled behind it, leaving the wild lands for the station country along the Victoria.

That station country is not settled as the southern lands are. Stations in the farthest north are generally thousands of square miles in extent, and, probably, there will not be more than two white stockmen and a white cook, working on a station of thousands of square miles. Exceptional stations support from six to ten whites. But the general rule is two white men, a white or Chinese cook, and a crowd of native stockmen. So that Nemarluk was not running into organized civilization when he approached the borders of settled country.

One brilliant morning he climbed the cliff range and stood surveying the outspread world falling away below. There gleamed the Victoria, a silver ribbon emerging from precipitous ranges in the west, to wind and twist and turn for twenty miles then merge into the ranges towards the south-east. Away across river the Whirlwind Plains were dotted with toy cattle, the cattle of Auvergne Station. Directly below, near that sombre winding snake that was the timber lining the Shaw River a little doll's house shone under the sun – Bradshaw homestead. Plains and flat topped hills and crumbled clefts and shadowed lines of cliffs filled Nemarluk with a feeling of great distances under a mighty sky. His chest swelled as he gazed out over this fair land, not really his land, for his own country was away towards the coast. But he lorded this land, every man in it was afraid of him, all except a few cursed white men. Then Nemarluk stiffened and stared. Far below, coming out of a clump of timber were horses and mules, small as a line of moving dogs.

A patrol! He vanished.

He had thought he was so cunning, doubling back here to the very country the patrol had started from. He did not realize that now it was a battle of wits, with the bush the playground, Fitzer, Nemarluk, and Bul-bul, the players. He thought they must have picked up the tracks of his women who, through carelessness, had left a track of his exposed. With a threatening snarl over his shoulder he started off parallel with the wild lands. He travelled swiftly and far and kept to rocky country, the women hurrying behind. Presently they began to get footsore. Always the women's, the piccaninnies', and the dogs' feet crack up first. As those whimperers behind began to hang back he sent them away one by one; they could seek the soft ground and rejoin the horde wherever they could find it.

Women and dogs when footsore leave tracks on rocky ground. They cringe from the heat of the rocks; from the sharpness of crack and flake and jagged pebble, their torn feet naturally seek any earth between, and there they leave a track. Very glad the women were to toil down from the ranges. Glad too because food is scarce among cliff and pinnacle. Gladly they and the dogs limped to the lowlands with its soft earth to walk upon, its cool billabongs and swamps, its plentiful plant-food.

At their own gossiping pace they could travel, very different from the speed of a powerful, hunted man.

Nemarluk sat upon a crag and watched the last one go. She was like a crippled black wallaroo as she groped her way down among the boulders. She would join her waiting mates somewhere in the lowlands, worn out, thin and starved. They would be feasting on water-rats beside some quiet lagoon. Well, they had been of use, and he could get others when he needed them.

His fierce eyes stared at an eagle far up in the blue.

He knew every action of that bird; could put his mind in its mind. He was an eagle too, a beast of prey far above all other beasts of prey. In all the world there were only two enemies he feared – the witch-doctor and the police patrol.

He snarled, his eyes sweeping far out over the lowlands with their hills and plains, grasslands and timber, silvered splashes of lagoon and waterways. His body all muscle and sinew, thinning rapidly, would thin faster now that he did not have those five women to feed him, to keep the body of Nemarluk in fighting strength. Ah, well, they were starved while he was still in the acme of physical fitness. He kept to the rocks a few days longer, until his feet warned him.

Those feet of Nemarluk's must *never* crack up.

He took to the lowlands.

From the range wall a broken stretch of spinifex country led to the plains. Spinifex grows in clumps. He leapt from clump to clump of the coarse, springy grass landing in such a way that each tussock crinkled upright again as he leapt to the next. For a human foot can leave its faint, detectable pressure even upon a clump of thick, coarse, springy grass.

Nemarluk scowled, thinking of Bul-bul. If Bul-bul drew near that range he would not climb it and seek upon the escarpments above. He would ride along the base of the range seeking tracks where a man might have come down. And Bul-bul would seek tales not only from the earth, but the rocks and grass and trees and bushes; from the ground upon which a man had slept, upon which he ate, the trees and logs from where he would chop sugar-bag or snake or frog; from the swamp where he dug mussel or water-rat-Bul-bul would seek for tracks upon everything. .

But Bul-bul was far away, seeking vainly with that wandering police patrol.

Nemarluk laughed and travelled faster, his eyes eager. He had quite lost the patrol. He sought now human comradeship; he wanted the welcome, the guttural voices of the horde; he wanted the smoke of the fires, the smell of roasting animals, the comradeship of sleeping bodies instead of the loneliness among the rocks with the Spirits of the night..

By many a subterfuge known to the cunning among primitive men Nemarluk evaded capture for a long time. He probably would still be free, certainly would have cost the country thousands of pounds, had not Fitzer worked with his head.

Fanny Bay Gaol, Darwin.

40
THE ARREST OF NEMARLUK

BUL-BUL, working independently with Splinter, travelled without all the disadvantages attendant on a long string of horses, of commissariat and other problems. He was a wild man hunting a wild enemy who pictured him as among the horses of a patrol. Whereas Bul-bul came and went with the night, he was here and was gone exactly as Nemarluk was here and was gone. But Bul-bul could look into Nemarluk's mind, which a patrol never could quite. And Bul-bul was sure Nemarluk would again come to Legune, his nostrils would turn towards Legune with a craving for tobacco. He would seek mates at the last, fighting mates who were not afraid of the police. All his best friends were in far away Darwin gaol, but in the ranges, somewhere around Legune, was Deven, Deven who cut horses' tongues out, Deven who swore he was going to spear white men, Deven who had broken out of Fanny Bay gaol. Nemarluk and Deven would join up and together collect around them another Red Band.

The Legune blacks were frightened of both Deven and Nemarluk, especially they would not dare to put Nemarluk away. But Bul-bul had his "secret intelligence," so, though the Legune folk dare not betray Nemarluk, neither would they warn him against Bul-bul.

Although Bul-bul travelled far from Legune, his secret friends were there and would quickly signal him of the return of Nemarluk.

Nemarluk did return. And Bul-bul knew. One night, while sleeping among those whom he counted as friends, Nemarluk rose up, silent as a shadow, and as silently stole away. Quite a distance, until his shadow vanished in the blackness of a thicket. There he coiled himself up to sleep.

But other shadows had followed as silently. Not clothed trackers, but naked, their bodies greased. They gave him time to lapse into real sleep. Then Bul-bul crawled in after him. Only Bul-bul, for the thicket was a mass of cane and vine. But when Bul-bul slung his great arms around his enemy the others leapt into the struggle and the thrashing canes, the uprooting vines, the splintering sticks, the hoarse snarls and maddened growls of those unseen fighters broke on the night like a fight in a tiger's lair. They handcuffed him eventually; the very vines that were to warn him of advancing enemies entangled him with those enemies without chance of breaking away.

Then came the travel up-river to meet Fitzer. One cold morning before the dawn they were sleeping on the bank of the Bullo River. The trackers were clothed now. Nemarluk was staring at the big form of Bul-bul beside him, snoring hoarsely. On the other side of him another tracker slept; around were the black forms of several of Bul-bul's friends.

Inch by slow inch Nemarluk wormed his way towards the river-bank. Just as slowly, the grey dawn came. Nemarluk's heart was pounding, he was very near the edge of the steep bank, he could see the icy gleam of water. Once in there meant freedom again. He drew a deep breath and took a last glance at the sleeping trackers. Bul-bul's eyes were open, a grin at the corners of his mouth. Nemarluk's wrists were handcuffed before him; he slung his legs over the bank as Bul-bul leapt. Nemarluk slid down into water up to his waist, but Bul-bul was leaping down as Nemarluk's manacled hands shot up and clutched Bul-bul's throat. Fearful realization glared from both men's eyes as Nemarluk strained to drag his enemy under, as Bul-bul strained to drag him back. Bul-bul could not utter a sound while those terrible fingers clenched on the grip that will never let go while consciousness remains. Bul-bul dropped his hand behind his belt and gripped a spare set of handcuffs. He swung the steel high and crashed it down upon Nemarluk's head. The grip convulsively loosened and Nemarluk slipped under water.

Bul-bul clawed his tortured throat, wheezed air into his lungs, shouted hoarsely, then slid into the water and groped for Nemarluk on the bottom.

But it was Nemarluk's surrender. When I saw him last in Fanny Bay gaol he was laughing again, with his hair cut and his beard shaved off, and good solid flesh on his ribs.

Milton Keynes UK
Ingram Content Group UK Ltd.
UKHW042147131124
451149UK00003B/386